Mothers, Mobility, Narrative

SUNY series in Multiethnic Literatures

Mary Jo Bona, editor

Mothers, Mobility, Narrative
Maternality in US Literature

MARY JO BONA

Cover art: Detail, *Crisis Scene*, carved oak bas-relief. Christine Perri, 2016, photograph and loan of image by kind permission of Christine Perri.

Published by State University of New York Press, Albany

© 2025 State University of New York

All rights reserved

Printed in the United States of America

No part of this book may be used or reproduced in any manner whatsoever without written permission. No part of this book may be stored in a retrieval system or transmitted in any form or by any means including electronic, electrostatic, magnetic tape, mechanical, photocopying, recording, or otherwise without the prior permission in writing of the publisher.

Links to third-party websites are provided as a convenience and for informational purposes only. They do not constitute an endorsement or an approval of any of the products, services, or opinions of the organization, companies, or individuals. SUNY Press bears no responsibility for the accuracy, legality, or content of a URL, the external website, or for that of subsequent websites.

EU GPSR Authorised Representative:
Logos Europe, 9 rue Nicolas Poussin, 17000, La Rochelle, France
contact@logoseurope.eu

For information, contact State University of New York Press, Albany, NY
www.sunypress.edu

Library of Congress Cataloging-in-Publication Data

Name: Bona, Mary Jo, author.
Title: Mothers, mobility, narrative : maternality in US literature / Mary Jo Bona.
Description: Albany : State University of New York Press, [2025]. | Series: SUNY series in multiethnic literatures | Includes bibliographical references and index.
Identifiers: LCCN 2024042808 | ISBN 9798855802009 (hardcover : alk. paper) | ISBN 9798855802016 (ebook) | ISBN 9798855801996 (pbk. : alk. paper)
Subjects: LCSH: American literature—History and criticism. | Mothers in literature. | Motherhood in literature. | LCGFT: Literary criticism.
Classification: LCC PS173.M68 B66 2025 | DDC 810.9/35252—dc23/eng/20250101
LC record available at https://lccn.loc.gov/2024042808

To mothers, othermothers, far and wide

Contents

List of Illustrations ix

Acknowledgments xi

Introduction: Mothers, Mobility, Narrative: Comparative Studies of Maternality in US Literature 1

1. Mother-Daughter Plots and Maternal Black Bodies: Jacobs's *Incidents in the Life of a Slave Girl* and Cather's *Sapphira and the Slave Girl* 23

2. Long-Distance Mothering and Generational Haunting in Morrison's *Beloved* and García's *Dreaming in Cuban* 55

3. Matrilineal Desire and Geographies of Return in Lorde's *Zami: A New Spelling of My Name* and Ragusa's *The Skin Between Us: A Memoir of Race, Beauty, and Belonging* 87

4. Queer Maternality in Maso's *The Art Lover* and Makkai's *The Great Believers* 121

Coda 151

Notes 159

Bibliography 201

Index 223

Illustrations

Figure 1.1	*Molly Horniblow's House.*	39
Figure 1.2	Typescript of Cather's first paragraph deletion in the epilogue of *Sapphira and the Slave Girl*, by Willa Cather.	51
Figure 2.1	Faith Ringgold, *Coming to Jones Road #4: Under a Blood Red Sky*, 2000.	63
Figure 2.2	Maria Faedo, panel from *The Birthing Album*, 1994.	78
Figure 3.1	Cover design, *Zami: A New Spelling of My Name*, by Audre Lorde, 1982.	95
Figure 3.2	Title page, *The Skin Between Us: A Memoir of Race, Beauty, and Belonging*, by Kym Ragusa, 2006.	100
Figure 3.3	Italian woman carrying heavy bundle of clothing on her head, by Lewis Hine, 1912.	116
Figure 4.1	ACT UP, designed by the SILENCE = DEATH collective, 1987.	134
Figure C.1	Christine Perri, *Detail, Shipwreck in a Tree, Figurehead with Cloth*, 2016.	156

Acknowledgments

My gratitude runs deep. Much of the writing of this book took place during the pandemic, when quarantines were in place and virtual meetings filled our days. During part of this period, a coveted sabbatical from Stony Brook University enabled me to begin thinking about maternal lives under constraint. I thank my former dean of the College of Arts and Sciences, Nicole Sampson, for her support of my scholarly work during this time. I also thank Amy Cook, then associate dean, who spearheaded the Faculty Writing Group, which afforded us meaningful ways to write under challenging circumstances. A fortuitous result of this initiative was an inspiring writing relationship I developed with my colleagues, Nancy Hiemstra and Kristina Lucenko, whose support of this book has been immense. Self-proclaimed "writing worms," we continue reading and revising drafts, supporting each other every step of the way.

A portion of chapter 3 on Kym Ragusa's *The Skin Between Us* was published in *Italian American Review*, vol. 13, no. 1, 2023, pp. 31–53. In a different and condensed form, an earlier analysis of Carole Maso's *The Art Lover* in chapter 4 first appeared in Mary Jo Bona's *By the Breath of Their Mouths: Narratives of Resistance in Italian America*, State University of New York Press, 2010, pp. 195–203. I would like to thank those academic organizations where I shared untested thoughts on literary representations of motherhood, including the MLA (Modern Language Association), AISNA (Associazione Italiana di Studi Nord-Americani, the American Studies Association of Italy), and MELUS (the Multiethnic Literature of the United States Association); I also thank those academic institutions which invited me to share my developing ideas about this project: University of Roma Tre, University of Georgia, Indiana University, the Italian Diaspora Studies Summer Institute, the John D. Calandra Italian American Institute/

Queens College, Santa Clara University, and the Center for Italian Studies (Stony Brook University).

I am grateful to the Stony Brook librarians, particularly those in ILL (Interlibrary Loan), who retrieved books and articles for me with alacrity and kindness. Thanks also to Provost Carl Lejuez and Vice Provost Mónica Bugallo for the Provost's Lecture series, which features talks by SUNY Distinguished Academy faculty members at Stony Brook University, allowing me to speak about Carole Maso's heart-rending novel, *The Art Lover*. To my former and recent graduate students, especially Dr. Yalda Hamidi, Dr. Stephanie Bonvissuto, Hayden Cuttone, Emillion Adekoya, and Kara Pernicano, whose intellectual contributions in the graduate seminars I taught on maternal praxis and narratives of diaspora, enabled me to broaden my thinking about the intersections between mothers, mobilities, and the stories they tell.

I have drawn great sustenance from so many scholars over the years and wish to honor those whose work came before mine and, as a result, has been a steadfast influence on my own: Nellie Y. McKay, Annis Pratt, Suzanne Gossett, Josephine Gattuso Hendin, Sandra Mortola Gilbert, and William L. Andrews. In particular, I wish to thank the following colleagues, whose work has informed my own: Sabrina Vellucci, Carla Francellini, Wenying Xu, Jessica Maucione, Loredana Polezzi, Fred L. Gardaphé, and Tracey Walters. In especial, I wish to thank Roseanne Lucia Giannini Quinn, whose expertise on experimental writers and feminist theory immeasurably enabled my own scholarly work in motherhood literary studies. And I wish to thank Jennifer Di Gregorio Kightlinger, whose support of this monograph and whose editorial expertise have been enormous.

I am deeply grateful to my editor at SUNY Press, Rebecca Colesworthy, not only for her keen editorial acumen, but also for her humor, kindness, and supportive conversations we had throughout this journey. For her expertise during the shepherding of this manuscript, I heartily thank my production editor, Diane Ganeles; and thanks also to editors Jenn Bennett-Genthner, Julia Cosacchi, Ryan Morris, and Camille Hale for their support. Finally, and always, I am grateful to Judy, who has made all this possible.

Introduction

Mothers, Mobility, Narrative: Comparative Studies of Maternality in US Literature

Motherhood Literary Studies Now

Mothers, Mobility, Narrative extends an analysis of maternal subjectivities across a swath of American narratives, exposing a generic blending in both autobiographies and novels, ranging from the mid-nineteenth century to the millennium. The narratives in *Mothers, Mobility, Narrative* encourage a paradigm shift in national consciousness about maternity and movement, especially as the authors represent mother figures physically moving or devising plans to move to other spaces. Mothers and daughters are simultaneously represented as refusing both literally and symbolically to stay in their places. They are compelled not only by a shift in perception about their roles but also by a recognition that they must physically leave untenable circumstances. The narratives I examine are not merely stories about mothering and movement; they reveal the authors' resistance to ideological constructs of maternity. Such figures are represented as deliberately deciding to move from unsafe spaces to ensure theirs and others' safety, a decision that stems from their centrality as mother figures who refuse to abide by norms that would otherwise destroy them.

A central aim of *Mothers, Mobility, Narrative* is to examine how motherhood is represented in US-based literary texts across different time periods and addressing urgent but distinct social concerns. While largely a transhistorical comparative project, I analyze narrative works through the lens of motherhood literary studies and argue all the writers narrate the activity of maternity, by which I mean both mothering and daughtering, under unforgiving constraints. The authors I discuss—Harriet Jacobs, Willa Cather, Toni Morrison, Cristina García, Audre Lorde, Kym Ragusa, Carole Maso, and Rebecca Makkai—theorize capaciously about motherhood, daughterhood, movement, and desire across a century and a half of literary expression in the United States. By using the critical lens of maternal feminism, alongside recent theories on time, space, and memory, I reengage motherhood studies in order more fully to explore the linkages between motherhood and movement, drawing on the tensions afoot in the arena of motherhood studies from its inception in the 1980s. By returning to the foundational discourses on motherhood, I draw out the interdisciplinarity of prominent studies, recognizing their limitations in focus, especially about race, but also highlighting the intersections between race, gender, and ethnicity from those early works that made possible future work, including my own.

I see maternal practice largely governed through spaces endangered by structural inequalities and obstacles to maternity. The authors on which I focus emerge from a variety of settings with different histories and cultural geographies. Placing them together invites a cross-cultural conversation about alternative maternalities[1] occurring within inhospitable contexts that compel a rethinking of normative understandings of time and space. My decision to pair texts emerges from a recognition of the intertextual connections between them, though my interest is not premised on an assumption that these pairings are uniquely determinative. As Mikhail Bakhtin has explained, "every age re-accentuates in its own way the works of its most immediate past" ("Dialogic Imagination" 421). By reprising and extending Paul Lauter's organizing principle of pairing texts,[2] I do so less to show radical similarities in literary origin (as interesting as that is), as to show how ideological understandings of maternal bodies shift in meaning and are dismantled before our reading eyes when set in largely segregated spaces as singular as plantation space and epidemic space. By pairing texts and placing them in relation to each other, I claim for them valuable nongenealogical inheritances as they achieve a kind of solidarity in company with each other.

In *Mothers, Mobility, Narrative*, I also theorize more fully the meanings of motherhood within and beyond natality, which includes affiliations beyond conventional understandings of family, kinship, and home. I argue that the authors of necessity disrupt traditional discourses of the maternal to challenge normative ideas about reproduction and to create spaces not only of resistance but also of difference in order to embrace more generous recognitions of maternal subjectivity. The works I consider in *Mothers, Mobility, Narrative* engage in multiple incarnations of mothering on a shifting maternal continuum. Nonetheless, specific conceptual patterns regarding maternality emerge, a partial list of which I offer here:

- An overidentification with and of the maternal;

- An erotic yearning for the maternal;

- A reframing of mother abandonment from perspectives of race, ethnicity, and diaspora;

- A reparenting of friends whose nonprocreative desires clear a space for connective work beyond the familial.[3]

Regarding the specific paired texts I examine, Harriet Jacobs's *Incidents in the Life of a Slave Girl* and Willa Cather's *Sapphira and the Slave Girl* represent divergent views on antebellum culture, but they forcefully highlight spatial and temporal practices that equip enslaved women with the means to escape their bondage, receiving covert help from maternal figures who perform connective work beyond the familial. Through movements away from plantation space and island space, Toni Morrison's *Beloved* and Cristina García's *Dreaming in Cuban* extend ideas about motherhood by employing haunting as a metaphor and a materiality to echo an irreversible trauma from which maternal figures suffer in these narratives, reframing ideas about abandonment and overidentification with the maternal. Audre Lorde's *Zami: A New Spelling of My Name* and Kym Ragusa's *The Skin Between Us: A Memoir of Race, Beauty, and Belonging* broaden ideas about motherhood, separation, and mobility to embrace a matrilineal diaspora and far-reaching definitions of erotic mothering. Finally, Carole Maso's *The Art Lover* and Rebecca Makkai's *The Great Believers* envisage a reproduction of mothering through a type of reparenting that identifies queer kinship from lesbians and sisters who mother dying men, helping to ease their crossing, recalling those nineteenth-century maternal figures who functioned covertly to actualize geographical crossings for enslaved women.

The linkages between these works are largely inflected by the narratives' various geographical trajectories, from antebellum antislavery genres represented by Jacobs, for example, in her rendering of 1820 through 1830s Edenton, North Carolina, to AIDS narratives revisited in the second decade of the millennium in Makkai's reimagining of gay life in 1980s Chicago.

By pairing US women-identified writers from different eras and cultures, I illuminate both connections and divergences in narrative forms and strategies related to both embracement and displacement of maternity. Two feminist scholars who have centrally guided my framework and interpretations, and have expanded the perimeters of motherhood studies in crucial ways, are Adriana Cavarero, an Italian philosopher, and Patricia Hill Collins, a Black American sociologist. Cavarero's probative reinterpretation of ancient myths of maternity invite me to examine how such figures as Demeter and Persephone implicitly and explicitly undergird the narratives under consideration. Likewise, I employ Collins's term *othermothering* to explore practices of maternity Collins locates in Black mothering, but I locate more broadly to examine mothering across multiethnic cultures and in contextual situations of people in racial, ethnic, and LGBTQ* communities unsupported by a political economy that separates family from public life. Below, I briefly examine how I will be using their work.

Cavarero and Collins in Tandem

In *Mothers, Mobility, Narrative*, I use the term *abduction* to discuss mothering, taking my first prompt from Adriana Cavarero's book, *In Spite of Plato*, whose reinterpretation of the myth of Demeter in particular guides my analysis. By representing societal structures enforcing rigid binaries between genders to ensure the inferiority of women, the authors implicitly engage the concept of abduction to examine how maternity operates both within mother-daughter dynamics and outside traditional understandings of the practice of motherhood. The narratives I analyze represent women-identified mothers and daughters as subject to multiple kinds of movement. I take as de rigueur the etymological roots of the word, *abduction*, to mean "robbing" and "to lead away," as the authors expose the underlying reasons for women's forcible separation from each other as a result of institutionalized oppressions that guarantee their abuse.[4] The authors illuminate how women both discovered and created ways to resist their objectification, fundamentally changing their conceptions of home and maternity while simultaneously increasing their insistence on mobility to ensure a safe place for themselves and their progeny. To demonstrate this idea, I use Cavarero's reinterpretation of the stories of ancient maternal figures, including the mythological tales of Demeter and her daughter, Persephone (Kore).

Cavarero shows how these mythic women resisted patriarchy by manipulating perceptions of time and space through seemingly innocuous activities as weaving and waiting. For example, when Demeter's daughter, Persephone (Kore), is "snatched out of her sight," this act brings to the scene a "nothingness," a "birth-no-more" (60).[5] By reinterpreting the myth of Demeter to focus on the matricidal qualities within it, Cavarero declares, "In fact the kernel of the myth is a disavowal of the maternal order of birth, an order that posits itself as a place from which human existence comes and takes signification" (63). In response to "this erasure," that is, not being able to see her daughter, Demeter refuses to generate. Forced into exile, Persephone/Kore "is no longer Demeter's *daughter* but Hades' *wife*. . . . The daughters will be destined to be wives of other men and objects of other deportations" (Cavarero 65–66).[6] In her Foreword to Cavarero's book, Rosi Braidotti argues that Cavarero separates maternality from the logic of patriarchy, explaining that the "maternal function, which, far from being reduced to a support of patriarchy, is turned into a structuring or foundational site for the empowerment of women" (*In Spite of Plato* xvi). Rather than supporting patriarchy, ancient maternal figures such as Demeter and Penelope manipulate perceptions of time, including halting time, to ensure their continuation of the mother-daughter bond. My project likewise demonstrates how these authors represent maternal figures resisting institutionalized practices of motherhood, engaging in care work that challenges traditional discourses that delimit how women function as maternal.

I connect Cavarero's discussion of women's experience of abduction to maternal work, taking my second cue from Patricia Hill Collins, whose creation and conception of the term *othermother* promulgates a contrast between the privatized nurturing expected of biological mothers and "interdependent, complementary dimensions of motherhood" that include women who "assist blood-mothers by sharing mothering responsibilities, traditionally . . . central to the institution of Black motherhood" ("The Meaning of Motherhood" 5).[7] I extend an exploration of depictions of abduction and practices of othermothering, arguing that the authors radically reinterpret motherhood through a persistent critique of institutional failures to support maternal work. Collins's trope of othermothering equips me then to examine a variety of maternal practices that take place under severe conditions, from the most trenchant context of slavery to immigrant maternity, and from mother abandonment to affiliative mothering beyond the consanguin.[8]

Collins approaches motherhood studies from a primarily sociocultural and matrilineal perspective, toppling discursive notions that the cult of true womanhood and the nuclear family are universal paradigms of family structure. Collins denaturalizes and thereby destabilizes "Eurocentric views of white motherhood" and in contrast outlines Afrocentric ideologies of maternity that opened new ways of interpreting interdependent dimensions of motherhood, introducing the concept of othermothers to demonstrate how children across cultures were in actuality nurtured ("Meaning of Motherhood" 3).[9] By recognizing the importance of highlighting experiential realities to effect social change, Collins and other feminist women of color moved away from psychological feminism and toward emphasizing (and redefining) familial concepts.[10] While I reference psychological feminist studies throughout this study, I will focus more fully on the social dimensions of motherhood that challenge ideologies of white, middle-class maternal representation. While my use of the term *abduction* deliberately recalls Jane Gallop's *The Daughter's Seduction*,[11] my book steers away from Gallop's focus on the interface between psychoanalysis and feminism. Although I recognize that this dynamic came of age for mostly white feminists in the late 1970s and 1980s as literary and gender studies began reinscribing the long-time erasure of motherhood as a topic of literary study and social significance, my approach foregrounds legacies of intersectional feminism.[12] As such, my project navigates the intertwined topic of mothering and daughtering across multiple intersections, including race, gender, ethnicity, sexuality, and expression.

Motherhood Studies across Intersections and Feminist Literary Criticism

Published thirty years after Marianne Hirsch's formative 1981 review essay on motherhood studies for *Signs* (to which I shall return), Samira Kawash's 2011 "New Directions in Motherhood Studies," also published in *Signs*, attributes the millennial marginalization of this topic to a conservative backlash to feminism and poststructuralist theories that largely left "motherhood to the side" (972).[13] Kawash nonetheless referenced a diverse and heterogenous scholarship that continues in motherhood studies, noting that inquiries on mothering and motherhood remain precariously "unbounded," and yet relevant work emerges from "literary studies, art history, psychoanalysis, [and] social theory" (995). Motherhood literary studies has always resisted backlash tendencies within academic discourse and in conservative circles and continues to centralize maternity within marginalized communities.

While the authors I discuss are dispersed across time and space, their works and my analysis are rooted in literary studies. Kawash rightly interprets the susceptibility characteristic of the unbounded nature of motherhood studies, rendering it vulnerable to too much dispersal and perhaps even endangering the efficacy of future studies. In response to that, I return to a relevant comment made by Judith Butler in her discussion of space vis-à-vis the epistemological closet. In her famous essay, "Imitation and Gender Insubordination," Butler revealed both a dissatisfaction with and support of a "new, unbounded spatiality" for gay or lesbian subjects (16). My study, which represents a comparative and multiethnic return to literary motherhood studies, contends that the authors promise and deliver upon an unbounded spatiality in their resistance to conventional maternality.[14] By entering this conversation under the auspice of motherhood literary studies, I also argue that the authors I discuss fundamentally compel a redefinition of how maternal praxis necessarily occurs within a larger matrix of connections. Andrea O'Reilly's *Maternal Theory: Essential Readings* highlights the sheer breadth of writing published on maternal theory over the course of several decades, many of which intersect with and have further influenced the field of feminist literary studies.[15] Such plenitude in motherhood studies continues to be the case in the third decade of the millennium, including interdisciplinary scholarship comprising feminist migration studies and feminist geographies, to which I shall return.

In her 1981 review essay, Hirsch argued that from its inception feminist studies on motherhood was fundamentally interdisciplinary: "Any full study of mother-daughter relationships, in whatever field, is by definition both feminist and interdisciplinary" (202). The interdisciplinary nature of motherhood studies from the outset demonstrated feminist praxis from second-wave feminist thinkers. For example, in the 1970s and 1980s, theorists from multiple disciplines developed far-ranging approaches to maternal studies, including landmark works by Nancy Chodorow, Adrienne Rich, Patricia Hill Collins, Luce Irigaray, and Marianne Hirsch, to name just a few of the scholars who have been deeply influential to the field at large and have guided my own thinking. These scholars may have emerged from different intellectual traditions, but the complexity of their work compelled further study. Extensive in their approaches, feminist theorists such as Rich, Chodorow, and Hirsch deployed a methodology of psychoanalytical feminism to explore mother-daughter dyads, elaborating accounts of women's psychological life by focusing on white female subjectivity in a patriarchal society.

While my intention in this section is not meant to be exhaustive, I do want to note that postmillennial feminist literary scholars continually reference maternal theorists who emerged from second-wave feminism of the 1970s and 1980s. And for good reason. Regardless of their disciplinary backgrounds, early theorists in motherhood studies not only cited literary texts to disseminate their theories but also enabled feminist literary scholars to interpret those texts through analyses of the socialization of girl children and mother-daughter relationships. For example, in discussing the mother's loss of self in (white middle-class) families, Chodorow writes in her 1974 precursor essay to *The Reproduction of Mothering* that due to boundary confusion, mothers and daughters experience guilt and self-blame for the other's unhappiness. To support her argument, Chodorow references women writers from Simone de Beauvoir to Tillie Olsen who portray an extreme sense of guilt mothers have felt for their "overwhelming responsibility for and connection to others" (59).[16] In a reflective essay published in 2000, Chodorow recalls that she was writing *The Reproduction of Mothering* at a time when "no one had really noticed the mother-daughter relationship," citing the continued feasibility of her book as it centralized largely white mother-daughter relationships as passionate, forming "the core of women's lives" but also as overwhelming and invading "both the mother's and daughter's psyche" ("Reflections On" 340). Declaring that *The Reproduction of Mothering* was written "from the daughter's point of view more than the mother," Chodorow's understanding of maternal subjectivity continues to recognize that "psychology and politics are not always homologous and that, as we imagine fulfilling lives, the relative claims of each are not self-evident" ("Reflections On" 348). Because mothers and daughters from different cultures and racial backgrounds have been traditionally separated by patriarchal divisions structured within the institution of the family and often the nation, for example, separations between them prevail. As Rocío Davis adds when discussing Latinx narratives, "while division prevails, there can never be completion" (61). Autobiographical narrators and their fictional counterparts, including those in my study, must travel far and search deeply for what Julee Tate describes are buried family and national histories, revealing "the lack of reliable maternal sources" (160).

Mothers and daughters must unearth their buried pasts in order to realize that connections are shared alongside differentiation.

Such connections between mothers and daughters are also reflected in adaptations to traditional genre forms, such as the autobiography, the novel, and the scholarly monograph. A mixed-genre approach aptly characterizes Rich's innovative *Of Woman Born: Motherhood as Experience and Institution*. As Rich explains, "for most of what we know as the 'mainstream' of recorded history, motherhood as institution has ghettoized and degraded female potentialities" (13). Incorporating her own experiences as a young mother, Rich placed feelings of "exquisite suffering" her children caused her in the larger realm of "the patriarchal institution of motherhood," weaving her personal story as only *one* story of motherhood "and by no means limited to the maternal function" (21, 40). In 1986, when Norton reissued the tenth-anniversary edition of her text, Rich scrupulously updated it with annotations and responses to her own exclusions. Rich's book was always an interdisciplinary inquiry into the experience of motherhood and a generic melding of the experiential and autobiographical with the scholarly.

Marianne Hirsch's 1981 review essay explores the interdisciplinarity of foundational works in motherhood studies, beginning with Rich's *Of Woman Born*. Describing as "revolutionary" both the content and methodology of Rich's study, Hirsch began her essay on mothers and daughters with Rich's now-famous proclamation: " 'The cathexis between mother and daughter—essential, distorted, misused—is the great unwritten story' " ("Mothers and Daughters" 202).[17] As O'Reilly explains, Rich's *Of Woman Born* influenced "the *way* feminist scholars theorize motheringmotherhood" (*From Motherhood* 2), and Rich's early interlocutors such as Audre Lorde mobilized "an exchange of voices spoken through differences of race" (Driver "Reading Adrienne" 110). In an interview with Rich, Lorde identifies her mother as one of the foundational sources for her understanding of the powerful world of nonverbal communication, "vital and protective information . . . beneath language. My life depended on it." ("An Interview" 83).[18] Thus, while Lorde clearly understood the role of motherhood as an institution that subjugated women in the manner of Rich's argument in *Of Woman Born*, she also identified as foundational her own Black immigrant mother's behavior (despite loss of power in America) as empowering in nuanced and nontraditional ways per O'Reilly's concept of the empowered mother.[19] Unsurprising to note here is that Lorde, too, activated her own theorization of motherhood by blending life writing with myth and history in her pathbreaking *Zami: A New Spelling of My Name*.

Hirsch continued her scholarly work on motherhood with her 1989 *The Mother/Daughter Plot: Narrative, Psychoanalysis, Feminism*, which critiques and reinterprets Freud's concept of the "family romance" by examining alternate plot patterns that surpass the story of Oedipus and serve as models for female writers. Hirsch explores mother-daughter plots in relation to specific classical origins, including such pairings as Clytemnestra/Electra, Demeter/Persephone, and Jocasta/Antigone.[20] Choosing literary texts across a range of racial, ethnic, and class categories, Hirsch maps out two paradigmatic stories—"Jocasta's missing story in the Oedipus narrative and a very recent black feminist re-vision of that story in Toni Morrison's *Beloved*" (*Mother/Daughter Plot* 3). Hirsch early recognized that applying an intersectional approach to study maternity would not only test her psychoanalytical framework but also exceed narratives of mother-daughter attachments within heterosexual romance in white families; less a study of the "daughter's developmental process" and more about "mothers *and* daughters," Hirsch concentrated on "narratives that connect or separate them" (*Mother/Daughter Plot* 27). Expanding Hirsch's interdisciplinary approach, my aim in examining autobiographical narrators and fictional characters in *Mothers, Mobility, Narrative* is to show how maternal figures manage time through everyday acts in order to control space. As a result of this practice, the authors claim other structures of belonging produced through innovatory writing modes that construct wide-ranging conceptions of maternality.

In 1986, Hirsch attended a public reading at Dartmouth where Toni Morrison read from the first chapter of what would become her magnum opus, *Beloved*. So crucial became Morrison's *Beloved* to Hirsch's analysis of an enslaved Black mother's subjectivity "not mediated by the daughter's narrative, . . . the unspeakable mother who cannot protect her child" (*Generation* 11), that Hirsch waited until Morrison's novel was published the following year to finish her own monograph. As Hirsch says in a later book, "I began and ended *The Mother/Daughter Plot* with Sethe" (*Generation* 11). Hirsch's decision to focus on "mothers *and* daughters" through an intersectional lens is also my own. As Morrison probes in *Beloved*, the daughter's abduction is always about the mother's daunting situation, redefining ideas about abandonment to highlight forced separation. And the one doesn't stir without the other.[21]

The heterogeneous quality that Kawash thus notes in recent scholarship on motherhood studies might also then be interpreted equally as an act of deferral, a resistance by many scholars and artists to centralize maternal representations any *one* way. Analyzing literary texts through multifarious experiences of maternity in diverse locations permits my own cognizance of the constitutive power of motherhood itself, changing over time and as a result of movement. Kawash reminds us that, at the outset, Adrienne Rich powerfully demonstrated the vital fact that "the problem of the institution of motherhood is not attitudes, it's power" (987). The writers qualify portrayals of turbulence between mothers and daughters by largely problematizing the practice of mothering under structural oppressions exacerbated by the economy of slavery and discourses of white patriarchal supremacy. These works push back against institutional oppressions that erase the mother-daughter cathexis, expanding maternal horizons through a variety of movements, both geographical and imaginary.

Constructing alternative maternal languages in response to a combination of desire and extremity, the authors intervene to repair damage caused by oppressive systems controlling their race, gender, and sexuality. In her thoughtful reconsideration of Rich's *Of Woman Born* from the perspective of a queer, feminist daughter, Susan Driver cites Rich's inspired intervention through subjective introspection and institutional analysis to imagine maternity as a "paradoxical locus of social control, creative labour, and corporeal pleasure" ("Reading Adrienne" 110). Examining the paradoxical locus of social control vis-à-vis predominating discourses on motherhood, Collins explains, "We must distinguish between what has been said about subordinated groups in the dominant discourse, and what such groups might say about themselves if given the opportunity" ("Shifting the Center" 314). Perhaps nothing can be more paradoxical than to imagine maternity under the domus of plantation space. The works I discuss reimagine women's positions on a maternal continuum as their radically unhoused[22] living situations require stealth and creativity so that they may continue to engage in maternal work under life-denying restrictions. Struggling to decide whether to stay put or go elsewhere, maternal figures are eventually portrayed in these narratives as leaving, exposing how such movement feels at times as though it were generated coercively. Notions of belonging are paradoxically nestled next to feelings of exile, compelling alternative maternal practices inclusive of reproducing culture somewhere else and challenging fundamental notions of mobility and stasis.[23]

Diasporic Space, Maternal Time

My turning to both feminist diaspora studies and feminist geographies in *Mothers, Mobility, Narrative* allows a fuller examination of maternal subjects and the problematics of their mobility. For purposes of my project, I define the uses of diaspora from the perspective of multiple kinds of movement, and, as Samantha Pinto explains, as a "set of aesthetic and interpretative strategies" the authors use to describe and redefine the spaces they inhabit (4).[24] Scholars in areas of feminist diaspora studies expand an interpretation of how mothers and daughters experience forms of abduction through separation and forced movement (especially the forced displacement of Africans by Europeans during the Atlantic slave trade), but also experience practices of othermothering through everyday acts of "embodied reproduction," as Irene Gedalof describes it within contexts of movement and migration (85). Equally useful to my thoughts on mothers and mobility is Avtar Brah's notion of how diaspora space itself intersects with narrative, inviting me to probe the concept of diaspora as a "critique of discourses of fixed origins," thereby distinguishing between accounts of a "homing desire" and a desire for a homeland, a distinction of note, since "not all diasporas sustain an ideology of return" (16). For the maternal subjects examined in this book, nativist discourses delimit their relationship to the nation, compelling them to imagine and reconfigure diaspora space through nontraditional social relations.

Ideas about diaspora and home remain in flux for women who have been radically unhoused. I agree with Gedalof, who asks us to reconsider "an over-privileging of movement" as it risks "celebrating rootlessness rather than attending to the complexities of inhabitance in the context of displacement" (87). Such complexities also occur when maternal figures must stay put, must wait for the right moment, and must find ways to halt time in order to control their everyday lives. Thus, both temporalities and spatialities intersect with what I call "maternal time," in which everyday practices serve to support others, reduce inequalities, and subvert structures of power.

Everyday activities practiced by women whose lives are circumscribed by oppressive structures are explored in Katherine McKittrick's *Demonic Grounds: Black Women and the Cartographies of Struggle*. McKittrick explains that "black women also *inhabited* what Jenny Sharpe calls 'the crevices of power' necessary to enslavement, and from this location some were able to manipulate and recast the meanings of slavery's geographic terrain" (*Demonic Grounds* xvii).²⁵ Employing an interdisciplinary methodology to examine Black women's geographies, McKittrick draws on a variety of past and contemporary literary texts by Black women writers, including Harriet Jacobs and Toni Morrison. Useful to my analysis is McKittrick's contention that oppositional geographic practices offer a "*public* genealogy of resistance, histories, names and places of black pain, language, and opposition" and a "black sense of place [that] communicates the terms of captivity" (xxvii–xxviii). While certain spaces are not only confining but barely habitable, they also simultaneously function as interstitial space, which, for example, Harriet Jacobs's garret becomes.

Such liminal space is paradoxical in that it enables the person confined not only to reside but also to linger, delaying movement until the time is right.²⁶ I add here Minrose Gwin's incorporation of theorists on space such as Michel de Certeau and Doreen Massey to interpret literary texts. Gwin examines multiple kinds of space, whether material or textual, to argue how space is "always in the process of being temporalized," making space "*a practiced place*" in which "aesthetic productions that make space never occur outside time because these productions are themselves temporal" (24).²⁷ From Jacobs to Makkai, the authors covertly and overtly make aesthetic decisions to challenge hegemonic structures regulating the temporal lives of maternal women in "practiced" places. Converting demonic space into loopholes of retreat, Jacobs portrays Linda Brent as (letter)-writing her way to freedom. Destabilizing the genre of autobiography, Lorde builds a house of fiction and myth, thereby producing a category of life writing that is textured, utilizing words that echo material art forms such as crazy quilting and scrapbooking. In their writing, these authors create and manage space where there seem to be only dystopian settings.

For the writers in the archive I examine, maternal subjectivity is transformed by historical trauma suffered by those divested of basic protections. Least equipped with resources to effect change, such maternal-identified figures in these works develop other terms of affiliation to resist their subjection. By doing so, they simultaneously create a new affiliative status between people who do maternal work, developing innovative narrative strategies within their purview to resist further endangerment. In these works, maternal practice is largely governed through spaces endangered by structural inequalities and obstacles to maternity, by which I mean both mothering and daughtering. The authors on which I focus emerge from a variety of settings with different histories and cultural geographies. Placing them together invites a cross-cultural conversation about alternative maternalities occurring in challenging contexts, compelling reconsiderations of conventional meanings of time and space.

Chapter Summaries

"Mother-Daughter Plots and Maternal Black Bodies: Jacobs's *Incidents in the Life of a Slave Girl* and Cather's *Sapphira and the Slave Girl*," the focus of chapter 1, examines overlapping representations of nonnormative maternal voices emerging from these narratives. Both works also function as "onset" narratives, appearing just before the breakout of catastrophic wars: the Civil War and World War II. In rhetorical terms, both writers are compelled by personal and political exigencies, discursively revealing and concealing a textual urgency bounded by specific historical and autobiographical moments in their lives. As such, Harriet Jacobs and Willa Cather manipulate temporality in their works, slowing down narrative time; however, unlike Cather, Jacobs recognizes that she cannot linger too long in that antebellum past. Jacobs's *Incidents* was published in 1861, when the Civil War began, determining slavery's abolition. Set in Virginia just before the Civil War, Cather's *Sapphira* was published in 1940, a year before the United States entered the Second World War, profoundly reshaping American attitudes about space, place, and global geographies. I first draw on historian Nora Doyle's discussion[28] of maternal bodies and motherhood in antebellum America in which the virtuous and orderly (white, middle-class) mother became a longstanding symbol that deeply influenced both narratives. While Jacobs's autobiography deftly deploys woman-focused genres such as women's domestic fiction (and the seduction plot central to this narrative), Cather succumbs to employing a seduction plot nestled pruriently alongside plantation tropes that stereotype Black lives.[29] Such narratives, which included the seduction plot, continued to influence cultural depictions of enslaved women under constant threat of sexual exploitation. Black mothers and daughters in Jacobs's and Cather's texts effect change by reorienting their perspectives about themselves as enslaved women experiencing untenable lives.

In addition, I analyze mother-daughter configurations by examining material cultures that spatialize maternal interactions, enabling a form of narrative diaspora space to function discursively, empowering these mothers and daughters eventually to escape grotesque forms of unbridled power. For Jacobs and Cather, letters and nondiegetic communication enact such narrative diaspora space, solidifying the eventual and albeit nontraditional reunion(s) between mother and daughter.[30] By examining the metanarrational quality of the authors' final chapters, moreover, I argue that Jacobs's anger and incredulity shift her autobiographical focus toward social activism, anticipating the postbellum work in which she and her daughter were engaged. As Jacobs's abolitionist activism is part of her narrative practice, her final chapters continue to focus on the human chattel slavery in American society, hammering home her unabated resistance to it throughout the narrative. By contrast, Cather's novel abruptly shifts from the genre of fiction to autobiography, the author portraying what I call a "faux reunion" of her own family's formerly enslaved mother and daughter, a separation fictionalized in the novel by a thwarted abduction and arguably a form of othermothering that enables the daughter's escape. Cather's shift in genre is simultaneously a reification of the genre of the plantation narrative with all its grotesque realities, including postbellum racial apartheid within Cather's family as spatial separations between Black and white family members are maintained. Cather's putative shift into autobiography, I argue, is both regressive and revelatory, illuminating the author's obeisance to white supremacy, which predetermined her inability to resolve the story of race and motherhood.

Chapter 2, "Long-Distance Mothering and Generational Haunting in Morrison's *Beloved* and García's *Dreaming in Cuban*," examines Toni Morrison's *Beloved* and Cristina García's *Dreaming in Cuban* through the lens of generational time. Morrison's and García's novels, published in 1987 and 1992, respectively, are what I call "projects of recovery." By this description, I suggest that both authors are engaged in what Collins calls "shifting the center," to probe "the experiences of women in alternative family structures with quite different political economies" *(Maternal Theory* 312).[31] Both authors communicate and extend ideas about generations through ties to plantation space and island space, and both writers use haunting as a trope to illustrate an irreparable trauma from which maternal figures suffer. Mothers in these works react to injury by manipulating and managing time, Sethe through Morrison's conception of rememory and Celia through García's conception of narrative diaspora space. Both practices are invested in nonsequential perceptions of time, a kind of time binding to use Elizabeth Freeman's felicitous term that both critiques temporalities and compels a rethinking of *how* "people are bound to one another, engrouped, made to feel coherently collective" (*Time Binds* 3). Hirsch's definition of postmemory also permits a more intimate clarification of Morrison's and García's representations of generational ties between mothers and daughters. These ties get performed elsewhere and are projected in different ways. For the maternal figures in both Morrison's and García's novels, daughters bear the burden of repeating their mother's maternal memories, even if they have not experienced their mother's suffering, or even if they have been afforded some means to escape their mother's situation and had children of their own in another place. I will employ Hirsch's useful description of postmemory as both novels portray the lingering effects of trauma for these maternal women.[32]

I argue that Sethe's manipulation of time in part 2 of *Beloved* and Celia's letters never sent in *Dreaming in Cuban* enable these mothers to weave a form of impenetrable time in their responses to traumatic maternal memories, their own and others. Sethe and Celia survive what Cavarero describes as "the house of unbearable death," by redefining generational time beyond conventional genealogies (65). By abolishing traditional linear narrative, both authors unburden themselves from typical generational structures, refusing to be ruled "tyrannically [by] genealogy," a criticism especially ascribed to immigrant sagas (Stavans 30).[33] Thus, these authors can explore maternal dynamics between mothers and daughters across borders, achieving more malleable conceptions of time and space.

Audre Lorde's and Kym Ragusa's reconceptualizations of maternality take place across borders and through diasporic histories and are the subjects of chapter 3, "Matrilineal Desire and Geographies of Return in Lorde's *Zami: A New Spelling of My Name* and Ragusa's *The Skin Between Us: A Memoir of Race, Beauty, and Belonging*." I call these autobiographical narratives "autoethnographies" because both authors excavate buried maternal histories that authorize their own personal redefinitions of maternal and erotic love. Developing their versions of "autohistoria" to use Gloria Anzaldúa's genre-bending concept, the authors broaden ideas about motherhood and mobility to embrace a matrilineal diaspora and erotic mothering. Anzaldúa describes her own commitment to creating new spaces of in-betweenness through an experimental form, which she describes as "the genre of writing about one's personal and collective history using fictional elements, a sort of fictionalized autobiography or memoir; and autohistoria-teoría is a personal essay that theorizes" ("now let us shift" 578).[34] Lorde and Ragusa create flexible narratives, crossing borders between memoir, poetry, and visual cultures. As a result, they critique specific spaces to illuminate racial dynamics vis-à-vis the bodies of women of color, who inhabit spaces that are a priori coded as white, segregated, and off-limits to the very people who have attained a positionality that requires them to enter those spaces. That a generation separates the publication of these works—1982 and 2006—may simulate the generational divide between mothers and daughters, but the gap also enables an examination of how racialized neighborhoods in Harlem continue to illuminate the dangers of hostile space for Black and mixed-race daughters across decades and after movements for social change.

Lorde and Ragusa explore situations of being radically unhoused from the Harlem homes in which each was raised, Lorde in the 1940s, and Ragusa in the 1970s. For the daughter of Grenadian and Barbadian immigrant parents, Lorde details urban spaces in 1950s New York City through an intersectional prism of race, class, and sexuality, especially in her life as a student at Hunter College and as a frequenter of the Greenwich Village lesbian bar scene. Barbara Smith asserts that in its structural form, Lorde's *Zami* "carves out a unique place in African American literature as the first-full length autobiographical work by an established Black Lesbian writer" ("The Truth That Never Hurts" 239).[35] Opening up an autobiographical space that invites more porous understandings of verisimilitude and authenticity as Smith puts it, Lorde's work made way for a writer such as Kym Ragusa, daughter of an African American mother and a Sicilian/Calabrian American father. The urban spaces of the 1970s remained remarkably similar to Lorde's generation regarding racial segregation. Ragusa travels between white ethnic and Black worlds, including Italian Harlem and Black Harlem.

Each writer creates new spaces of in-betweenness through travel where borderland spaces and cultures rub against each other. Lorde and Ragusa redefine the maternal through relationships established because of their mobility. Chinosole's definition of matrilineal diaspora ably describes how Lorde's and Ragusa's movements qualify them to redefine their bodies' positionality vis-à-vis other women of color. Matrilineal diaspora establishes "the links among Black women worldwide enabling us to experience distinct but related cultures while retaining a special sense of home as the locus of self-definition of power" (Chinosole 379). Re-producing heritage cultures through travel, both Lorde and Ragusa offer narratives of border crossings that help redefine and contextualize relationships to their birth mothers and more largely to their expanded comprehension of the maternal erotic and othermothering.

In my final chapter, "Queer Maternality: Maso's *The Art Lover* and Makkai's *The Great Believers*," I argue that the authors envisage a reproduction of mothering through a type of reparenting that identifies queer kinship from lesbians and sisters who mother dying men. As such, these novels function as queer maternal (meta)fictions. Maso and Makkai represent young men sickened by the AIDS virus, and, as a result, prematurely forced into a "disidentification from the promise of futurity," as Lee Edelman has claimed, though neither author portrays her ill character identifying with a negated future nor imagining "an oppositional stance" in all instances (27). An opposing stance in these novels is less about a negative future and more focused on how both authors construct maternal narratives through what Blau du Plessis has called a "critical dissent from dominant narrative," employing metafictional techniques that challenge ideas about narrative and aesthetic construction (5).

Analyzing the activity of reparenting through reappraisals of maternity in both novels, I focus on how maternal plots get reconfigured during the AIDS crisis and how nontraditional art is portrayed through the central female characters, Caroline of *The Art Lover*, and Fiona of *The Great Believers*, who support the artistic ambitions of their loved ones by engaging visual artforms to memorialize the era of AIDS. Overlaying each novel is a recurring story about ruptured mother-daughter bonds due to forms of abduction and exacerbated by the AIDS pandemic but not defined by it. In contrast to ideas about reproduction of cultures through childrearing and family culture, Maso and Makkai practice a form of mourning and mending through distinctive incorporations of visual artforms. These extraliterary materials appear in both novels to challenge the limits of narrative itself, specifically the genre of the novel, in order to represent the unspeakable. To explore the idea of the unrepresentable more fully, I return to Hirsch's analysis of the intersections between narrative and visual culture after the Holocaust to argue that both authors incorporate counterhistories to "engage in alternative patterns of affiliation beyond the familial, forming alternate attachments across lines of difference" (*Generation of Postmemory* 16). Alluding to the atrocities of the Holocaust from the perspective of neither survivors nor their descendants, both authors nonetheless establish metonymic comparisons between victims from two periods of social history to engage in a filiation beyond the heteronormative.

Published during the height of the AIDS epidemic in 1990, *The Art Lover*'s feeling of immediacy becomes a searing present tempered by Maso's insertions of dozens of graphics, including art details, photographs, posters, recipes, and astronomical updates from the *New York Times*. Maso's protagonist, Caroline, experiences her body as overwhelmed by memory: she tries to testify for a *"body* that is overwhelmed" by disease and for her own body's unspeakable sorrow (Frank, *The Wounded Storyteller* 139).[36] Maso portrays her narrator's body serving multiple roles: as the lesbian-friend-sister-othermother to her beloved friend as he lay dying and as the writer whose lamentation is a reflection of this experience in "excess of any language that testimony can speak" as Arthur Frank describes the position of the wounded storyteller (140). Desperately mourning her dying friend while simultaneously trying to write her novel, Maso shifts midway in *The Art Lover* to memoir in contemporaneous response to this devastating reality. Maso's use of extraliterary visual material helps her to retell the story of the Passion as the story of bodily suffering during the AIDS epidemic.

Similar to Lorde's and Ragusa's dates of publication, a generation intervenes between the release of Maso's *The Art Lover* and Makkai's *The Great Believers*, which was published in 2018. Neither a survivor of AIDS nor a descendant, Makkai's approach to this period allows her to portray radically altered relationships between young adults through the lens of sexuality and disease. To trace the fallout of a period marked by the tragedy of young men dying in their prime, Makkai alternates chapters, toggling between two periods of social history—1985 through 1992 and 2015. This narrative structure—which typifies metafiction generally—permits the author to examine maternal bonds beyond normative conceptions of motherhood *and* to represent gay/queer life into the second decade of the millennium, which continues to vivify the repronormative, to use Freeman's term, that is, "living aslant to dominant forms of object-choice, coupledom, family, marriage, sociability, and self-presentation, and thus [remaining] out of synch with state-sponsored narratives of belonging and becoming" (*Time Binds* xv). Firmly ensconced within both novels are versions of mother-daughter plots that are profoundly affected by the epidemic crisis. To give one instance: the daughter's abduction in Makkai's telling fluctuates recursively and refers both to mother and daughter in this novel; their "reunion," if it might be called that, transpires within a reimagined diasporic queer community in Paris at the narrative's end. Revising ideas about generational time and queer space, Makkai centralizes the work of two artists who span two periods of social history in *The Great Believers* at the beginning of the twentieth century and in the millennium. In addition, by centralizing othermothering as the means by which these stories of extremity are told and retold, Maso and Makkai enlarge the protagonists' experiences of maternal caretaking, thereby enabling them to embrace a queer maternality, which may inspire them to search if not find their mothers again.

Mothering Narratives

The works I explore in this book proclaim daughterhood as a radical idea, both in its etymological sense of being rooted in the maternal and in an alternative sense of being marked by movements that restrict this fundamental mother-daughter relationship between women. While these authors do not overtly interrogate the fluidity of gender, their willingness to portray daughterhood under various kinds of disguise and by flouting various forms of binary constructions of gender advances the field of motherhood literary studies further. Daughters, like their mothers before them, must develop a radical sense of alterity to survive their *mother's* circumstances, which does not always or entirely rupture their relationship to the maternal, but it certainly changes it forever. Mothers who are daughters, daughters who may or may not be mothers, are required by the exigencies of their lives to separate from each other, moving elsewhere and taking covert and coerced routes, triggered by twin (and often opposing) desires: to survive and to reunite. By refusing a "reductive identification of the feminine with the maternal," Cavarero declares that the "'substance' of being woman with the act of generating *alone*" is forbidden (64). The narratives I examine in the subsequent chapters illuminate the infinite variety contained within the whys and wherefores of abduction, such as those people displaced by the trauma of enslavement and others suffering from the effects of dictatorship; these authors expose injustices and employ divergent narrative forms to illuminate the power of maternality through various practices of othermothering to enlarge the discourse on belonging, navigating a safer space to call home.

Perhaps the ghost in the cupboard of American literary histories is the centuries-long resistance these authors waged to challenge ideological prescriptions about motherhood and maternal love. In the chapters that follow, I hope to centralize the enduring if not at times haunting effects of maternal lives on the move. Mothers in these narratives are always forever daughters, and by continuing to seek maternal love, they expand limiting ideologies regarding the roles inhering in motherhood. As Cavarero writes, "The theme of this resemblance [between mother and daughter] . . . is the engendering that comes from maternal power" and "not the necessity of imposing biological reproduction on women" (63). The authors illuminate the kinds of maternal loving that occurs under circumstances of extremity. Daughters, who may or may not become birthmothers themselves, neither repress nor surpass their need for mother love, though many such women must search for it through movement elsewhere, emerging from outrageous situations that cause their flight. As flying is a woman's gesture, as Hélène Cixous famously wrote,[37] the women-identified writers who portray maternality in these narratives suggest the trope of flight through language and action, both gestures of mobility enabled by the dismantling of daughterly abductions on patriarchal terrain. The following chapters show how far, however haltingly, these women flew.

Chapter 1

Mother-Daughter Plots and Maternal Black Bodies

Jacobs's *Incidents in the Life of a Slave Girl* and
Cather's *Sapphira and the Slave Girl*

Maternal Plotting in Jacobs and Cather

Seventy-nine years separate the publications of *Incidents in the Life of a Slave Girl* (1861) and *Sapphira and the Slave Girl* (1940), but readers devoted to a teleological progress narrative might be hard-pressed to choose which narrative came first. A fast-paced narrative, Jacobs's antebellum autobiography reads by turns as a classic fugitive narrative of enslavement and a modern jeremiad that challenges racial injustice. Underlying the abolitionist intention of Jacobs's antislavery narrative is its dedication to antiracism through the author's focus on motherhood. Nothing could be further from Jacobs's focus on motherhood than Cather's twentieth-century novel, which, I read paradoxically as antimaternalist. I qualify a definition of this term, *antimaternalism*, to examine how an author such as Cather exposed the hypocrisy of white Victorian woman/motherhood, especially those ideals of self-sacrifice and republican motherhood.[1] At the same time, Cather erased the subjectivity of Black mothers and daughters to delimit the intersection between constructions of maternality and slavocracy in antebellum America. Cather is involved in both efforts throughout *Sapphira*.

Cather's erasure of maternity between Black women is deliberate. By linking *Incidents* and *Sapphira*, I argue the following: Southern-born white writer Cather, likely because of her literary acclaim, reinforced entrenched white supremacy despite her significant insertion of a counterplot to enable othermothering ministrations with abolitionist support. Ultimately, however, unlike Jacobs's subscription to the genre of the abolitionist slave narrative, Cather's novel partakes in plantation nostalgia. Unlike the minor characters working covertly to enable successful escapes from the institution of slavery in Jacobs's text, the majority of minor characters in Cather's novel, who are not plantation owners, are literally suffocated by the whiteness redounding in her fictional agrarian world. In contrast to Cather's novel, Jacobs's *Incidents* provides a retrospective corrective to Cather's *Sapphira*, including portrayals of maternal care among a community of people dedicated to helping unfree people escape from the South, thereby protecting daughters from a foreseeable future of abduction, sexual violence, and forced reproduction.

Published on the eve of the Civil War, *Incidents in the Life of a Slave Girl* reflects an American South on the brink of a regional war, the likes of which the nation had never experienced. Published a year before the United States entered World War II, *Sapphira and the Slave Girl* recursively interweaves a foiled rape plot within a plantation setting, interspersed with Cather's insertions of isolated stories that resolutely distract from the immediate horror, as though the author refuses to reconcile the munificent Virginia landscape with the violence of chattel slavery. In addition, Cather's novel features plantation staples that look back nostalgically to antebellum America, but it is also contrastive to the most egregious local color stereotypes about idealized behavior among free and enslaved people. Regardless, the bonds of loyalty in *Sapphira* are both reified and undone in this disturbing novel that takes a backward look at the American South, obscurely (and paradoxically) showcasing her own family's Confederate and abolitionist past. Reading Jacobs's canonical autobiography alongside Cather's final, largely untaught novel enables a further reckoning of the misreadings of *Sapphira* through a dismissal of the work as an artistic failure rather than what it really is: an assertion of white supremacy.[2]

Jacobs's and Cather's onset narratives do in fact share features of maternal practice that intersect with portrayals of the inner workings of local communities instrumental in coordinating the movements of Black women in the American South. Jacobs and Cather represent interracial communities of men and women whose abolitionist leanings are never fully revealed but whose covert support of Black women help to facilitate their escape north through what I will call maternal plotting. The genres in which each author is engaged supports underground methods to activate scenarios of movement toward escape. Mothers and daughters in *Incidents* and *Sapphira* manage to escape "the house of unbearable death" through their own maternal plotting with help from other figures who deploy covert measures of support to enable these women to escape intolerable lives (Cavarero 65).

Jacobs represents maternal practice in radically innovative ways, introducing a model of maternal womanhood based on a renunciation of slavocracy and an embracing of social equality. I argue in this chapter that Jacobs is quite aware of her era's cultural conceptions of sentimental motherhood and exploits them to service her goal of changing perceptions of Black motherhood under the institution of slavery. Placing Jacobs's narrative of a formerly enslaved woman next to Cather's novel written through the lens of privilege allows me to examine opposing portrayals of Black maternal bodies in antebellum America. Cather cannot represent Black women's subjectivity, obscuring ideas about those white enslavers who claimed people as property in favor of representing variations of propriety for Black and white women, especially mothers.[3] While Jacobs's narrative never strays from a voice simultaneously autobiographical and didactic, Cather's novel registers doubt and imprecision when shifting to memoir in her epilogue.

While both authors include many mother-daughter dyads, my focus on Jacobs's Linda and Cather's Nancy permits me to examine how these resisting daughters are a product of their authors' expansive definition of motherhood, which encourages activist arguments for dismantling racial and sexual hierarchies. For my purposes in this chapter, I focus on Jacobs's adopted literary persona, Linda Brent, the pseudonym she chose to tell a harrowing tale of dissent and escape.[4] Similar in age to Linda Brent when she experiences sexual stalking on plantation space, Nancy of Cather's *Sapphira* must drastically consent to abrupt change in her life, which requires acceding to a planned escape to circumvent imminent sexual violation. To accomplish these goals, Jacobs and Cather redefine concepts of time and space within their narratives, accelerating and/or arresting movement. Radically unhoused, Linda and Nancy must make painstaking decisions that will expedite their ultimate escape from slavery, repudiating abduction and promoting autonomy. Jacobs and Cather incorporate interracial maternal figures who support abolition, subversively destabilizing the long-established infrastructure of slavocracy supported by egregious forms of patriarchy. I want to clarify a separation between interracial maternal figures and female enslavers, insisting here that gestures of maternality organized within mother-daughter configurations are not to be equated with the grossly unequal relationship represented by white women enslavers and enslaved women.[5] While I will discuss, as Toni Morrison has written, "the reckless, unabated power" of a white woman over unfree Black women (*Playing* 25), I will also focus on how resisting daughters, who are often also mothers from Black and white communities alike, implement measures to enable movement for these women.

An ideological framework about motherhood undergirds *Incidents* and *Sapphira*, influencing how each author responds to the crisis of female enslavement in antebellum America. Motherhood as a cultural concept was fully available to Jacobs, who was writing just before the Civil War, and the author skillfully implements a version of this through the cult of true womanhood, to which I shall return in the next section. While set primarily in the American South during the 1850s, Cather's novel nonetheless reflects the contemporary exacerbations of the Great Depression of 1930s America. This period of intensified heterosexual coupling and reproduction also saw the construction of motherhood as a prized subjectivity referred to as "The Good Mother."[6] Cather responds to this "narrow range of maternal values and attitudes" (Fullerton 3) in her own era by originating a new role for a white, Southern daughter of the Confederacy. Neither surrogate nor entirely othermother, Rachel Blake's maternality in antebellum Virginia functions outside dominant norms and certainly in opposition to her mother, Sapphira. Both Jacobs and Cather simultaneously espouse and critique ideological standards of motherhood while portraying how movements are made possible for Black women in the American South. How well each author succeeded in showcasing alternative portrayals of motherhood remains debatable for Cather in my view, but both authors created more complex meanings of maternity for women who mothered during the antebellum period.

Jacobs's Enslaved Mother: True Womanhood, Moral Motherhood

Jacobs's *Incidents* is a foundational American story about Black mothers and daughters.[7] The relationship between mother and daughter in Jacobs's narrative invites a careful reconsideration of maternal subjectivity as the author's life story takes us well beyond the pages of her book and into the social and civic realm where she and her daughter continued their abolitionist and educational work.[8] Jacobs's representation of mothering under enslavement engages with ideas about caretaking across race, region, gender, and sexuality and stands as a testimonial to how a writer such as Jacobs navigated space and time through a carefully nuanced use of language that both highlighted the centrality of a redefined practice of motherhood and simultaneously challenged the ideological rigidity of Northern white women's codes of maternal conduct.

Jacobs represents her literary persona, Linda Brent, as a moral mother. She also projects an imagined maternal body for her Northern female audience by juxtaposing an enslaved woman's corporeal body to a refined maternal body through her constructed persona, Linda Brent. Jacobs represents Linda Brent as encompassing both subjectivities: a Black body and a transcendent mother's body, both of which literally disappear in the text.[9] As Nora Doyle explains, by the beginning of the nineteenth century, ideas about motherhood become centralized within a discourse about "American notions of virtuous womanhood," marking "a significant departure from long-standing notions of female corporeality. By emphasizing emotional and moral qualities, cultural representations of sentimental motherhood contested the ways [white] women had been defined as inferior and corrupted by their bodies" (N. Doyle 4–5).

Significantly, Jacobs characterizes Linda's mothering as encompassing traits of sentimental motherhood, that is, the narrator recognizes the "power of feeling" as central to the definition of the good mother. Despite exhibiting moral and emotional qualities of mothering, Linda Brent cannot entirely efface her body as she is neither white nor free; her seven-year captivity compels her to acknowledge a corporeally enslaved woman who is also a maternal self. Jacobs's creation of a literary persona in Linda Brent allows the author vital privacy: she can establish a spatial separation that is both emotional and corporeal. Thus, Jacobs's narrative itself, as Miranda Green-Barteet explains, functions as an interstitial space, "an in-between location arguably more public than private, in which she is able to discuss private matters, such as motherhood, sexuality, and abuse, in a public forum" (55). Jacobs recalls incidents in the life of an enslaved "girl," and, at fifteen, that girl must make unavoidable decisions about her body to escape the further trap of becoming her enslaver's sex slave. In this way, Jacobs's portrayal of Linda's struggle to maintain her virtue parallels Nancy's in *Sapphira*: both girls take extreme measures to resist being treated like sexual fodder by white enslavers.

Throughout *Incidents*, Jacobs clarifies that Linda Brent's maternal authority ultimately emerges from her status as an unfree woman; as Stephanie Li explains, "It is precisely through her flesh as both mother and slave woman that Harriet A. Jacobs . . . claims the insurgent ground of her social identity and formulates her resistance to human bondage" ("Motherhood as Resistance" 14). Jacobs continues to represent Linda as claiming the "moral and emotional" high ground that comes with being a good mother (N. Doyle 7) by counterpoising Linda's steadfast maternal affections against those of an unrestrained and disorderly woman enslaver. In choosing a literary persona in Linda Brent, Jacobs redefines the cult of true womanhood through a variation of sentimental motherhood: portraying not only the physical victimization of Linda's body under slavery but also her affective life as a mother.[10] As a result, Jacobs enlarges conceptions of motherhood to include a definition of maternity that transcends solely biological relations. As Li writes, for Jacobs, motherhood "encompasses an entire worldview: a belief in the liberation of all people, a commitment to human equality, and an establishment of viable, egalitarian economic opportunities" ("Motherhood" 21).[11] This worldbuilding view is promulgated throughout Jacobs's narrative.

Jacobs's first four chapters of *Incidents* offer important details of her early life in North Carolina, where she was born during slavery in 1813. These introductory chapters serve as both an overview and a prediction of Jacobs's simultaneous focus on abusive power, maternal love, and Black agency. Jacobs details an enslaved girl's upbringing at the beginning of the nineteenth century in the port town of Edenton, North Carolina. According to the 1790 census, Edenton comprised about 150 houses and a population numbering about "1,000 black slaves—and 600 whites, a third of whom owned no slaves," a ratio more starkly established in Cather's novel (Yellin, *Harriet Jacobs* 5; Inscoe n. 26). Closely analyzing Jacobs's introductory chapters establishes an understanding of how the author enfolds her literary enslaved narrator into a structure of belonging that enables her resistance and eventuates in her escape.

Chapters 1 through 4 of *Incidents in the Life of a Slave Girl* offer in microcosm an organizational structure and rhetorical style that epitomize Jacobs's dual goal: to narrate an enslaved female's life as a mother and an enslaved person and to critique the manifold hypocrisies and cruelties of slavocracy. Jacobs's narration significantly begins before Linda reaches puberty, but the content within exposes a genealogy of miscegenation, repeated attempts by family members to escape slavery, and the deaths of both her mother and father. An orphan by the age of thirteen, Jacobs clarifies in chapter 1, "Childhood," that despite being enslaved, Linda remained unaware of her status until aged six.[12] Loved and cared for by her parents and extended family, including instrumental othermothers, especially her maternal grandmother and Aunt Nancy, Jacobs offers her Northern female audience a portrayal of family life disrupted, exploited, and abused by slavery. Bequeathed to the five-year-old daughter of her female enslaver's sister after her death, Linda's former status as "free from care as that of any free-born white child" is a myth quickly dispelled by the facts of her life in the Flint household (*Incidents* 7).

By introducing and then undercutting such comparisons between unfree and free children as ineffectual euphemism, Jacobs prepares readers to question the rhetorical ploys of white slavers who make promises they never keep. Despite being recognized as never more than a valuable piece of property, Linda blesses the memory of her female enslaver for teaching her to read and spell, which will permit her later to control time when in hiding. Nonetheless, Linda is unable to blot out of her memory of "that one great wrong" from an enslaver who facilitated her literacy and taught her to sew but whose empty promise is illuminated by Linda's grandmother and two members of her family who are summarily placed on the auction block after the death of her female enslaver (8).[13] Chattel slavery is buttressed by the deathbed codicil of an enslaver, and, under the "perversions of judicial power," the peculiar institution impels enslavers to "*treat* the enslaved as property, not as person" (Spillers, "Mama's Baby" 78). A poignant example of Jacobs portraying how a person becomes property occurs in chapter 2, "The New Master and Mistress." Linda learns from her grandmother that her father has suddenly died, but she is prohibited by the Flint family from going to her father's bedside. Jacobs sets this prohibition against chapters 3 and 4 that focus on auctions of enslaved peoples and consequences of enslaved persons who make escapes, "The Slaves' New Year's Day" and "The Slave Who Dared to Feel Like a Man." In these chapters, Jacobs places her literary persona in juxtaposition with her uncle Benjamin, whose multiple attempts to escape slavery eventually led to success. Recognizing by age fourteen that the "war of her life had begun," Linda explains, "I had not lived fourteen years in slavery for nothing." Shored up by her uncle's example, Linda resolves "never to be conquered," modeling herself on the manhood she sees displayed by Benjamin in her early years of life (*Incidents* 19).

These first chapters of *Incidents* recall situations in which Linda regularly resists being transformed from "personality into property" (Spillers 78). Learning how to survive with little or no control over how and where she spends her time, Jacobs represents Linda as regularly resisting dehumanization, biding her time carefully by visiting her parents' gravesite on the day before her escape, all the while knowing that she is entering a phase of her life that feels like death but that will ultimately secure a new life in freedom (*Incidents* 90). Jacobs keeps silent in *Incidents* about the name and location of this gravesite. Bought communally by free blacks, Providence was "their crowning effort to create their own space"; and Jacobs portrays this "providentially inaccessible plot" (Yellin, *Harriet* 19) during a time when Linda Brent is precariously located on one of the Flint family's plantations. Sharing this information bodes well for Linda, who remains determined to escape slavery *and* maintain her commitment to motherhood as she has given birth to two children by this time. Having refused Dr. Flint's advances to ensure her entrapment by building a separate "cottage" for her to live in (inverting the public-private dichotomy by taking the idea of separate spheres to suggest sexual enslavement), Linda subverts his plan through pregnancy with a white man of "higher status than Norcum [Flint]."[14] Gloria T. Randle explains that Brent's decision to enter into a sexual liaison with a white man in her community "is clearly a preemptive move on her part, painfully borne, not of a lack of moral values, but of a fierce resolve to spare herself from the dreaded Dr. Flint's sexual advances at any cost" (49). Jacobs's decision to include this excruciating response by Linda to her untenable circumstances is also her refusal to abide by a definition of true womanhood that excludes enslaved Black women.

By admitting to taking a "headlong plunge" into a sexual liaison with a white man, Linda recognizes that she shocks and disappoints her virtuous white readers. Within the same paragraph, however, Jacobs as the older interlocutor interprets her persona's youthful decision through the lens of race: "I feel that the slave woman ought not to be judged by the same standard as others" (55, 56). By which Jacobs means to say without pointing a finger: you white women up North who are free should not make a judgment against Linda Brent, who has rhetorically castigated herself and fallen on her knees in shame to her readers. Issuing a statement through Linda that sounds rhetorically more like a casual comment than a manifesto—enslaved women ought not to be judged by the same standard as free women—Jacobs proclaims a radical alternative to the sexual ideology that informs her confession. Virtuous motherhood has undergone radical revision by Harriet Jacobs: it will assist her fictionalized persona, Linda, in plotting her way toward freedom.

Cather's Unimagined Black Motherhood

In stark contrast to Jacobs's presentation of Linda's interior thoughts, *Sapphira and the Slave Girl* succeeds in replicating Cather's inability to access Black women's personal experiences of unfreedom. When Toni Morrison describes the mother-daughter relationship between Till and Nancy as "wholly unanalyzed," she illuminates Cather's decision to ignore any attempt at "historical discourse on slave parent-child relationships and pain" (*Playing* 21). After Rachel Blake (Sapphira's daughter) arranges for Nancy's escape through the underground railroad, Nancy's history as an enslaved person ends. We do not hear from or about Nancy until the epilogue of the novel, which Cather advances twenty-five years later in the 1880s. The one "furtive exchange" (Morrison, *Playing* 21) between Till and Rachel occurs when Till asks after her daughter, rhetorically using indirection to phrase her question: "You ain't heard nothing, Miss Rachel?" (245). As Morrison explains, "The contemporary reader is relieved when Till finally finds the language and occasion to make this inquiry about the fate of her daughter. But nothing more is made of it" (*Playing* 22). Morrison attributes this silence to an assumption shared by many whites in antebellum and postbellum culture that enslaved women are "not mothers; they are 'natally dead,' with no obligations to their offspring or their own parents" (*Playing* 21). Of course, Jacobs's autobiography gives the lie to this belief by refusing to allow institutionalized slavery to thwart her faith in the efficacy of maternal love, her own and that of her parents. While Cather scholars have offered other explanations for Till's silence, including feigning lack of care about Nancy's disappearance as a form of protection for both mother and daughter, Cather's representation of enslaved mothers and daughters leaves no doubt to my mind that the author was ill equipped to access or imagine Black Americans existentially.[15] As Ann Romines suggests, Cather's ambivalent position replicates "the strain and difficulty—if not the impossibility—of accessing African Americans' experience of slavery in a novel by a white Virginian who was born in 1873" ("Historical Essay" 317). This white Virginian was a heralded, canonical American writer by this time, so Cather's lack of imagination seems deliberate and racist.

What *Sapphira and the Slave Girl* purports to be about and what it is are two very different things. The front-cover endorsement on the paperback edition reads, "A novel of jealousy set in pre–Civil War

Virginia," which utilizes a well-known trope of narratives about enslaved persons, the irrationally jealous "mistress."[16] While this focus is arguable, it clearly misses the point as Sapphira is entirely rational in her desire to maintain her power from her wheelchair. Her cruelty emerges less from what Morrison calls a "feverish imagination" (*Playing* 19) than from her refusal to cede power to anyone, including her husband, a miller from the remote region of Back Creek, who has allowed his wife's aristocratic position (coming from an elite planter family) to go unchallenged until the narrative begins. While the novel is about a female enslaver's machinations to maintain power, Morrison and other scholars approach this focus through a critical-race lens, arguing that Cather struggled to "address an almost completely buried subject: the interdependent working of power, race, and sexuality in a white woman's battle for coherence" (*Playing* 20).[17] It seems that all editions of Cather's novel, including the scholarly edition, continue to bury the subject of race, which, by contrast, is patently the focus of Jacobs's abolitionist narrative.

In its summary announcement of the novel, the Willa Cather scholarly edition of *Sapphira and the Slave Girl*, published in 2009, mostly manages to ignore a critical-race focus but does offer a persuasive description of the author's narrative intentions: "Set in Cather's Virginia birthplace in 1856, the novel draws on family and local history and the escalating conflicts of the last years of slavery—conflicts in which Cather's family members were deeply involved, both as slave owners and opponents of slavery. . . . Cather powerfully and sparely renders a Virginia world that is simultaneously beautiful and, as she said, " 'terrible.' " In "Willa Cather's Civil War: A Very Long Engagement," Romines explains the possible meanings of the something "terrible," describing it as an "estranging force beneath the surfaces (often pleasant) of domestic life" (19).[18] Neither a novel solely about a vengeful woman enslaver nor about the flora and fauna of a slave state before the Civil War, *Sapphira and the Slave Girl* reenvisions white Southern womanhood within a classical paradigm of the mother-daughter plot. In doing so, Cather attempts to redefine Southern women's emergence from a plantation economy to a more egalitarian society by using what I call an ethics of maternality, displaying subversion by abolitionist-leaning characters who work within the patriarchal regime. By tracing Cather's progressive vision of racial progress in *Sapphira*, Nghana Lewis promulgates an aesthetics of civil rights: "By subverting the imbrication of white dominance and black oppression in a cultural system, . . . Cather—via Rachel—revitalizes the myth of Southern Womanhood, affirming its authority to promote racial progress in a modern southern context" (54). Cather arguably achieves this revitalization through Rachel, the daughter of Sapphira.

The conflict between this mother and daughter remains unresolved throughout *Sapphira and the Slave Girl*, emerging at the novel's beginning but remaining just beneath the surface, hidden by outward manifestations of decorum to which Sapphira subscribes.[19] The "fixed ways" of plantation slavery found to be satisfying to Sapphira are anathema to her daughter, Rachel, and ambiguously tolerated by her husband, Henry Colbert (*Sapphira* 19). As Romines reminds us, "This tradition of selective silence is part of the southern inheritance Willa Cather brought to her last novel" ("Historical Essay," *Sapphira* 320). Cather's canny description of the Mill House nonetheless reinforces the subterranean impulse informing how she will narrate the story: "All was orderly in front. . . . Behind the house lay another world; a helter-skelter scattering, like a small village" (*Sapphira* 23). Cather's silence on the interior lives of this "small village" of enslaved people on plantation space does not prevent her from displaying in grotesque detail the malevolence of the enslaver character, Sapphira, whose plotting contradicts all understanding of moral motherhood, starkly contrasting Jacobs's multiple depictions of moral mothers in *Incidents*.

In the first two chapters of *Sapphira and the Slave Girl*, Cather creates a twice-told tale, both told Southern style. Book 1, "Sapphira and Her Household," encapsulates the racial, gendered, and regional conflicts accentuating the entire novel. Conflict between Sapphira and her husband is introduced immediately in the first chapter as Henry refuses to sign the deed to "sell" the Black girl, Nancy, which is Sapphira's request. Although he is beneath his wife in station, his gender supersedes her class status as he has the power of the pen.[20] Henry's refusal—"we don't sell our people"—sets in motion the sexual assault plot Sapphira designs to fight against her husband's patriarchal prerogative. Sotto voce, Sapphira says, "Then we must find some other way" (13). Unbeknownst to herself, but clearly not to her author, Sapphira instigates the novel's trajectory toward the redefined American South of her daughter, Rachel.

This route toward change is made apparent when Rachel visits her mother in chapter 2 of *Sapphira*. Cather juxtaposes opposing world views through her descriptive characterizations of each woman's behavior. Functioning both recursively and subversively, this chapter sets the plot on a collision course: Rachel's unstated advocacy of republican motherhood, which is "responsible for raising worthy citizens, a recognition of the intersection of women's private actions and the public interest of the nation"

(Kennedy 15), directly contradicts her mother's dehumanizing treatment of those enslaved. Sapphira's dropsical condition, which leaves her bound to a wheelchair, is immediately counterpoised by her daughter's outdoor movements. Serving as a skillful nurse to the community, Rachel's perambulations about town and through "back doors" where Sapphira's enslaved persons come and go, constitute a care-driven ethic not solely or merely based on maternity. Rachel's very being disrupts her mother's racial and class biases, and her status as a widowed mother herself inoculates her from being socially distrusted, but it also positions her to inhabit spaces that will engender the advent of a revisionary interpretation of autonomy for Black women on plantation space.

In chapter 2, Cather describes Sapphira sitting at her "dressing table before a gilt mirror" evoking the nineteenth-century fairy tale of "Snow White" about a wicked and vain woman in front of her magic mirror.[21] Readers acquainted with the queen's plan to have Snow White killed in the forest will immediately apprehend how Sapphira's plot and Cather's novel will end, though the author spares Sapphira the queen's death dance in red-hot iron slippers. Linked to this type of folktale is an earlier Italian tale entitled "The Young Slave," in which a wife jealous of the beauty of her husband's niece enslaves her.[22] Key features in both folktales include mirrors, coffins, forests, and combs: all references Cather makes in chapter 2, an antebellum American version of the angry stepmother and the young enslaved girl. Rachel Blake will interrupt this narrative on behalf of her commitment to abolition.

In fact, before Rachel enters her mother's boudoir, she hears the smacking sound of a wooden hairbrush striking the arm of Nancy, Sapphira's waiting maid. Cather's first description of "Mrs. Colbert" in her daughter's presence includes Sapphira sitting at her "dressing table before a gilt mirror, a white combing-cloth about her shoulders" (17).[23] When Rachel takes leave of her mother, she goes "the back way," which immerses her in spaces of captivity. Rachel Blake is tactless and insensitive about Black space. With injudicious abandon, Rachel enters the backyard and locations of captivity of enslaved people.[24] The laundry cabin is part of the slave quarters, a border space that functions interstitially between private and public acts. Like the kitchen space, it is separate from the main house and the location where Nancy both completes domestic work (ironing, washing) and privately cries after being verbally and physically abused by Sapphira. Rachel's intrusion into this space is also propitious as it is in this scene that she sees Nancy's eyes, "still red from crying." Rachel's observations briefly focus on Nancy's feelings, having fallen "out of favor" with Sapphira; in this space, Cather racializes Nancy as a "yellow girl," but where Cather sees yellow, Rachel sees pale gold, a beautiful girl child, whose skin tone also reveals a genealogy of miscegenation (21). What Rachel further observes is an innocent girl, an expert ironer with red marks on her arm and whose situation is precarious.[25] In an attempt to validate Willa Cather as a socially aware critic of Southern issues, Traci B. Abbott argues that Nancy's situation is best understood through the work of Black activists and journalists in the 1890s who promoted "imagery of non-sexual, modest womanhood" to reinforce "middle class standards of female propriety" by encouraging "female agency over their bodies and homes, utilizing progressive and scientific rhetoric to redefine black female" sexuality (31). Both Jacobs and Cather spatialize the struggles of Black characters, especially through depictions of the girlhoods and early womanhood of Linda and Nancy, under plantation domination, which Jacobs refuses to normalize, but which Cather naturalizes through a homage to the Virginian countryside. How and where Linda and Nancy inhabit liminal spaces in settings where white people held Blacks in slavery prepares them for movement elsewhere.

Space Matters: Jacobs's Garret

To escape the miscegenistic culture of sexual violence that threatens their bodies, Linda and Nancy must negotiate spaces under extreme forms of geographic domination. In her interdisciplinary analysis of Black women's geographies in the diaspora, Katherine McKittrick writes that "black matters are spatial matters" (xii).[26] Jacobs and Cather represent Linda and Nancy under siege and in spaces racialized by "seemingly predetermined stabilities" set by infrastructures of plantation slavery in the antebellum South (McKittrick xi). Despite their hypervisibility, these young women hide in plain sight, occupying enclosed and bounded spaces, both inside and outside, to inhabit what Jenny Sharpe calls " 'crevices of power' necessary to enslavement and from this location some were able to manipulate and recast the meanings of slavery's geographic terrain" (as qtd. in McKittrick xvi). Taking her lead from what Doreen Massey calls "space-time," Minrose Gwin maintains that aesthetic productions, "themselves temporal," "make space never occur outside time" (24). In their daring escapes, these young women enter spaces that profoundly alter their conceptions of time, enclosing them within maternal structures of belonging that enable their mobility. While both authors use the idea of delay in diametrically different ways (protracted versus accelerated), they simultaneously challenge linear conceptions of time by depicting less segmented notions about progress in their portrayals of Black women's escape from slavery. In doing so, Jacobs's Linda and Cather's Nancy enter a space-time continuum that is more cyclical and recursive than straightforward, allowing each woman to bond with othermothers and underground communities who enable their healing and mobility. Within their constrained spaces, Linda and Nancy manage to create a diasporic space (a waiting space that enables eventual movement) to subvert the "perimeters [of their] bondage" (McKittrick 40).

Early in *Incidents,* Harriet Jacobs characterizes Linda's refusal to be sexual prey for Dr. Flint through references to spaces within the Edenton community, including her grandmother's house, to which I shall return. Recognizing the ruinous desire involved in Dr. Flint's having built a "cottage" for her, Linda does not need expertise in domestic architecture to know its fundamentally antidomestic meaning: sexual enslavement.[27] Given the false choice to live with her children in the cottage or be sent to the plantation gifted by Dr. Flint to his son, Linda chooses the latter. Recognizing the spurious nature of Flint's promise of "a home and freedom!" (83), Linda leaves with her children for Auburn, a "435-acre plantation near Albemarle Sound that produced cotton and corn" about twelve miles away from her grandmother's house (*Incidents* 274, note 2). On plantation space, Linda carefully plans her escape, subverting conventional ideas about motherhood and true womanhood in order to "foil my master and save my children, or I would perish in the attempt" (84). Modeling herself on white, male subjectivity, Linda takes her cue in this passage from Patrick Henry, whom she directly quotes in chapter 18, "Months of Peril," selecting as her motto the founding father's famous declaration "Give me liberty or give me death!" (99). Jacobs regularly depicts her literary persona, Linda Brent, as well-versed in political history as she is in Bible stories and literary notables. In addition, as Joanne M. Braxton suggests, for a brief period, Jacobs portrays Linda Brent as an "American Maroon, a rebel and a fugitive from slavery," taking to the woods with help from her maternal grandmother and others in the community who support her efforts (301).

Jacobs presents Linda as willing to risk familial and community disapprobation by seeming to abandon her children when she escapes from the plantation. This plan is motivated by her desire to secure her children's freedom through a sale to Mr. Sands.[28] In order to assure her children's freedom, Linda relies on and upends the cult of true womanhood to manage her escape. She says, "They thought my children's being there would fetter me to the spot, and that it was a good place to break us all in to abject submission to our lot as slaves" (93–94).[29] Guided by the unswerving objective of freeing her children, Linda escapes at night, concealed in predetermined and improvised places and supported by white and Black members of the community. Before she is concealed in a detached kitchen, Linda is hidden in attic space in the main house by her friend, Betty, the cook-slave, whose female enslaver supports this measure and maintains friendly ties to Linda's grandmother. Katja Kanzler describes such liminal domestic spaces as "too small or too slippery to control (in material as well as epistemic terms) for slavery to fully colonize" (349). After Betty swiftly removes Linda from the attic to the kitchen for safety's sake, the detached space serves as the one room where "the operations of slavery become most readily intelligible" (Kanzler 344). There, Linda is given shelter under a floor plank, which she describes as close to the grave as death: "In my shallow bed I had but just room enough to bring my hands to my face to keep the dust out of my eyes; for Betty walked over me twenty times in an hour. . . . [A]nd as she walked back and forth, in the performance of her culinary duties, she talked apparently to herself, but with the intention that I should hear what was going on" (*Incidents* 103, 110). From this "polymorphous space," the kitchen functions as both "contact zone" and "perfect seclusion" (Kanzler 348) while Linda is kept updated on the status of her children and the false leads regarding her whereabouts, which Flint continues to follow.

Jacobs foreshadows Linda's narrative trajectory toward enclosure by focusing on close calls in detection and multiple moves (including a short stay at the Dismal Swamp) before her final relocation to her grandmother's garret.[30] For Jacobs, both the local swamp and the garret space function simultaneously as dismal holes and subversive spaces for survival. Jacobs's narrative shifts from characterizing Linda's escape pattern of cloak-and-dagger concealments to what Georgia Krieger calls "live entombment, . . . a protracted encounter with death" (610). Entering a nonsequential form of time and a spatial crevice that permits her to resist racial and sexual degradation, Linda describes the dueling perceptions she has of her garret space as both a "dismal hole" and a "loophole of retreat" (113, 114). Sarah Stefana Smith references Spillers's description, the "not-quite space," alongside McKittrick's verbal, "garreting," to highlight the "implausible, but real acts of seeing and overhearing that take place" when Linda is in hiding: "Thus the importance of Jacobs's story in the pantheon of the [Liberation] narrative and Black study—we are made privy to a moment of not-quite space and not-quite temporality, the loophole of retreat, whereby a life, Black life, exists in extreme violence and power" (15).

Jacobs characterizes Linda's seven-year ordeal through her paradoxical creation of diasporic space and not-quite space through repeated acts of maternal love. In doing so, Jacobs portrays Linda as resisting domination and mothering her children while inhabiting "a third mediating space, . . . neither slavery nor freedom," as Randle explains (50). Prepared for by her carpenter Uncle during Linda's perilous movements to stay undetected, the narrator's multiple nomenclatures to describe this space—shed, den, cell, retreat, concealment, hole, dungeon—according to Green-Barteet, is Jacobs's conscious decision to "position the garret as a border space . . . a makeshift space, . . . The least desirable location in her grandmother's house" (53, 54).[31] By using actual measurements to describe her loophole of retreat, Linda illustrates the exacting nature of her focus to achieve freedom for her children and to undergo extreme forms of sensory deprivation and physical debilitation to ensure her own sexual autonomy while guaranteeing her children's ultimate freedom from the institution of slavery, both of which she achieves.[32] In chapter 21, "The Loophole of Retreat," Linda describes the small shed to which she will be confined for seven years as "only nine feet long and seven wide. The highest part was three feet high, and sloped down abruptly to the loose board floor" (114).

Jacobs's inclusion of the actual measurements of the shed is a literal and figurative calculation on her part, reminding her Northern white readers of the extremity to which she will go to escape an intolerable system. Linda takes up her tomblike residence with the same exactitude she demonstrates for her motherhood: she will survive her living death to attain freedom for herself and her children.

Steadfastly supporting her physical and emotional needs, Linda's family conceals her in a space that is as uninhabitable as it is incongruously empowering. Hollowing out three holes with a gimlet near the trap door of her shed, Linda bores out "the interstices" between, allowing her loophole of retreat to become a material presence and physical fortification through which she will negotiate the terms of her freedom as a woman and a mother (115) (see figure 1.1). As Green-Barteet argues, the interstitial nature of the garret itself will allow Linda to "empower herself," as

Figure 1.1. *Molly Horniblow's House: Reconstruction to Scale of Elevation and Floor Plan Jacobs's Hiding Place*, designed and drawn by Carl L. Lounsbury, Colonial Williamsburg Foundation, image #D2022-COPY-1017-0001.

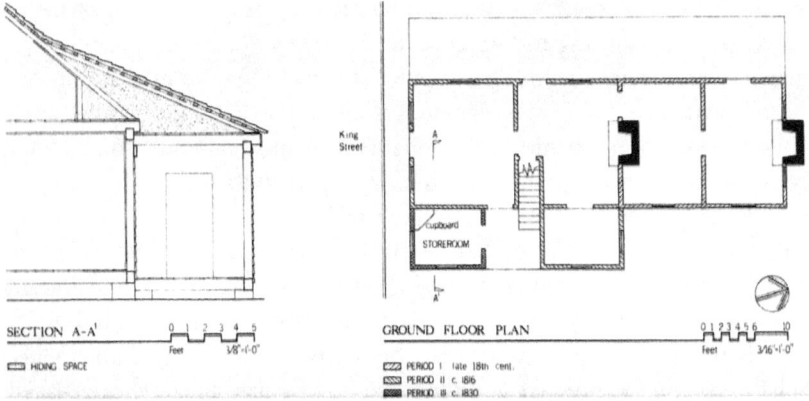

such spaces, according to Margaret E. Farrar, "intervene between things, especially things considered to be opposites, in such a way as to unsettle them both" (as qtd. in Green-Barteet 56). As Jacobs's mouthpiece, Linda's narrative permits the author to gain emotional respite from the deeply disturbing parts of her story under slavery, claiming "a space of her own and openly engag[ing]in public debates surrounding slavery and womanhood" (Green-Barteet 66). Within that space, however, Jacobs shares with her readers that Brent's garret life is an ongoing struggle with despair, the deadliest of sins in Christian belief and only diminished by her prayers to God: "Alone in my cell, where no eye but God's could see me, I wept bitter tears. How earnestly I prayed to him to restore me to my children and enable me to be a useful and a good mother!" (133) Conditioned on hope despite a "dark past" and "the uncertain future," Linda's prayers to God focus unabatedly on her commitment to a cardinal virtue of true womanhood: motherhood within domesticity and Christian piety (133).

A little over midway through her garret internment, Linda employs her literacy to good effect. In chapter 25, "Competition in Cunning," Jacobs inserts letter writing to create diasporic space, further anticipating Linda's migration north and ultimately beyond national borders, when she visits England for ten months in 1845. From her garret space, Linda writes letters to her grandmother and Dr. Flint, arranging for a friend to transport her letters to New York to be posted from there, manipulating the enslaver into believing she is living in the North. The ruse successfully assures Linda that there remains "no suspicion of my being anywhere in the vicinity," permitting her to leave her "cell, sometimes and exercise my limbs to prevent my becoming a cripple" (132). Using what little storeroom space is available, Linda's regular exercising prepares her for escape north when the occasion permits. As Stephanie Y. Evans contends, though "far from the notion of yoga for fitness as it is perceived today, stretching is described by Jacobs as necessary and desirable for basic health," and, along with other freedom fighters like Sojourner Truth and Harriet Tubman, "Harriet Jacobs's story is one of the earliest examples of self-empowerment narratives," but in this case, explicitly about "sexual violence" (180–81).

During her captivity, Jacobs implicitly alludes to her first slave "mistress," whose "one great wrong" in not freeing those she enslaved has resulted in years of confinement and bodily torture for Linda, who nonetheless manages to use her literacy skills to gain advantage over those in power, winning the competition in cunning. As William L. Andrews explains, "Jacobs's first experiments in writing let her play the role of slave trickster lodged in the interstices of a social structure that she pries apart with her spying eyes and her ventriloquist voice. She takes the power that comes with the point of a pen to project an alter ego in freedom up North. . . . In her garret, where she reads and sews, she wields a literary needle that injects her master's mind . . . with poisonous 'delusions.'" (259). Always aware that virtuous womanhood means guiding children's "moral and intellectual development" (N. Doyle 4), Jacobs represents Linda as wielding more than a literary needle as she uses both literal pen and needle in material and manipulable ways. Just as she uses the pen to pronounce that she would be free in the North to set an example of virtuous motherhood for her children (129), Linda uses the needle to sew "some new garments and little playthings for my children" (118). Performing this sartorial ritual under egregious conditions reinforces Jacobs's subscription to the cult of true womanhood for a Black mother, who understands the importance of clothing to shelter and protect Black bodies too readily exposed by slavocracy. Jacobs's focus on the material realities of moral motherhood extends throughout *Incidents* to Linda Brent's maternal narrative as she continuously attempts to embrace the dominant ideology of sentimental [white] motherhood to illustrate her commitment to her Northern female readers who uphold feminine ideologies of maternal superiority and the importance of emotional sensibility. At the same time, Jacobs employs the intersecting activities of writing and sewing to manage unsegmented time; like Penelope, "her job is to weave, not to unweave. . . . As long as she can delay . . . she does not belong to him, even though she is under siege" (Cavarero 11). Jacobs's letters north serve to manipulate the plot by both delaying detection and putting in place measures of escape. Jacobs represents the summit of moral motherhood in Linda's final interview with her daughter, Ellen, who is thereafter sent north to one of Mr. Sands's relatives.[33]

Jacobs utilizes the mother-daughter interview as a tableau to showcase virtuous motherhood. Linda holds her daughter, Ellen, in her arms throughout the night, embodying sentimental motherhood, resonating with qualities of the *Pietà*. Within the span of one night, Linda must (re-)introduce herself as the mother to her young daughter *and* inform her daughter of her mother's status as an enslaved person; it is the only night mother and child share together. Refusing to allow her daughter to see her mother in her "wretched hiding place," Linda begs permission to return to her grandmother's upstairs bedroom, where she gave birth to both children. Recognizing the risk in exacting a promise of silence and secrecy from her young daughter, Linda's maternal feelings about her child prove to be true; as Ellen promises, "Mother, I will never tell," Linda replies, "And she never did" (141).[34] Seeking to liberate those enslaved, Jacobs deploys interstitial spaces and nonsequential forms of time invisible to slavocracy, focusing in microscopic detail on Linda's determined commitment to escape slavery in order to practice maternal love in freedom.

Space Matters: Cather's Double §

Harriet Jacobs offers her readers an unblinkered view of what domesticity looks like in the North for an enslaved person who must redefine conceptions of home in light of her dispersal. Once she has escaped, Linda Brent's precarious position continues unabated, separating her from her children. In contrast, Willa Cather elides information about the complexities of Nancy's displacement after she escapes the Colbert plantation. Readers wait twenty-five years before Nancy reappears in *Sapphira and the Slave Girl*. This reputed reunion between Till and Nancy is constrained by a first-person white narrator (purportedly a prepubescent Cather) who is unable to represent Black women's subjective feelings, maternal or otherwise. Scholars have largely accepted Cather's artistic subscription to the "thing not named," to examine the reticence or "unfurnished" quality in many of her novels, though *Sapphira*'s devotion to detail belies this in so many ways. What becomes quite apparent is Cather's explicable focus on slavery which has a distinct surface feel for those who suffer on its terrain. That texture is the thing "felt and not heard."[35] Cather inserts both topographical and typographical references to slavery's ubiquity, inscribing chattelism through literal and figurative spaces that intersect with local and national antebellum history.

In addition, though Cather scholars have examined mother-daughter dyads in *Sapphira*, they have tended to focus on familial bonds or, falsely, on interracial bonds between women slavers and enslaved women. As Lisa Marcus writes, the one interracial relationship that is not about "a white subject who needs that degraded other to consolidate his or her own white subjectivity," is that between Nancy and Rachel, notwithstanding their unequal status (113). The alternative maternality Cather proposes in *Sapphira* occurs through the creation of this coupling, which comprises the following: a disclosure of maternal plotting mapped onto the ancient Greek story of Demeter-Persephone; and a legerdemain performance of racialism and classism on Southern soil before Nancy makes her escape. Abetted by a tacit though one-sided agreement between a frightened young woman and a privileged white woman, Nancy's escape results from Rachel's radical protest as she privately denounces slavery. Only by having refused to abide by "plantation proprieties," relating to her gender, race, and class, is Rachel able to effect Nancy's escape through the underground railroad.[36]

Set twenty-five years later in the 1880s and written as a first-person epilogue, book 9 of *Sapphira and the Slave Girl* is still typographically flanked by slavery. The iconography of the double § precedes each of the two chapters, suggesting a perverse form of intransigence that relies on white supremacy rather than on critique to maintain antebellum conventions of white Southern womanhood. Cather does attempt to disrupt those conventions through Nancy and Rachel's brave act, to which I shall return.[37] As Patricia Yaeger explains, "These double *Ss* are re-created typographically, in Cather's own text, marking the space before each numeral that denotes a chapter heading, suggesting that we should read each chapter as 'Slavery 1,' 'Slavery 2,' et cetera." (147). Like it or not, we cannot get away from it: it's in the air, like the particles of dust from Henry Colbert's flour mill. Similar to her repeated references to "land-and-chapterscapes rutted with Ss," Cather spatializes this plantation economy through an excess of botanical delights and flour particles, "at once too mimetic and too hyperbolic in its duplications of this world's sociology of color" (Yaeger 147). The landscape of *Sapphira* tells the story Cather cannot tell through characterization as it would require her to create, as Marilyn Mobley McKenzie explains, "a requisite interior life for her slave girl or her mother" (86).

Sapphira's topography, however, "reproduces the problem driving Cather's novel—that the black labor of enslaved persons like Sampson and Nancy continually reproduces the 'unearthly' whiteness of the air-drifting flour as well as the ether of white capital that keeps them enslaved" (Yaeger 147–48). Black labor is made invisible by their separate cabins on the farm—the kitchen, the laundry room, the smokehouse—segregated spaces that buttress the plantation economy, as Cather makes few overt references to the ceaseless labor of Colbert's enslaved persons. Instead, as her jacket-copy description of *Sapphira* advertises, this novel is about "the subtle persecution of a beautiful mulatto by her jealous mistress," thus reducing Black women's labor "from 'visibility' as a context," and replacing it with a "rubric of sexualized competition between mistress and female slave," sexualizing Nancy's labor itself.[38] As a result, the assault plot that constrains Nancy's movement "explicitly dramatizes the manner in which Sapphira ruthlessly extracts a kind of sexualized labor from Nancy, by acting the 'pimp' to Martin's 'john'" (Wald 93). Using the language of indirection permits Cather to talk about what she cannot talk about with regard to race and sexuality. In her vicious effort to maintain power, Sapphira's violent scheme grotesquely contributes to the stereotype of Black female sexual immorality. Yet this effort stands in stark contrast to Cather's depiction of Nancy as a nonsexual young woman who epitomizes the cardinal virtues of true womanhood! It makes this plot scenario pathologically obscene.

Sapphira successfully arranges for Martin Colbert, Henry's nephew, to visit Back Creek, knowing that his reputation as a sexual predator precedes him. Book 6 of *Sapphira*, "Sampson Speaks to the Master," occurs more than halfway through the novel, after Nancy screams for help and is rescued by her stepfather and Sampson, the head mill hand, from the clutches of Martin, who tries to accost her in the cherry grove. After Sapphira sets in place the sexual assault plot in book 1, three other books intervene before Martin's visit in book 5 and Sampson's admission to Henry Colbert of Nancy's taking "sick" after the cherry-picking scene (190). Cather's interpolations of other stories in books 2, 3, and 4 redirect the novel's plot to focus on the back stories of Till and Rachel and the relationships between landed whites and the larger Blue Ridge communities of mountain folk. This disruption might charitably be read as Cather's systematic decision to "displace the seduction plot" as Lewis explains, thereby undermining "Sapphira's authority, and authoriz[ing] Nancy's release through Rachel's activism" (45, 44). Thus, in book 6, when Cather reprises the sexual-assault plot through the formulaic ritual of daily breakfast between Sapphira and Henry, it has a remarkably different effect than at the beginning of the novel as now both enslavers are sexually implicated as immoral and indecent. Ostensibly, Henry wants his nephew's protracted six-week visit to end while Sapphira plays the Southern-hospitality card by contrasting plantation cordiality from Northern customs. Their conversation is truly obscene. Husband and wife are incapable of speaking directly to each other, but they are both talking obliquely about Nancy's body: will the "slave girl" be sexually violated (Sapphira's endgame) or saved (Henry's desire, though the jury's out on how long he can repress his desire by projecting Nancy onto allegorical Mercy from *Pilgrim's Progress*).

Throughout *Sapphira*, whenever Cather refers to flowers and flour, she is also always discussing gender and race. Witness the breakfast scene between husband and wife, which is a master class in indirection and innuendo. Within this scene, Cather inserts a heuristic device at the end of chapter 2, book 6, to assist readers in interpretation. "Sapphira laughed softly. It was almost as good as a play, she was thinking; the way whenever she and her husband were thinking of Nancy, they invariably talked about Bluebell" (198). The cook's daughter, Bluebell, is represented by Sapphira as mendacious and of loose character, though she is neither of these. Bluebell is crafty and no-nonsense. That bluebells are a sign of humility and gratitude is something Cather would have known as she carried a "heavily annotated" personal copy of Schuyler Matthews's field book of American wildflowers on her treks in the Virginia countryside.[39] Evidently the author assigns this appellation deliberately to Bluebell, associating her with a gorgeous perennial wildflower and aligning both enslaved girls with strong mother figures.

Cather radically revises the ancient Greek story of Demeter/Persephone by inserting a maternal plot that organizes Nancy's escape in plain sight, releasing her from an abduction that would occur on plantation space. While she never asks her mother anything personal about her parentage, Nancy knows that her mother was a victim of sexual assault as her own mixed-race status attests, as were her maternal ancestors, beginning with her great-grandmother, Jezebel.[40] Despite all that has been written by Cather scholars of Nancy's lack of any distinguishing features, right down to her bones, when Nancy feels that her sexual safety is imminently threatened, she demonstrates volition and seeks help from Rachel Blake.[41] Because the author refuses to portray Black subjectivity and the Black woman's body under the system of slavery, the horrifying fact is this: Cather minimizes Nancy's determination to maintain the sanctity of her body. Despite Cather's flattening of her character, Nancy maintains a night-by-night heroic vigil against sexual predation. At her wit's end, Nancy tells Rachel in book 7 that she would rather drown herself than be assaulted. The cherry-picking scene in book 5 epitomizes Nancy's strength and her resistance. She is accosted by Martin Colbert after she has climbed up the cherry tree to pick ripened blackhearts. Before he distracts her and catches her bare ankles, Martin taunts her verbally: "'Who's your beau, anyway Nancy Till?' 'Ain't got none.' 'You going to be a sour old maid?' 'I reckon I is'" (179). After he catches her legs and attempts to sexually assault her, Nancy manages to scream for Pappy's help, which is immediately provided by Old Jeff and Sampson, who breaks protocol and risks his position as head staff person of the mill, by looking at Martin directly in the face (180). A young girl maintains her sexual virtue despite a predator actively preparing to assault her. Cather overrides her own seduction plot to establish, albeit anachronistically, Nancy's "good-girl" credentials, ascribing white, Southern womanhood virtues to an innocent Black girl.[42]

Cather also implements a modern version of the story of Demeter and Persephone, which is initiated by Nancy's visit to Rachel's house in book 5, "Martin Colbert." The severity of Nancy's situation on the Colbert farm is lessened by Cather's distancing measures, but it is also inscribed in landscape spaces and through the author's botanical references: both distracting and lifesaving. Until now, Sapphira would take seasonal trips in her carriage to the Double S to partake in laurel-picking season, observing the beauty of the landscape while Nancy gathered flowers. That she sends Nancy *alone* to the Double S in chapter 3 of book 5 testifies to Sapphira's perverse determination to harm her. Before Sapphira puts the assault plot in action, Nancy has within her an equally strong resolve to "escape from something," as the narrator writes early in *Sapphira*: extending to Nancy "a delicacy of feeling," Cather endows the young woman with what becomes a version of sentimental womanhood (43–44). Nancy overtly expresses to Rachel her fear of being sexually accosted by Martin Colbert and obliquely suggests that Sapphira masterminded this opportunity, knowing that her nephew was "goin' ridin' this morning" (167). Twice confessing her fear that

Martin will "overtake me in the woods," Nancy simultaneously expresses her shame in revealing this news to Rachel. Rachel's response sets in place the counternarrative that will override Sapphira's sexual assault plot. Cather employs interior monologue to disclose Rachel's ruminations about the depths of her mother's pathology; by the chapter's end, the rhetorical questions in Rachel's mind are dramatically answered in the flower-picking scene that follows: "Did her mother really want to ruin Nancy? Could her spite go so far as that?" (168) Of course, of course.

Cather's flower-picking chapter distracts as much as it anticipates. Using the conventional trope that unites snakes and slaveholders, Cather inscribes what Cynthia Griffin Wolff describes as the "serpentine horror" (227) of slavocracy through the landscape of the Double S, about which Cather, slipping into white nostalgia, describes as "the unstained loveliness, the pleasant feeling one had there." But the reader also hears the hissing on those "now-naked hills . . . rich in verdure" (170). As Jacobs writes in *Incidents*, "hot weather brings out snakes and slaveholders" (174), and this scene is no different in Cather's novel. When she hears hoofbeats come closer, Rachel holds up a "warning finger" to her sister laurel-gatherer, Nancy, preparing her for their encounter with Martin Colbert, which will foil the rape plot. Cather uses synecdoche as a sartorial decoy to describe what Martin sees: "two sunbonnets over there in the green bushes" (171). Rachel's lack of propriety regarding her gender also extends to her class as well: the sunbonnet symbolizes "simple, practical attire" and is no different in appearance from Nancy's: both their heads are covered by bonnets disguising their race (Romines, "Explanatory Notes," *Sapphira* 419). This staging is buttressed by Cather's use of the myth of Demeter and Persephone, but with a fundamentally different outcome than that of the primeval story. As Cavarero explains, "Demeter has the merit of naming a mother who not only posits her relationship with her daughter as primary, but, more importantly, wants her daughter to be what she is. Demeter wants a Kore who is a girl, the virgin to whom she has given birth. She does not want a pregnant daughter in an uninterrupted act of regeneration" (90). While Rachel is neither Nancy's biological mother nor entirely an othermother, she wants Nancy to be a girl-child who will enter womanhood without being sexually violated. In Nancy's case, this also means occupying a body that her mother, Till, would have desired for herself. At the end of their encounter with Martin, Rachel offers protection to Nancy: "Nancy girl, if I was you I wouldn't go off into the woods or any lonesome place while Mr. Martin is here. If you have to go off somewhere, come by, and I'll go along. If I happen to be away, take Mary and Better [Rachel's daughters] with you. I'll give them leave" (174). Rachel revises antebellum customs of chaperonage for uniquely defensive aims, authenticating the maternal plot that validates separation from the mother to maintain one of the preeminent cardinal virtues of white womanhood for a Black enslaved woman: purity.

In book 7, "Nancy's Flight," Cather reiterates the maternal plot by setting it at harvest time. While the fall season traditionally indicates the separation of mother and daughter in classical myth, Cather's version in *Sapphira* remarkably alters the script to denounce slavery and serve the goals of abolitionism. Rachel implements measures that will ensure Nancy's escape through the underground railroad, thereby revisioning space as a form of movement in time. Rachel's implicit connections with abolitionists, including Quakers, reinforce her belief in "racial progress in a modern southern context" as Lewis asserts (54).[43] In this way, Rachel guarantees that Nancy will be enfolded into a structure of belonging on her journey away from the violence endemic to plantation slavery.

Rachel and Nancy must align themselves with customs of the country, and together, they commit racial and class transgressions to pass as normative. Cather theatricalizes Nancy's escape through a wardrobe sleight of hand in the scene that portrays Rachel escorting Nancy across the Potomac. Both dress for their parts and present themselves in disguise. Playing Rachel's waiting maid, Nancy is dressed in town apparel, wearing an "old black turban of Mrs. Colbert's" with a red-feather flourish, perhaps Cather's homage to Till's maternal presence in this scene as Till had been the one who inserted the feather for her daughter when Nancy first accompanied Sapphira to Winchester (227). Mrs. Blake, attired in her "Sunday best, even to black gloves" passes as an affluent Southern lady, parodying the plantation "mistress," a role writ large by her mother, Sapphira, but supplanting it for a righteous cause (228).[44] Cather's references to apparel in *Sapphira* are a more nuanced illustration of cross-dressing than what is seen in Cather's own biography.[45]

Nancy's escape from human bondage, fraught with danger, requires extreme care lest she be exposed. Apparel may disguise the high risks involved in their passage toward safety, but this version of cross-dressing ultimately, as Jack Halberstam explains, "positions itself against an aesthetic of nakedness" (99) symbolized by the sparsely covered bodies of those enslaved on plantations. Cather's decision to manipulate dress codes to effect Nancy's escape parallels features of other slave narratives, including Harriet Jacobs's *Incidents*. Disguised in a sailor's outfit, Linda Brent walks in broad daylight and passes several people whom she knows (112). While

Linda's method of duplicity through cross-dressing does not eventuate in escape, it does illustrate the operational quality of what Anne Bradford Warner explains was an "active Underground Railroad as well as a powerful, invisible maroon community" (40).[46] Ubiquitous and invisible, networks of support flourished in Edenton, North Carolina, and Frederick County, Virginia. Linda and Nancy are supported by these well-organized interracial communities that make movement for escapees possible.

Harriet Jacobs and Willa Cather portray Linda and Nancy, respectively, suffering versions of living death. Both young women strive to preserve the sanctity of their bodies; in doing so, they endure living deaths on plantation space and within the contexts of their movement toward liberation. Jacobs describes Linda's garret space as equivalent to live entombment, and Cather reprises the fairy-tale feature of the coffin to highlight Nancy's brush with death during her escape. This scene in *Sapphira* occurs in the wagon driven by the local carpenter, Mr. Whitford, who transports Nancy out to the ferry. To ward off drunken marauders at the edge of town, the carpenter announces: "I'm Whitford, of Back Creek, and I'm carrying a coffin home" (230). Represented by the coffin, Nancy's "loophole of retreat," symbolically suggests live entombment, a diasporic space that enables movement elsewhere. Both Linda and Nancy seek freedom from sexual assault of their bodies: both narratives discuss the terrorizing details of this liberation for Black women who strive to establish the safety of home space in other places, centralizing a maternal ethos.

Homes without Dread: Jacobs's "Free at Last" and Cather's Faux Reunion

Jacobs and Cather revise ideologies about true womanhood for nineteenth-century Black women. Despite the conservative nature of this domestic ideology, the authors portray, albeit Cather unevenly, maternal practices that insist upon equal protections for all women regardless of race. In this way, Jacobs and Cather advance progressive views on women's autonomy, promoting mobility as an exercise of basic civil rights, which have yet to be allotted to them during the time periods in which they are representing Black women's movements. Focalizing on a reconceived understanding of maternal love compels a concomitant reconsideration of sexuality and motherhood as a result of women having been forced into the institution of slavery at birth. Both Linda and Nancy escape from Southern soil but suffer further from the consequences of the Fugitive Slave Act: Linda's freedoms are curtailed as she continues hiding in the North as a "runaway." She remains a single mother of two children; her son eventually migrates to Australia with his uncle, "sheltered by British law, more colorblind than the American legal system" (Yellin, *Harriet* 113).[47] Nancy migrates to Canada in order to escape the most baneful aspects of the 1850 law. She becomes an immigrant mother, married to a "half Scotch and half Indian" husband with whom she has three children (278). Like many immigrants, Nancy sends a yearly remittance to her mother, Till, every Christmas.

The final chapters in *Incidents* and *Sapphira* offer intersecting versions of diasporic space, which, according to Avtar Brah, is a site of creative tension between dispersal and "staying put." (242). For these formerly unfree women, the idea of *going home* is an exercise in grotesque nostalgia. Neither has such an intention. Neither will ever return to live in her natal home. Having found safe(r) spaces, Linda and Nancy may long to possess a home of their own, but it is a dream deferred. Due to the persistence of race and class inequities in North America, Linda and Nancy continue to perform domestic work in white people's houses, Linda as an au pair for the Bruce [Willis] family in New York and Nancy for an English family in Montreal, where she and her gardener husband live in a *cottage* on the grounds of the estate.

Both authors carve out literary spaces for their characters to claim a "disembodied, metaphysical will in an era denied such a possibility for women of color," ultimately proposing that corporeality can be "transcended" (Sorisio 203). Both authors take special account of their readership in their final chapters, maintaining awareness of a white Christian, female audience but swerving away from them as well. While the enslavers who hobbled Linda's and Nancy's lives are mercifully dead, as Jacobs writes, "There are wrongs which even the grave does not bury," and such wrongs are confessed overtly in Jacobs's final chapter (196). In "Free at Last," Linda must reckon with the fact that without her knowledge, her employer, Mrs. Bruce, buys her freedom in order to put a stop to the Flint relatives seeking to reenslave her.[48] By turns indignant and relieved, Linda must steer a fine line between gratitude toward her white benefactress, Mrs. Bruce, and irate incredulity that she was trafficked as chattel in the "free city of New York!" (200). In the final two pages of her narrative, Jacobs mindfully blurs distinctions between her literary persona, Linda, and herself. Like a cinematic flash forward, the literary persona has now caught up with her author. Jacobs's penultimate paragraph demonstrates this conflation between obligatory resignation and unconcealed resistance, which bears reference here:

> Reader, my story ends with freedom; not in the usual way, with marriage. I and my children are now free! . . . The dream of my life is not yet realized. I do not sit with my children in a home of my *own*. I still long for a hearthstone of my *own*. However humble, I wish it for my children's sake far more than for my *own*. But God so orders circumstances as to keep me with my friend, Mrs. Bruce. Love, duty, gratitude, also *bind* me to her side. (201, emphasis added)

Paying rhetorical homage to white readers and their literary habits, Jacobs subtly critiques their institutions, which subscribe to compulsory heterosexuality through marriage and motherhood, forgoing an explicit reminder of the sexual predation that occurs because of slavocracy: "Reader, my story ends with freedom; not in the usual way, with marriage" (201). Jacobs inserts her larger criticism of institutionalized slavery between her first and last sentences, claiming that racial slavery's sexual brutality sought to prevent Black women from being maternal mothers *but has failed*. Jacobs clarifies in her concluding remarks, that, as a mother of two children, slavocracy did not control her maternal relationships because such women established close bonds with their children and close bonds with othermothers across races. As Grace McEntee explains, Jacobs's goal was to utilize an ethos of motherhood in order to "change a national culture," employing motherhood to "illustrate a vision of racial equality [. . .] [I]t helps to highlight the frequency with which Jacobs describes friendships she formed across race lines, and how often these seem inspired and fueled by the power of mother love" (200–1).[49] Jacobs's repeated use of the possessive first-person pronoun *own* in the final paragraphs of her autobiography illuminates her determined will to protect her children by providing them with a home as a single mother. Jacobs then juxtaposes this radical alternative for women with another reference to gratitude, but this time linking it with the verb *bind*, reminding readers that bondage by the very white people for whom she is writing continues to constrain her as a result of her race.

Cather's epilogue, written as autobiography, obscures more than it reveals. In an edited typescript of "Nancy's Return" (book 9), Cather deletes a first-person explanation in order to shift into what Romines calls "the innovative autobiographical epilogue" (404) (see figure 1.2).

Cather then strangely adds an italicized "postscript" after she typographically inserts "The End" underscoring her final line of "Nancy's

Figure 1.2. Typescript of Cather's first paragraph deletion in the epilogue of *Sapphira and the Slave Girl* by Willa Cather. Drew University Special Collections, Cather Collection.

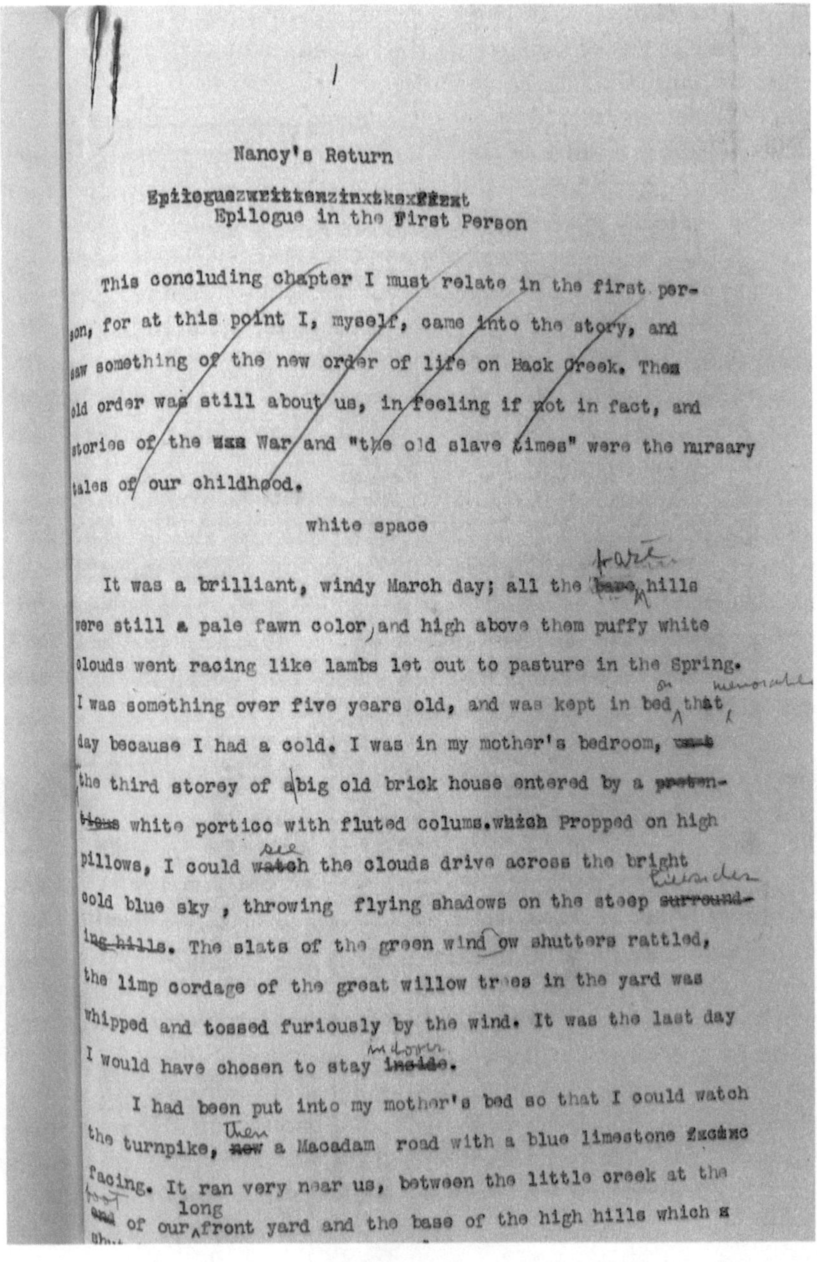

> Nancy's Return
>
> ~~Epilogue:written:in:the:First~~
> Epilogue in the First Person
>
> ~~This concluding chapter I must relate in the first person, for at this point I, myself, came into the story, and saw something of the new order of life on Back Creek. Then old order was still about us, in feeling if not in fact, and stories of the War and "the old slave times" were the nursary tales of our childhood.~~
>
> white space
>
> It was a brilliant, windy March day; all the ~~bare~~ hills were still a pale fawn color, and high above them puffy white clouds went racing like lambs let out to pasture in the Spring. I was something over five years old, and was kept in bed that day because I had a cold. I was in my mother's bedroom, ~~on~~ the third storey of a big old brick house entered by a ~~pretentious~~ white portico with fluted colums. ~~which~~ Propped on high pillows, I could ~~watch~~ see the clouds drive across the bright cold blue sky , throwing flying shadows on the steep ~~surrounding hills~~. The slats of the green window shutters rattled, the limp cordage of the great willow trees in the yard was whipped and tossed furiously by the wind. It was the last day I would have chosen to stay ~~inside~~ indoors.
>
> I had been put into my mother's bed so that I could watch the turnpike, ~~now~~ then a Macadam road with a blue limestone facing. It ran very near us, between the little creek at the ~~foot~~ long ~~end~~ of our front yard and the base of the high hills which

Return," in effect, opening up the frame narrative instead of closing it.[50] This endnote was a late addition to the novel, suggesting that Cather might have been unable to conclude *Sapphira* to her (or the reader's) satisfaction. Such an oddly constructed frame narrative also alerts readers to the unreliability of its narrator, who happens to be a child whose adult self relies on self-indulgent memories.

Inscribing racist conventions throughout *Sapphira*, Cather continues in her epilogue to portray a postbellum culture that preserves segregation during the midday dinner where a "second table" is set downstairs for Black domestic workers, including the mother-daughter duo, Till and Nancy (279), who are presented minimally during their six-week visit. Of the two chapters comprising Cather's epilogue in book 9, only the second chapter focuses on this mother-daughter reunion, but it rings false. Unlike Jacobs's concluding chapter in which she claims an identity that transcends her former status as an enslaved person, Cather's Black characters never "own the story," as Wolff explains (221).[51] Instead, the mother-daughter reunion of Till and Nancy, who have been separated for twenty-five years, is narrated by a *five-year-old* Cather. Such a literary decision permits the author religiously to diminish and devalue Black women's lives. Sharon O'Brien understates, "An adult's memories of childhood experiences do not, of course, constitute an objective record of the past" (46). One of the earliest scholars to take on Cather's *Sapphira*, Elizabeth Ammons, argues that the most disturbing feature in this epilogue is Cather's "appropriation of Nancy's story, . . . the heroism of a black woman," explaining that "the novel in fact steals the black woman's story to give it to white women" (135).

Unable through characterization to portray a forty-four-year-old Black woman possessing a disembodied metaphysical will, Cather instead reprises an "epistemology of the wardrobe" (Halberstam 89) paradoxically to suggest Nancy's transcendence. In doing so, Cather both disguises and expands a social reality for Black women that was inconceivable to her in antebellum (or postbellum) America. It will be the closest the author gets to advancing resistance *from a Black woman* to institutionalized structures of racism and sexism. While not overtly oppositional, Cather's description of Nancy's attire is her version of a politics of "disavowal . . . so that change becomes conceivable" (Grosz 153). Abbott argues, "Despite, then, the novel's nostalgic tone or evocation of Cather's ancestors, its plot hinges on a modern definition of black female sexual propriety" (33). After a wordless reunion between mother and daughter, Nancy is described as laying aside a fur-lined black coat, removing a "turban and brush[ing] back a strand of her blue-black hair. She wore a black silk dress. A gold watch-chain was looped about her neck and came down to her belt, where the watch was tucked away in a little pocket" (276).[52] In contrast to donning Southern women's apparel for cross-dressing purposes to escape slavery, Nancy presents herself as a Northern, highly stylized urban self, a Canadian immigrant woman in command of her performance. Cather's reference to the watch fob showcases Nancy's demonstrable control of time, which she keeps tucked away as both assurance and safety. She will never be as vulnerable again after migrating to and relocating in Montreal, where she found a safer space and created her own family. While her six-week visit remains largely determined by her employers' schedules, Nancy, like Jacobs's Linda, will continue to move forward as a mother whose mobility enabled freedoms unspeakable and unimaginable in the plantation spaces of racial captivity. Neither woman suffers from this kind of sexual vulnerability again, but they know other Black women do and will; nonetheless, their movements elsewhere are attempts to ensure (more) safety for their children. While still largely defined by their racial and gendered status, both women nonetheless achieve social and spatial liberation as working mothers who exemplify autonomy as Black maternal women.

As I briefly discussed at the beginning of this chapter, each author's narrative was published at the onset of catastrophic wars: the Civil War commenced in 1861, the same year Jacobs's *Incidents in the Life of a Slave Girl* was published; and America entered the second World War in 1941, a year after *Sapphira and the Slave Girl*'s 1940 publication. The archaic definition of the word *onset*, is a military attack. The agitated tone of Jacobs's *Incidents* suggests that the narrator has frequently experienced attack by whites both to her physical body and to the members of the community where she lived in Edenton, North Carolina. That Civil War is on the horizon perhaps came as no surprise to Jacobs, who was working as a domestic and secretly writing in a Northern home whose white employers exemplified the division in the country, with her white, female employer, covertly protecting Harriet as she wrote, knowing that her husband felt otherwise. Cather's response to imminent attack reverts to a nostalgia available to someone whose family moved away from plantation culture early in the author's life. Her recreation of antebellum culture is ultimately retrograde, but by portraying a white abolitionist woman in Rachel Blake, Cather manages to highlight the surreptitious efforts of some Southern white women who engaged in abolitionist activities.

Although nearly eighty years separates the publication of these narratives, Jacobs and Cather, albeit in different ways, portrayed Black women's lives in mortal danger. Without the efforts of othermothers and community members, Linda and Nancy would not have survived the onslaught of racist violence against their bodies, having seen their maternal elders abused by the reckless and cruel system of slavery in antebellum America. Regardless of the intensity of their motherlove, Linda and Nancy must escape unbearable circumstances through movement away from their loved ones, resulting in permanent separation from their mothers, families, and communities. The daughters' love for their mothers remains constant, but forever one of long-distance yearning. Chapter 2 examines the aftershocks of maternal suffering by daughters whose escapes intensify their mothers' ghostly incarnations in Toni Morrison's *Beloved* and Cristina García's *Dreaming in Cuban*, respectively, and compels daughters to develop a form of long-distance mothering in response to their separation.

Chapter 2

Long-Distance Mothering and Generational Haunting in Morrison's *Beloved* and García's *Dreaming in Cuban*

Mothers and Daughters Longing for Less Distance

Beloved and *Dreaming in Cuban* are projects of recovery. Toni Morrison and Cristina García advance a postmodern aesthetics to examine motherhood under erasure. By "shifting the center," as Collins writes, to examine "the experiences of women in alternative family structures with quite different political economies" (312), both authors communicate and extend ideas about generations through ties to plantation space and island space, utilizing actual and metaphorical haunting to echo an irreversible trauma from which maternal figures suffer. While Morrison narrativizes the concept of rememory, and García spatializes notions of diasporic time, both authors reexamine such ideas through women characters whose motherhood is experienced under extremity. To disclose layers of oppressions intrinsic to motherhood under slavery and dictatorship, both authors utilize nonconventional means of communication to expose maternal realities that exceed traditional notions of time and space. Ascribing an order of long-distance mothering permits the authors to dismantle limited configurations of generational rhetoric typical in American culture in order to recover bonds of maternal lineage heretofore silenced. Linking generations, Morrison and García also literalize the ghosts in their novels. These ghostly incarnations not only cause but also enable radical forms of unhousing for mothers and daughters as a result of continued maternal anguish across generations.

The revolutionary vehicle through which both Morrison and García explore the effects of repressive authority is through motherhood. To examine the aftershocks of maternal suffering, Morrison and García employ metafictional techniques inclusive of nonlinear temporalities, simultaneous points of view, and polyphonic voices[1] to explore the ongoing trauma from which generations of mothers and daughters continue to suffer.[2] *Beloved* and *Dreaming in Cuban* feature tripartite structures, advancing narratives about individual families divided by the institutional arrangements of slavery and dictatorship, both of which eradicate distinctions between the home and the world.[3] As a result, we see multiple examples of unhoused women from several generations, finding ways to resist their oppression. Rewriting Western accounts of history through maternal stories, these women-identified authors represent maternal characters seeking lasting escape from patriarchal subordination. Merging the realistic with the fantastic, Morrison and García intersperse surreal sequences, intersecting plots, and nonchronology to execute a maternal plotting of rebellion in both novels. Both authors commit their works to a maternal praxis that strives to exemplify the autonomy women seek in their natal or adopted countries.

As if in response to Willa Cather's "wholly unanalyzed" relationship between Till and Nancy in *Sapphira and the Slave Girl*, Morrison's *Beloved* illuminates a multilayered discourse on maternal relations, inspired by the source story of Margaret Garner, an enslaved woman who killed her daughter rather than have her return to slavery (*Playing in the Dark* 21).[4] Morrison expands the conceptual terrain about mothering under the confines of plantation slavery; in doing so, she not only pays homage to Harriet Jacobs's antebellum *Incidents in the Life of a Slave Girl* in her dedication to portraying an enslaved woman's claim that she possesses the maternal authority to nurture her children, but she also advances a maternal standpoint that reconstructs matrilineal bonds in postbellum America.[5]

With a similar focus in mind, García reinstates broken bonds between women through communal stories shared in nonconventional ways in *Dreaming in Cuban*. Depicting entrenched conditions of inequality between men and women within one family and exacerbated by a dictatorship, García portrays how bonds of mothering are ruptured a priori, thwarting women from establishing bonds with their children before they are even born. Morrison and García retrieve those "private and particular" spaces of captive communities to recover buried voices (Spillers, "Mama's Baby" 67). To disrupt dominant discourses that erase the experiences of mothers, both authors invoke pivotal historical periods in America and Cuba, permitting them to retrieve matrilineal histories based on the proficiency of storytelling mothers and daughters.

The failures of both the American Reconstruction and the Cuban Revolution nonetheless hover over these novels, triggering representations of maternal agony and rebellion and ushering in the haunting presence that scaffolds their works. While I partially agree with Homi Bhabha, who declares a hastiness in Morrison's approach to historical events of the 1870s, Morrison rather chooses to focus on how one woman, Sethe, resists structures of power aimed at destroying her children.[6] Likewise, the Cuban Revolution of 1959 shadows the Del Pino family and arranges their lives, but García chooses to centralize this family's dislocation by focusing on how the matriarch, Celia, responds to restricted domestic spaces and virulent forms of male power.[7] Ghostly company enters *Beloved* and *Dreaming in Cuban* to evoke the malleable borders between those domestic spaces and the world, revealing the interstices between human and spectral forces. Bhabha explains that "the recesses of domestic space become sites for history's most intricate invasions" (9). For mothers in both works, in private and particular spaces, as Spillers explains, "biological, sexual, social, cultural, linguistic, ritualistic, and psychological fortunes join. This profound intimacy of interlocking detail is disrupted, however, by externally imposed meanings and uses" ("Mama's Baby" 67). In *Beloved* and *Dreaming in Cuba*, there is no freedom in private or public space until ghosting makes it so. Morrison and García set their novels before and after national failures, setting in motion the voices behind the maternal stories that fundamentally upend historical events conventionally told.

Where and When They Enter: 1873

Toni Morrison sets *Beloved* in 1873, the same year as Willa Cather's birth.[8] The Panic of 1873 ushered in America's first economic depression. The Freedmen's Bureau ended the year before, destroying any strides made during Reconstruction, which Harriet Jacobs personally confronted in her attempt to establish schools in the South.[9] Avery Gordon explains, "Radical Reconstruction had tried to combine the formal, legal freedom of Emancipation with the political self-rule and social resources that would make freedom secure and powerful. By 1873, these efforts were dead" (172). In their wake, Morrison begins the first section of part 1 of

Beloved (3–19) with a numerical nomenclature and personality: "124 was spiteful" *(Beloved* 3). This is the problematic that shadows the house on Bluestone Road. After an "excessively demanding" in medias res opening, Morrison enlists readers to orient themselves to a dislocation "completely foreign," ensuring that the novel's "underground life" engenders a mindful relationship between author and reader and "facilitate[s] making it one's own" ("Unspeakable Things" 228, 229). Orienting myself to *Beloved* permits an analysis of Morrison's maternal plotting accompanied by a generational haunting that reaches well beyond tracing lines of descent or capturing genealogy through family trees. Though, as I examine in the subsequent paragraphs, trees perform multiple functions and link all the living characters in *Beloved*.[10]

By 1873, when the novel begins, the reader gathers the following: it has been eighteen years since Sethe, pregnant with Denver, escapes without her husband from a Kentucky slave plantation called Sweet Home.[11] Sethe reunites with her three other children and preacher mother-in-law, Baby Suggs, on the outskirts of Cincinnati, Ohio, a free state. It has been twelve years since Denver remembers having any visitors come to their door; and, for Denver, eleven years since she has left the house. Eight years have elapsed since Baby Suggs has died. Sethe's sons, Howard and Buglar, ran off just before their grandmother's death. For nearly all those eighteen years, Sethe has been ostracized by her community, the root causes of which are hinted at in this first section. Within the first paragraph of *Beloved*, Morrison reduces the cast of characters to the mother-daughter dyad: Sethe and Denver. Only two of them remain in the house. But they are not alone, for they brave the company of a spiteful ghost beside them, whom they both know is Sethe's firstborn, "crawling already?" daughter, whom Sethe had killed twenty-eight days after her arrival on free soil. Morrison deftly deploys her sleight of hand in *Beloved* through a "fully realized presence of the haunting" so that she can supply "a controlled diet of the incredible political world" ("Unspeakable" 229). Morrison, however, encloses that world within a formerly enslaved mother's sense of time and space.

Morrison centralizes the mother-daughter bond to formulate a maternal ethos that reifies the persistence of motherlove after the trauma of slavery and the failures of Reconstruction. The political ramifications of this incredible world are narrated through maternal voices. Such aftershocks are transhistorically relocated within the house on Bluestone Road. As Bhabha asserts, memories of those enslaved obscure "the historical narrative of infanticide only to articulate the unspoken: that ghostly discourse that enters the world of 124 'from the outside' in order to reveal the transitional world of the aftermath of slavery in the 1870s, its private and public faces, its historical past and its narrative present" (15). The volcanic response to Paul D's 1873 entrance into this transitional world of *Beloved* is testimonial to Morrison's aesthetic repositioning of the mother-daughter plot. By intervening against "the racial-patriarchal story," as Laura A. Doyle explains, Morrison "exposes the self-displacing, mother-appropriating effects of a hierarchical metaphysics as institutionalized and lived in slavery; and she uncovers as extramaternal phenomenology by which to retrieve and find strength in a painful slave past" (209–10). The unhousing that takes place in 124 transcends Paul D's displacement in part 1 of the novel.[12] Morrison reconstructs a maternal logic that defies conventional notions of time and space and inserts a maternal language that challenges if not replaces discursive theories of race and gender.

Morrison ultimately claims for Sethe a subjectivity marked by the traumas she endured under slavery *as a mother* and conceptualized through a type of thought imagery, which Sethe describes to her daughter as a "floating picture" and refers to as a "rememory" (36).[13] For this reason, Denver is subjected to maternal memories she personally did not experience. In fact, she sees the ghost before her mother does, "holding its arm around her mother's waist" in the keeping room (35). As her mother's daughter, Denver will assume maternal practices in her own right. As Morrison said in an interview, "A woman has to be a daughter before she can be any kind of woman" (Taylor-Guthrie 184). Andrea O'Reilly explains that all of Morrison's oeuvre "challenges the received view, or what [Morrison] calls in another context, the master narrative of motherhood" in order to reformulate "motherwork as a political enterprise," aligning her with autobiographical predecessor, Harriet Jacobs (*Toni Morrison and Motherhood* 29, 25, 132). For this enterprise to prove effective for Denver's generation, Morrison "creates an alternative, subversive discourse of black motherhood" (O'Reilly 128). First, however, Sethe must experience herself as the "wildly unmothered" daughter she is before reentering Black motherhood in postbellum America (Rich, *Of Woman Born* 225).

For Sethe, milk is thicker than blood in and out of slavery. While she bears four children with Halle and manages to arrange their escape from slavery, Sethe's subjectivity as a former captive continues to violate and haunt her memories. Wresting herself from the logic of the captor takes much time, requiring her to redefine the maternal according to a logic in which her integrity as a person is maintained. She cannot achieve a "liberated subject-position" without help from phantom and human worlds (Spillers "Mama's Baby" 67). As a result of the assaults she suffered under slavery, Sethe recalls the primal scene of wounding that unites two intersecting tropes in *Beloved*: milk and trees. Morrison raises the possibility of uniting past and present for Sethe, allowing her to move into a future potentially less harmful yet necessarily overladen by memory. This possibility must exist for mother and daughter so that space emerges to include a less isolated future for Sethe and mobility for Denver.

The first pages of *Beloved* reveal that Sethe's nearly empty house is stuffed with plantation memories of maternal trauma. Early in *Beloved*, Sethe accuses Baby Suggs of willfully not remembering any details about her eight children except her firstborn's love of "the burned bottom of baked bread." "That's all you let yourself remember," Sethe remarks to her mother-in-law, a transference of vast proportion (5). With Paul D's entrance, Morrison sets up the potential uniting of Sethe's primal scene with Paul D's, as both characters are invested in the same tropes, milk and trees, intersecting as shared antebellum memories of Sweet Home. Before this, however, Morrison inserts a recursion to the classical plot of Demeter and Persephone with a late-blooming daughter's rebellion, occurring only after Paul D enters the scene, threatening to separate Denver from the mother she knows. A massive understatement, Sethe asks Denver "Did something happen?" because her daughter is "shaking now and sobbing so she could not speak. The tears *she had not shed for nine years* wetting her far too womanly breasts" (14, emphasis added). Denver's banishment by proxy from the community results from Sethe's unspeakable act of infanticide that occurred eighteen years earlier, to which I shall return.

Denver's emotional life has been entirely eclipsed by her mother's maternal suffering. Yet, Paul D's entry into the plot positions Denver as a *normative* daughter, which exposes an incarceration to a past she did not personally live but nonetheless experiences transgenerationally. By normative, I am referring to a family structure which Denver can neither relive nor experience again as a child, and this includes her father in the household. Denver's needs are basic: she wants her dad and wants to have friends. Despite her own stunted development, Denver clarifies a positionality from the outset: "I can't live here" (14). This assertion eventually enables Denver to step off her mother's porch to seek help and guarantee a postbellum mobility that will differ from first-generation parents, like Sethe, who experienced and survived slavery.

Denver's "far too womanly breasts" are Morrison's early reminder that, despite time passing, mother and daughter are locked inside the bodily memories of Sethe's past trauma. Denver's emotional eruption occurs before Sethe informs Paul D of the events that transpired shortly before she escaped from the plantation. In an effort to stop Paul D from questioning her choices, Sethe says this: "I got a tree on my back and a haint in my house, and nothing in between but the daughter I am holding in my arms" (15). As Morrison is fond of literalizing metaphors in *Beloved*,[14] it is likely that Sethe's maternal gesture of cradling a fully grown Denver is literal. Regardless, Sethe's role as *mater dolorosa* positions her as maternally static and perpetually out of emotional reach for her daughter.

Sethe repeatedly clarifies that her primal wounding is always maternal. Sexually assaulted when she is pregnant with Denver and then brutally beaten by schoolteacher's nephews, Sethe delays discussing the chokecherry tree on her back to repeat declaratively a reenactment of her maternal subjectivity, a memory located on her body: "And they took my milk" (17). Insisting upon her position as a nurturing mother, Sethe's litany-like reiteration of this violent abuse not only reinforces the psychic recurrence of traumatic memory but also focuses deliberately on Sethe's chronic response to that wounding: "And they took my milk." Sethe's maternal subjectivity is duty-bound to her understanding of motherhood. As O'Reilly explains, Sethe "not only speaks as a mother, she secures subjectivity through her mothering" (*Toni Morrison and Motherhood* 132). Only after thrice declaring the fact of this maternal theft does Sethe allow Paul D to see her back and touch the "decorative work of an ironsmith too passionate for display" (17). Spillers describes undecipherable markings on an enslaved person's body as "a hieroglyphics of the flesh" ("Mama's Baby" 67), which correspondingly represents Sethe's scarified back. Part and parcel, Sethe's memories of her lacerated back intrude upon her alongside the rememory of the nephews' assault on her breasts. Portraying the reproduction of violence against mothers and daughters in *Dreaming in Cuban*, García also references hieroglyphic markings and maternal violation of the flesh, to which I shall return.

In her final trimester of pregnancy, Sethe withstood a sadistic whipping. Sethe shuns her back as it has been appropriated by patriarchal codes of enslavers by which she refuses to abide. Her survival requires that she emotionally distance herself from white, male power. Paul D's question in response to the nephews' savagery—"They used cowhide on you?"—links the maternal to Halle also, whom Sethe later learns witnessed her assault in the barn, breaking him emotionally and reducing him to sitting next to the churn, smearing butter all over his face (69). When he disrobes Sethe to bear witness to her back, Paul D says privately to himself, "Aw, Lord, girl" (17). For him, Sethe's mutilated back bears more resemblance to actual markings that enslaved bodies sustained during brutal beatings in antebellum history than any sort of tree.[15] Nonetheless, Sethe's willingness to use Amy Denver's metaphor of "chokecherry tree" bears further commentary. Amy Denver, the white girl and indentured servant (also likely on the run), helps Sethe deliver her baby (Denver) on the shore of the Ohio River after Sethe escapes the farm shortly after her assault and beating.

Eighteen years later, Sethe continues to refer to her healed back lacerations as a tree, specifically a chokecherry: "Trunk, branches, even leaves" (16). Indigenous to the southeastern United States, chokecherry trees recall the cruel paradox of Southern history which makes Sethe want to scream out the truth: "The fire and brimstone all right, hidden in lacy groves" (6). Those groves are filled with trees: sycamore, cherry, and oak trees, all recalling for Sethe the unbearable beauty that was only made possible by the laboring bodies of enslaved persons. Perhaps a nod to Cather's cherry-picking scene when Nancy is spared a full-on assault from another lecherous nephew, Morrison's reference to the chokecherry tree also ensures further connection with Paul D, whose association with trees is integral to his postslavery survival, as flowering trees serve as his north star. Doyle explains that "trees have functioned in Paul D's life . . . to counter his displacement" (214). By linking both characters through the "rhetoric of trees," Morrison "clears a space for their future" (L. Doyle 214, 225) (see figure 2.1).

Morrison clarifies that Paul D can never replace or match the maternal bond: he may be a strong suitor, but he's no match for the daughter's desire. Nonetheless, the wound inflicted on Sethe's back may be read as a sign of "trauma's incommunicability," but the gap is bridgeable between Paul D and Sethe, having shared Sweet Home legibility and suffered the persistent aftershocks of its brutalities (Hirsch, *The Generation of Postmemory* 80). Paul D's physical presence yet requires further reckoning on the part of mother and daughters in *Beloved*. Once incarnated, Beloved's return compels Sethe's memories to extend beyond her primal scene of maternal violation to embrace an understanding of mothering that returns her to her daughterhood, which I will discuss later in this chapter.

Figure 2.1. Faith Ringgold, *Coming to Jones Road #4: Under a Blood Red Sky*, 2000. Acrylic on canvas, fabric borders; 78½ × 52½ × 1 in. (199 × 133 × 3 cm) Colby College Museum of Art, Museum purchase through the Jere Abbott Art Endowment and Jette Art Acquisition Fund 2021.276.

When and Where They Enter: 1959

Cristina García features unmothered daughters front and center in *Dreaming in Cuban*. An abandoned daughter and an abused wife, Celia's story is hardly sui generis, but it is amplified by further losses sustained after the 1959 Cuban Revolution. Celia's individual response to her wounding illuminates an imaginative consciousness as gorgeously visual as Sethe's heartbreaking rememories of Sweet Home, offering balm in a violent society in which the family microcosmically repeats the colonizing practices of Cuba's imperial history. As a result of her unmothering, Celia's later response to the Cuban Revolution has been augmented by a maternal body tyrannized by her husband and his family. Subjugated by male power, Celia suffers early in her marriage from familial and medical mistreatment bordering on the homicidal. García unearths the roots of internal familial colonialism within the Del Pino family, and by doing so, she illuminates the stories of women's lives before and after the failures of the 1959 Cuban Revolution. As García declared in an interview, "Celia is the spiritual guide as well as the backbone and strength of the novel," and Celia's story frames the text (López 611). By setting the story in 1972, García examines the steep consequences of the six-year armed conflict that resulted in Castro's installation of a Communist regime and the flight of a "massive flow of Cuban refugees" to the United States, including Celia's firstborn daughter, Lourdes, whose story I will return to below *(Dreaming* 3).

Traumatized by maternal abandonment and an insidiously punitive husband, Celia's scarification cannot be witnessed by an empathic interlocutor like Paul D, who reads "every ridge and leaf of [Sethe's back] with his mouth, none of which Sethe could feel because her back skin had been dead for years" (*Beloved* 18). Yet, by 1972, Celia is prepared to make the following declaration privately to herself: "Because of this, Celia thinks, her husband will be buried in stiff, foreign earth. Because of this, their children and their grandchildren are nomads" (6–7).[16] An exile herself, Celia has lived in a house by the sea since 1937, removed from the institutional harms imposed on her mind and body, García describing her skin a "cicatrix" (8). Attempting to kill Celia emotionally in order to compel her submission, Jorge's original sin precedes the Cuban Revolution by decades. As a result of such mistreatment, Celia's experience of maternal love will be delayed a generation as she has been unable to nurture, protect, or save any of her three children.[17] Referencing Benjamin's angel of history, Ibis Gomez-Vega focuses on writers such as García who attempt to translate the wreckage of their country's history, unsettled it seems beyond repair, by the "chaos created by dictatorial governments" (231). By filling in the gaps of where her history might be located and highlighted, García faces the chaos head-on by exposing maternal realities in nonconventional ways, expanding, like Morrison, notions of space and time in order to advance a maternality that exceeds generations and travels across boundaries.

For example, in "Ordinary Seductions (1972)," García begins the novel with Celia's story of multiple losses incurred over a lifetime and her compensatory modes of security to enable her psychic survival. In the first section, "Ocean Blue" (3–15), we meet a sixty-three-year-old Celia, sitting outside her house overlooking the sea. Like Sethe, Celia is stopped in time, and she too comes to realize that "memory cannot be confined" (47). Yet, Celia continues to pursue her memories through reiterative activities and an abiding acceptance of spectral forces she deems natural to her artistic sensibilities. While a decade has passed since the failed military invasion of Cuba by American forces, Celia del Pino, "equipped with binoculars and wearing her best housedress and drop pearl earrings," continues to guard Cuba's north coast from her wicker chair (3). While Celia's continued patriotism to El Líder seems counterintuitive (and anachronistic by 1972), it is understandable in light of a backstory revealed through Celia's memories of abandonment and García's implementation of the epistolary genre. Written between 1935 and 1959 to her former Spanish lover,[18] Celia's letters, like her piano playing, serve as her creative response to maintaining a subjectivity that promises some control over a life dominated by interlocking systems of oppression upheld by family and state. Celia's never-sent letters function as an expressive art that both encodes resistance and serves as a cautionary tale. Ultimately the letters encapsulate one Cuban woman's pre-Revolutionary autobiography that illuminates the collusion between domestic and exterior spheres, stressing inevitable correlations between domesticity and the political realities of race, class, ethnicity, and religion in Cuban history.

Stowed in a satin chest, the cache of letters Celia has treasured for twenty-five years evokes a voyage across the sea as now grandmother Celia concludes her letter writing on the day of her granddaughter's birth on January 11, 1959, which, auspiciously, is also Celia's fiftieth birthday. García intensifies the magic of transmitting Celia's story by accentuating a revolutionary past that begins and ends in private space. Similar to other material reminders stowed in traveling chests, Celia bestows on her granddaughter an inalienable possession, a gift that eschews appropriation as it can only be handed down as "a possible future claim, and [a] potential source of power" (Weiner 10). After Jorge institutionalized a young Celia, who endured electroshock therapy *during* motherhood, García describes a resultant docility that temporarily stilled Celia's expressive hands, illustrated by her letter writing and piano playing. By 1972, however, Celia's widowed hands epitomize the flexibility of her artistic mind, and the reader realizes retrospectively that, like so many abused women, she was biding her time.[19] Penelope-like, Celia has made waiting into an art: "The waiting began in 1934. . . . It seems to her that she has spent her entire life waiting for others, for something or other to happen. . . . Waiting for her husband to leave on his business trips so she could play Debussy on the piano" (*Dreaming* 35). After a quarter century of writing letters to her never-returning Spanish lover, Gustavo, Celia no longer needs him as she has found maternal love closer to home with a kindred spirit who "keeps a diary in the lining of her winter coat," awaiting a spring in which Pilar will be reunited with her grandmother: "She will remember everything," Celia writes in her final letter, which concludes the novel (7, 245).

Invoking the classical Demeter-Persephone myth enables García to position Pilar's hidden diary as part of "the complex discourse of the mother-daughter relationship as well as the imaginative inscription of the lost homeland" (Davis 60). Pilar longs for the lost mother country and its matriarchal representative, her maternal grandmother, Celia. That García chooses the verb *remember*—she will remember everything—suggests that Pilar can summon up the maternal discourse as she recalls "word-for-word conversations," sitting in her grandmother's lap when she was an infant in Cuba before her mother (Lourdes) moved the family to Brooklyn when she was two years old (26). Symbolized by the satin chest, the archive is awaiting her in Cuba, but Pilar has already lived her future. As Rocío G. Davis, explains, "The need to 'go back to the future' implies the urgency of appropriating the intricate truths about one's self and history as part of the process of self-affirmation" (61). Celia's letters ultimately provide her granddaughter with an archive that Pilar will steward into her adulthood as the daughter of a wounded immigrant mother, Lourdes, whom she does not yet understand. Celia's letters preserve a cultural archive that simultaneously records and traces collective memory and becomes a repository of gendered knowledge. To rephrase Sue McKemmish's felicitous expression: evidence of Celia becomes evidence of the divided Del Pino/Puente family.[20]

Celia spends the final decades of her life examining the consequences of an exile as far-reaching and dislocating as Lourdes's decision to flee Cuba and resettle in New York motivated by her own twin traumas of maternal abandonment and paternal abduction. As a result of the rape and miscarriage she experiences during the Cuban Revolution, Lourdes chooses migration over matrilineal ties to her homeland. Celia's letters will nonetheless travel toward the maternal, constructing narrative diaspora space, which potentially may reconstitute the mother-daughter configuration through which some movement toward healing may be experienced. Before she travels to Cuba in 1980 with her mother, Pilar has already established a telepathic connection with Celia.

What we learn in these first pages of *Dreaming in Cuban* is the fact that Celia has been separated from her husband well before his death. Fearlessly regarding her own mortality, Celia's swim in the sea fully dressed prepares us for the novel's watery conclusion. Before she learns of her husband's death in New York, where he was being treated for cancer, Celia sees her husband emerge from the sea, colossally oversized, "walking on water." Though he is speaking, Celia "cannot read his immense lips," García's parodic gesture delimiting the power of his resurrection—and, vitally, limiting his ability to haunt *her* (5). Before her marriage to Jorge, Celia had a passionate love affair with a Spanish businessman, who visited her department counter at the prestigious store in Havana where she worked selling photographic equipment. The ending of their affair left her bedridden and immobile, close to death. Celia recalls the prescient words of a santera brought in by her maiden great-aunt, Alicia, the woman who serves as her othermother and who refuses to let her die. García twice recalls the santera's words of assurance to Celia—"Miss Celia, there's a wet landscape in your palm"—aligning her less with the heavens than with the sea (7, 37).

Unable entirely to compensate for mother abandonment, female figures such as Celia's great aunt and the santera function importantly in Celia's young life not only as othermother models but as alternative ways of being. As such, though she remains untraveled, Celia's creativity enlarges her spatial sensibilities, linking her to an aesthetics of movement in her life-long dedication to the music of Debussy and the poetry of Federico García Lorca, expanding her embrace of racial and sexual differences inscribed also within Cuban culture. Thus, Celia's counterrevolution against family and patriarchal tyranny is established early in life and it enables her survival in "the house of unbearable death" (Cavarero, 65) with her traveling husband and his mother and sister, Berta and Ofelia, whose machinations nearly kill her.

Similar to Willa Cather's incorporation of the Grimms' version of the Snow White fairy tale in *Sapphira and the Slave Girl*, García incorporates folktale motifs in her novel, inclusive of Snow White and Cinderella, to exemplify women's service in collusion with patriarchal family mores. She also exposes the legacy of colonialism within families as both Berta and Ofelia use whitening cream in response to their self-loathing and torment Celia as a result of their colorism.[21] Despite her promise to stay put if she has a girl child, Celia's subsequent abandonment of her firstborn, Lourdes, is in direct proportion to the malice she endures on the domestic front from Berta and Ofelia, with their partner in crime, Jorge, an accomplice par excellence in absentia. That Celia renounces her daughter after giving birth, declaring, "I will not remember her name," is tragic but unsurprising, given the determined level of malevolence from which she suffered, especially during her first pregnancy (*Dreaming* 43).[22]

Mother abandoned as a young daughter herself, Celia's responses to her in-laws, despite their repeated cruelty, is a continued desire to please them to which they respond with more punishment. Inadequately loved by all the adults in her life, the abandoned daughter, Celia, cannot transfer motherlove to her first daughter, Lourdes. As Winnicott declared, "Babies do not remember being held well—what they remember is the traumatic experience of not being held well enough" (142).[23] Daughters, who may or may not become mothers themselves, respond to their own traumatizing experiences of inadequate maternal love, a kind of mis-love[24] that leaves daughters vulnerable to reactive responses without full consciousness of their mother's cultural contexts.

Reconciling daughterhood with maternal memories of abandonment, both Celia and Sethe ultimately teach their own daughters a "morphology of survival" through a pedagogy of gender, training girls to "read columns of blood and numbers in men's eyes" (*Dreaming* 42). Sethe endures sexual assault because a white "book-reading teacher" applies pseudo knowledge to feed his own carnality—"watching and writing it up"—while his nephews, "two boys with mossy teeth," attack a lactating Sethe (*Beloved* 70).[25] After their traumas, Celia and Sethe encounter ghostly spirits that emerge from water and serve to naturalize their understanding of the uncertain boundaries between the self and other, the living and the dead. The wounds that result from practices of abduction from which Sethe and Celia have suffered are the focus of the next section, with reference also to the daughters of abduction: Denver and Lourdes.

The Daughter's Abduction, the Mother's Wounds

How far back does it go, the daughter's abduction? As though in answer to this question, Morrison and García expand the conceptional terrain of generational rhetoric so endemic to American literature. In doing so, both authors move away from a rhetoric that is teleologically oriented in favor of a genealogical impulse, that, as William Boelhower explains, "generates a radical interrogation of the authority of the official cultural scale" (88).[26] Neither novel is solely constructed along genealogical lines as their narrative excavations illuminate a "crisis of foundations within a different set of historical facts" (Boelhower, "Ethnic Trilogy" 7, 8). Those foundations harken back to transatlantic voyages and colonizing processes that submerged subordinated cultures in America and Cuba. Both authors interrupt the genealogical principle by expanding the typical orientation device of three generations to reach beyond that paradigm to unearth foundational ideas about heritage cultures: African, Afro-Cuban, and European.

Through a rewriting of the Demeter/Persephone maternal plot, I argue that Morrison and García return their narratives to a place before abduction occurred, where all the women are daughters: before the drought and before the mother loses the daughter, who will be forever encumbered by patriarchal control. For Morrison and García, 1873 and 1959 underscore specific eras that illuminate the limitations of traditional archives to examine the failures of Reconstruction and the Cuban Revolution, largely told from the point of view of white males.[27] Rather, these novels ask: Where do radically unhoused women go when the ability to leave or to move is prohibited by the very institutions under which they were forced to live in these eras? And how and why did the mothers of these unhoused daughters leave, rending the mother-daughter bond? How do these authors go about reconstructing matrilineal relationships when so much has been eradicated? Neither author is a fantasist, though both use metafictional devices to share knowledge—nontraditional forms of expression—communicated between mothers and daughters, through ghostly measures, telepathy, and the natural world.

For example, in *Beloved*, the ghost's return instantiates a genealogy that is more rhizomatic than root tree.[28] When Beloved engages Sethe in storytelling, she does so to receive maternal sustenance, simultaneously generating Sethe's memories of her mother, Ma'am. Four weeks into her incarnation, Beloved has Sethe talking about crystal earrings, a crazy-quilt wedding dress, and the stigmata of a burned cross branded under Sethe's mother's *breast*. Remembering and deflecting, Sethe's silence regarding the whereabouts of those earrings is a Spivakian withholding for Denver's sake, the living daughter she ultimately saves from abduction.[29] Before her death, Beloved remembers Sethe jingling her earrings "for the pleasure of her crawling-already? girl" (94); like Pilar's toddler memories of sitting on Celia's lap, playing with her grandmother's drop-pearl earrings, Beloved craves her mother's memories as they extend the breadth of her earthly existence, reaching further back into a collective history that includes the "Sixty Million and more" of Morrison's epigraph, those unnamed humans erased by the transatlantic slave trade. O'Reilly argues that Morrison's ghostly reincarnation of Sethe's murdered baby girl is also the "flesh and blood personification of the motherline, or more appropriately, given that she is a spirit, a 'beyond-the grave' reincarnation of it, . . . developed and sustained throughout the text" (*Toni Morrison and Motherhood* 85). As a composite identity, Beloved is both Sethe's daughter "from beyond the grave and the captured and orphaned African daughter from 'the other side'" (O'Reilly, *Toni Morrison and Motherhood* 86). Expanding the conceptual and geographical terrain of generations by expanding genealogy through assemblage, Morrison embraces all the lost Africans who died—who were not counted—on the crossing; as Gordon explains, Morrison inscribes a "genealogy of the anonymous" (188).[30] Morrison reinvests the motherline with communicative powers that recover lost voices.

Through the narrative plot and nondiegetic references to a whole lineage of people, Morrison thus records the "disremembered and unaccounted for" (*Beloved* 275).[31] One such person is Sethe's mother, whom she only knows as a respectful salutation, Ma'am. Beloved's question to Sethe about her mother—"Your woman she never fix up your hair?"—bears further commentary. Once Sethe clarifies that Beloved is referencing her mother, she reveals aloud the following facts in earshot of a protesting Denver, whose hair she is fine-tooth combing: Sethe's mother worked in the fields, cultivating rice in paddies and harvesting indigo, thus suggesting an earlier location further south than Kentucky. Unable to nurse Sethe for more than a couple weeks, Sethe's mother, like other enslaved women working the fields, depended on wet nurses, Black enslaved women who fulfilled that role; and, finally, Sethe's mother reveals to her daughter the imprinted mark under her breast, branding her as chattel, but this scene is recalled here to indicate Ma'am's maternal relationship to her daughter: "'This is your ma'am. This' and she pointed. 'I am the only one got this mark now. The rest is dead. If something happens to me and you can't tell me by my face, you can know me by this mark'" (61). The story Sethe shares here continues to accumulate in detail, increasing in significance in different ways for mother and daughter. Denver, whose interest in the past only concerns the story of her miraculous birth, discovers that she had a maternal grandmother, which links her to a matrilineal history abridged by slavery. In response to seeing her mother's mark, Sethe naïvely says to her Ma'am: "'Mark me, too,' I said. 'Mark the mark on me too.' Sethe chuckled. 'Did she?' asked Denver. 'She slapped my face.' 'What for?' 'I didn't understand it then. Not till I had a mark of my own.'" (61). Sethe's response to Denver's own naïve question, "Did she?" takes her to memories she cannot divulge to Denver, though she utters aloud the horrifying fact that her mother was hung to death. Triggered by Beloved's maternal question, Sethe's storytelling activates a queer combination of fragmented memories and postmemories, as she starts to realize that her "privately shameful" feelings are not solely her own.[32]

Beloved's ghosting sparks Sethe's recursion to a centuries-long past she barely knew she remembered, inclusive of othermothers and a mother tongue she once understood but has lost, living with multiple women on a plantation elsewhere before Sweet Home: "Nan was the one she knew best, . . . who nursed the babies, cooked, had one good arm and half of another. And who used different words." Without the language, Sethe manages to break the code: "She told Sethe that her mother and Nan were together from the sea. Both were taken up many times by the crew. 'She threw them all away but you. . . . You she gave the name of the black man. She put her arms around him. The others she did not put her arms around. Never. Never. Telling you. I am telling you, small girl Sethe" (62). Unimpressed by this information as a girl, the adult Sethe inchoately recognizes that her unmothered status emerges from the abduction and enslavement of an African woman whose language and customs were nearly eradicated but for the ministrations of the ghostly presence in *Beloved*.

The daughter's abduction goes as far back as the sea. Morrison makes this claim in her requiem, the most polyphonic section of the novel, in which the women of 124 share "unspeakable thoughts, unspoken" (199). By inserting Beloved's testimonial of the sea voyage alongside references to captives on the slave ship, Morrison portrays the women partaking in a tradition of lamentation, in which, unlike traditional protocols of grieving, their lament is "intimate, private, oral, and informal" (Gilbert 31). In addition, the unspeakable and unspoken thoughts are Morrison's attempt to portray a dis(re)membered past. Saidiya V. Hartman explains, "The violence and dishonor and disaffiliation constituitive of enslavement and the radical breach introduced by the Middle Passage are articulated in these everyday practices and the possibilities or the impossibility of redress." (*Scenes of Subjection* 72). During this interlude, Morrison also records a maternal history in which Sethe functions as both Demeter and Persephone: the mother guarding her daughter and the daughter carrying the basket, a repeated allusion to Persephone gathering flowers. In fact,

Beloved sees Sethe as "the one that takes flowers . . . and puts them in a round basket;" it is Sethe who "picked flowers, yellow flowers, in the place before the crouching" (210, 214). Ultimately, matrilineal history is reconstructed as we learn that Sethe is also akin to and kin of abducted daughters of the Middle Passage.

In part 2 of *Beloved*, Morrison widens the maternal plot to invoke a Penelope-like delay and a Persephone-like return.[33] In this threnodic section of the novel Sethe, Denver, and Beloved first speak separately and then as a triadic voice of maternal longing (200–17). Morrison portrays these three characters reacting to "injury by coming to a standstill" (Cavarero 60). In the Demeter myth, "it is precisely the mother who stops generating when the daughter is snatched out of her sight. This act brings nothingness onto the stage as 'birth-no-more.' . . . Consequently, the maternal power to generate is coextensive with the reciprocal visibility of mother and daughter" (Cavarero 60). All three women are again visible to each other, permitting them to enter a home space in order to reenact "the complexities of inhabitance in the context of displacement" (Gedalof 87). Utilizing interior monologue as a form of confession, Morrison reveals Sethe's recognition of her displacement after she is released from jail, and, Hester-like, exiled from her community.[34] Sethe divulges more details of the maternal story to her ghostly interlocuter by revealing the shattering possibility that her Ma'am's death by hanging may have been the result of attempting to escape from slavery *without her*. Sethe disbelieves but simultaneously rationalizes its distinct possibility. Ma'am's rough choice to escape without her daughter reveals Sethe's enlarged maternal empathy as she examines the effects of trauma, realizing that her mother's body has been wrecked by relentless punishment: "She'd had that bit so many times she smiled," Sethe confesses (203). Her mother's daughter, Sethe's own rebellion and its consequences reveal her struggle to mother her living children at the same time as she longs to be with her dead girl. Admitting that her grief-stricken behavior gave her access to the world of the dead, Sethe chooses life even though her "mind was homeless then" as she endured community exile and came close to becoming a "Saturday girl," after her release from jail (204). Suffering the aftershocks of maternal abduction, Sethe confesses that her Ma'am, and all the women of her kinship group before her, can hope for no permanent "disinvestment from the polis" but only temporary reprieve (Cavarero 84). Like Penelope, Sethe reweaves impenetrable time by establishing "a boundary that demands an absolute separation between *home* and *polis*" so that she and her daughters can exist "in a separate and impenetrable space" (Cavarero 84). Before she hears the click and locks the door, however, Sethe speaks to Paul D, who leaves 124 Bluestone Road after she narrates a vertiginous story about the perfect death (163–65, 99).

Morrison examines the consequences of Sethe's unspeakable act of murdering her child in an effort to prevent her daughter's abduction. Though she cannot put her child's death into actual words, Sethe's reasoning for doing so is crystalline: "I couldn't let her nor any of em live under schoolteacher. That was out," she explains to Paul D (163). Morrison further narrates Sethe's internal thoughts to convey a maternal subjectivity that embraces death as the ultimate form of parental protection: "And if she thought anything it was No. No. Nono. Nonono. Simple. She just flew. Collected every bit of life she had made, all the parts of her that were precious and fine and beautiful, and carried, pushed, dragged them through the veil, out, away, over there where no one could hurt them. Over there. Outside *this place*, where they would be safe" (163, emphasis added). For the maternal to become a space and not a place, Morrison reprises the myth of Demeter in order to name, as I have quoted before, "a mother who not only posits her relationship with her daughter as primary, but, more importantly, wants her daughter to be what she is. Demeter wants a Kore who is a girl, the virgin to whom she has given birth. She does not want a pregnant daughter in an uninterrupted act of regeneration" (Cavarero 90).[35] That daughter is Denver, who is not destined for deportation by the novel's end. Denver's future trajectory directly results from the paradoxical outcome of Sethe's action. Neither woman nor child, Denver fully participates in the threnody, demonstrating a daughter's troubled response to her mother's trauma.[36] Denver is both her mother's daughter in her capacity to withstand her mother's memories and a disidentifying teenager who longs for her "angel man" Daddy, who will finally protect her from a murdering mother and her own recurring nightmare of suffering decapitation by her (206–7). Sethe's withholding of wrenching details of the sexual assaults of her and her Ma'am potentially ensures a certain distance to keep Denver from overidentifying with her mother's traumatic and shame-filled memories. Denver's embrace of Baby Suggs's postbellum commandment to "listen to my body and love it" corroborates a new dispensation coming her way (209).

Morrison revises the classical story of Demeter and Persephone through reversal: the interlude begins in January with Sethe's mothering her girl children and ends in April with Sethe regressing, reverting to the dying daughter, weak and without a mother's milk. Through this backsliding movement, Sethe mourns the loss not only of her dearly beloved daughter but also of her own unmothered daughterhood. Though eighteen years old, Denver's own stagnation has arrested her development, keeping her in a liminal state of childhood, which she will surpass as a result of this winter of maternal consent, this mother-daughter plot also hinging on Denver's reversal. Constitutionally unable to be sated, Beloved is the always-devouring daughter. During this maternal lockdown, Denver realizes that she's in an underworld not of her making. By leaving the house, Denver reenters the community as a maternal supplicant: she begins the process of saving her mother and setting in motion the reconvening of othermothering women in the community. Denver's leaving the house in which she has been incarcerated a dozen years is abetted by the ghostly presence of Baby Suggs, whom Denver accesses and who admonishes her to step off the porch, despite her feeling defenseless (244). Rendered mobile by an act of will spiritually sanctioned by her paternal grandmother, Denver will not relive her mother's antebellum history nor remain radically unhoused as have the women before her.

Daughter-Mother Wounds

Like Morrison's *Beloved*, the maternal stories García recovers centralize and redefine the primacy of the maternal line. Radically unhoused early in life, Celia's traumatized response to injury in *Dreaming in Cuban* is to stand still, a form of stopped time not dissimilar to what occurs at 124 Bluestone Road. Celia's rejection of Lourdes occurs after a brutal combination of abandonment by her mother, abuse by her in-laws, and institutionalization by coconspirator Jorge, whose punishment reflects a prerogative of superiority that falsely masks his misogyny and jealousy of his wife. In 1972, when the narrative begins, Celia ponders the degree of difference between separation and death, unable to choose which situation is worse. Separation is familiar, but Celia has yet to "reconcile it with permanence," yet through nonconventional means of expression, she communes with the dead (Jorge) and the living (Pilar), managing time and expanding space. Conversant with the del Pino family's sundry dissensions, Celia ponders the "unknown covenants" of her country, which forced their separations. These covenants reflect the political realities before and after the revolution and largely accounts for Celia's continued fidelity to Gustavo, Jorge, and

El Líder. Celia's own dispersal begins and ends on Cuban shores, with the spectral presence of Gustavo substituting also as a loyal confidant, increasing her capacity for travel unbound by traditional conceptions of time and movement (6). Celia's affiliative dedications also enlarge over time, taking her beyond the family tree and into the community. Honed on the razor edge of injustice, Celia's sense of fairness is reflected in the work she does as a *guardia civil*, a civil family court judge, which permits García to enact her own sleight of hand regarding the institution of family, spousal relationships, and insights about family lines. Like Morrison, García also inserts a maternal plot that reunites generations of women, focusing on the reproduction of violence against women, which begins and ends with the breast.

García frames the del Pino family tree between an epigraph by Wallace Stevens and the first part of *Dreaming in Cuban*, "Ordinary Seductions (1972)." Employing a form of narrative diegesis through her use of a genealogical tree, García sets the terms for how readers *might* engage the figures within the pages that follow. García's family tree follows in the footsteps of many Latinx writers, not the least of which is Gabriel García Márquez, whose family tree in *One Hundred Years of Solitude* is patrilineal and multigenerational, but distinguishes itself through its sparsity of detail and, in allegiance with a fluid notion of time, offers no dates of birth or death.[37] Presenting only dates of birth, García's family tree in *Dreaming in Cuban* pays homage to Márquez, especially by using the same name—Pilar—as a comic nod to the local prostitute whose nontraditional ways and clairvoyance give her powers to influence the patrimony of the Buendía line, the patronymic surname introducing Marquez's family tree.

García's family tree begins with Jorge del Pino (b. 1897), the patriarch whose name caps the ancestral line. Directly below, the author includes the maiden name of Celia (née Almeida) to signify at the outset multiple ethnic cultures, including this local origin name found in Portugal, Sardinia (Italy), and Spain, a derivation from the Arabic, *al'maida*, plateau, of the city. Read between the lines, García's version of the del Pino family tree might also be a resistance to bordered constructions about Cuban family genealogy and notions about their racial purity. In addition, by inserting a family tree, the author extends traditional versions of Cuban family life before and after the revolution, thereby aligning herself with other Latinx and racial/ethnic-heritage writers who have utilized family trees for a variety of purposes, some of them parodic.[38] That García inserts two lines from a Wallace Stevens poem as her epigraph before the standard fare of a family tree is equally noteworthy. Stevens's poem "Someone Puts a Pineapple Together" remained on García's desk as she was composing *Dreaming* (López 614). The epigraph reads, "These casual exfoliations are / Of the tropic of resemblances." In the poem, Stevens presents twelve (numbered) one-line metaphors on the pineapple, "an object the sum of its complications," as the poet writes (3.34). As though giving advance warning to her readers that metaphors will abound, García prepares us to accept the metafictional technique undergirding *Dreaming in Cuban*, which is also employed as a form of critique regarding rigid notions of genealogy.

Similar to Morrison, García's *Dreaming in Cuban* extends ideas about lineage beyond blood and borders. Rafael Dalleo draws on the work of Édouard Glissant, who forcefully rejects filiation and genealogy, arguing that "the concept of relation points to the limits of tradition and the historical dynamics tradition can obscure" (9). By using the metaphor of the rhizome to present an alternative to the family tree, Glissant unfixes ossified ideas about root identities, "imagining identity as both rooted and in process and of drawing attention not only to the vertical connections of genealogy but to horizontal relations as well" (Dalleo 9). By way of concluding this section, let me suggest, echoing Dalleo, just one such a horizontal relation: Sandra Cisneros's image of the woman at the window watching the outside world in *The House on Mango Street* is metamorphosed into a tropic of resemblance, in which we see an image of a woman sitting in her wicker chair by the sea, Celia del Pino, "equipped with binoculars and wearing her best housedress and drop pearl earrings" (3). By 1972, Celia's separation from men with power is nearly complete. Though her repetitive behavior may suggest otherwise, Celia persists in tying motherlove to her homeland island, which will partially bridge the gap between generations and across the sea, securing a connection with Lourdes, the daughter whom she abandoned. As Davis explains, "The process of reconciliation typical of mother-daughter ethnic novels is here presented . . . as incomplete" (67). While blame can be cast on the government for its role in dividing families, García focuses on the effects of trauma incurred as a result of Castro's seizure of power, the wreckage writ large within the del Pino family, engendering the rupture of the mother-daughter bond.

Celia's originary wound loops back to pre-Revolutionary times and to *her* mother, whose name is unsurprisingly absent from the patrilineal family tree. A victim of a bigamist husband whose second family lives less "than a mile away," Celia's mother abandons her children after her parents' divorce. On the train ride to Havana, Celia loses "her mother's face, the lies that had complicated her mouth" (92). At age four, Celia is "dispersed" to Havana to live with Great-Aunt Alicia, "known for her cooking and her iconoclasm" (92). As though she were inanimate, Celia's dispersal makes her a diasporic subject long before she moves to the house by the sea, after her return from the asylum. Celia's traumatic response to unceasing acts of abandonment is reflected in her decision to abandon her firstborn daughter, though she does not physically leave: "She held their child by one leg, handed it to Jorge, and said, 'I will not remember her name'" (42–43). Lourdes's Achilles heel stems not only from Celia's abandonment of her but also from Jorge's abduction, an act that occurred in utero, all but guaranteeing Celia's rejection of her firstborn child.

Similar to Sethe's response to her wounding, Lourdes's struggle in *Dreaming in Cuban* is all about milk. Her feelings of grief, which she attributes to her father's death, are actually about mother loss, inscribed on her body, imbricated within Cuban family culture, and dramatized in New York by eating and sexual disorders.[39] Lourdes's physical struggles to control her body's basic urges are fundamentally related to the unfinished feeling she gets from not being nurtured well enough by Celia. Like Sethe, Lourdes is both fully a woman and also an abandoned daughter; like Denver, Lourdes is frozen in a liminal state of childhood, feeling orphaned and denying her exilic status. As Julee Tates explains, Lourdes's estrangement from her mother reflects and "symbolically conditions the daughter's relationship with her Cuban motherland" (146).[40] Lourdes's maternal losses as both a daughter and a mother impel her migration to America. Before her exodus, Lourdes demonstrates an Amazonian brand of courage as she stands "like a shield before her husband," jumping "from her horse," in order physically and verbally to defend *a man*: she will be punished for her strength when the soldiers return to rape and mutilate her while her husband, Rufino, is away in Havana ordering a cow-milking machine for their farm (70). Unlike Halle in *Beloved*, Rufino does not witness the sexual assault and remains unaware of his wife's trauma. Significantly, García describes Lourdes's miscarriage as symbolic of patriarchal violence against the maternal, symbolized by the seat of its nurturance, the breast: "Lourdes felt the clot dislodge and liquefy beneath her breasts, float through her belly, and slide down her thighs. There was a pool of dark blood at her feet" (70) (see figure 2.2). This maternal trauma travels with Lourdes to the United States.

Figure 2.2. Maria Faedo, Panel from *The Birthing Album*, 1994, graphite on paper sewn to wool; steel wire, 72 5/8 x 168 1/4 x 1/8 in. (184.5 x 427.4 x 0.3 cm), Smithsonian American Art Museum, Museum purchase through the Smithsonian Latino Initiatives Pool and the Smithsonian Institution Collections Acquisition Program, 1995.

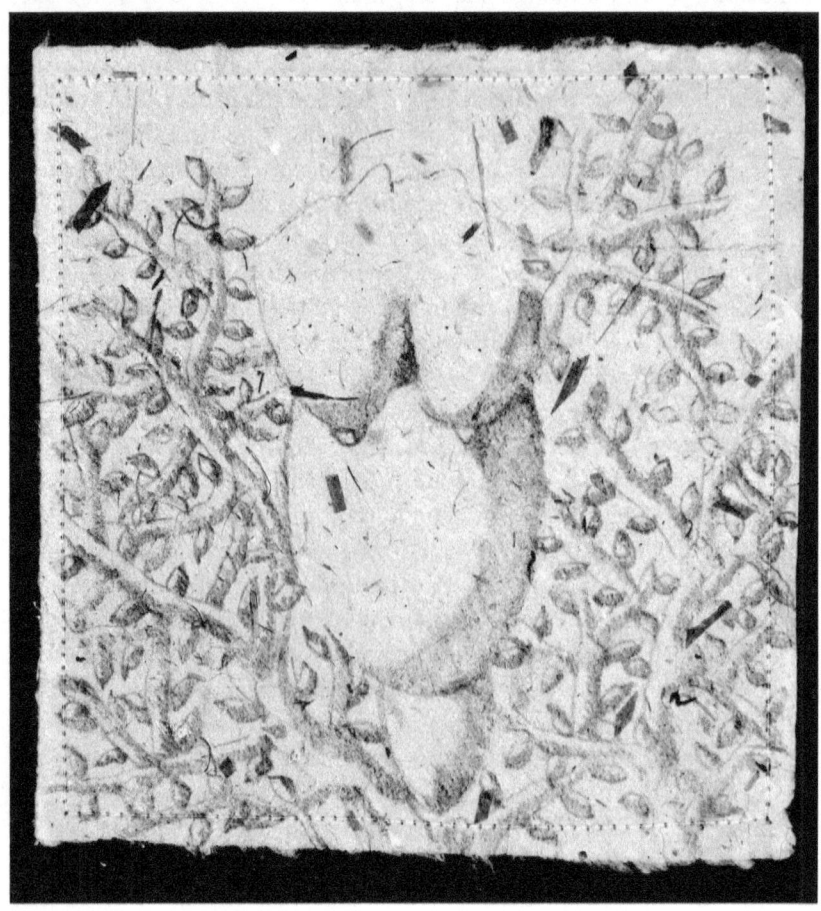

With the help of regular visitations from her ghostly father over a seven-year period, Lourdes moves closer to healing, preparing her to return with Pilar to the island she renounced. As salutary as these visitations are for Lourdes, they are a necessary *purgatorio* for Jorge, who waits to the eleventh hour to make his final confession. Borderland ghost, Jorge confesses his unforgivable transgression; he admits to his beloved daughter his intention to destroy her mother. Let me add here that Gustavo (Celia's lover before her marriage to Jorge) is Jorge's bête noire and becomes the ghost who haunts Jorge's entire life. Though disguised, Jorge never overcomes his jealousy, even on his deathbed, where he is still fighting with "the Spaniard," as he invariably calls Gustavo (*Dreaming* 32). He discloses to his daughter the malicious motive underlying his intent, leaving Celia with "my mother and my sister. I knew what it would do to her. A part of me wanted to punish her. For the Spaniard. I tried to kill her, Lourdes. I wanted to kill her. . . . I wanted to break her, may God forgive me" (*Dreaming* 195). He adds, "I wanted to own you for myself. And you've always been mine, *hija*" (*Dreaming* 196). A form of possession that mimics master narratives of slavocracy, Jorge's guilt-filled admission illuminates an extremity supported by infrastructural powers of family and state.

In chastened recognition of the murderous implications of his intentions, Jorge twice declares, "Your mother loved you," compelling Lourdes to retrace the mother-daughter bond as it has been subject to violent erasure from the start (195). Denied and severed by the father's abduction, the daughter's bond to her mother suffers a fissure from the start: the gap is as wide as the sea. Lourdes's maternal loss is incalculable, making it nearly impossible for her to comprehend what her father is saying. Merely parroting his words, but not fully grasping them, Lourdes echoes, "She loved me" (196). Regular visitations from Jorge recall the geographical place-name her father gave her: Lourdes is a heralded town in southwestern France and a famous pilgrimage site, a sanctuary for believers in ghosts, *Marian apparitions*, which Lourdes may one day experience, too. Inscribed within both her place name and her married name, Lourdes Puente will make strides by leaving New York to drink from the healing waters of Cuban springs. García's maternal plotting puts in place the daughter's return in April, which is not only Lourdes's favorite month but Demeter's too.

Jorge's final admission to Lourdes is simply bone chilling. He flatly confesses to having known that his daughter was raped by Cuban revolutionaries: however, Lourdes's mother, Celia, never knew. Jorge's disclosure illuminates the forever unacceptable story in which paternal law permits a father to abduct an innocent girl-child in plain sight of her mother because of his uncontrolled jealousy. Ellen McCracken explains that "her father's visit becomes the site of a feminist recuperation when he admits to Lourdes his misogynistic treatment of Celia and attempts to heal the rift between mother and daughter that his actions instigated. He admits in an 'even' tone to knowing about his daughter's rape by the government soldiers, suggesting at the very least that he engaged in the complicity of silence with his crime" (26).⁴¹ Perhaps that is why Lourdes cannot respond to Jorge's entreaty before his final departure: "Please return and tell your mother everything, tell her I'm sorry," a request that is not her duty to fulfill (197).⁴²

Lourdes may come to realize that the trauma she suffered as a mother-abandoned child is directly related to her subsequent miscarriage and rape by government revolutionaries, who usurped her husband's land. *And Jorge knows this.* Because the matrilineal bond was prematurely severed, all of Lourdes's ensuing behavior is in reaction to and compensation for this abandonment, including her marriage and migration to America. Hyperassimilating American culture,⁴³ Lourdes's behavior threatens to erode all Cuban heritage customs as Lourdes develops compensatory modes of security to enable her psychic survival as a traumatized immigrant mother in America. It will be Lourdes's decision to probe this paternal betrayal further, but her return to Cuba is instigated by her daughter, Pilar, who also experiences a sexual assault, this time, on American soil. These linked events reinforce three generations of women whose losses are inscribed on their bodies, specifically on their breasts. Mary S. Vásquez explains, "The mother-daughter parallels multiply in threads of connection that bind characters ever more tightly" (25). By the time she is in college, Pilar is in the process of formulating a feminist intervention, recognizing that both her gendered and national destinies have been dominated by "men who had nothing to do with me [but] had the power to rupture my dreams, to separate me from my grandmother" (200). Insisting on recovering matrilineal bonds, Pilar returns with Lourdes to the motherland.

García symbolizes separation between women through repeated references to the maltreated breast, solidifying an intertextual connection with Morrison as separations between women are inscribed through violent severances to their bodies. Clearly, García is aware of her readers, nodding intertextually to Morrison's primal scene of Sethe's assault in the barn which her husband witnesses. In *Dreaming*, Celia undergoes a radical mastectomy; Lourdes feels her miscarriage begin in her breasts after she is raped; and Pilar is sexually assaulted under knifepoint by boys who suckle her breasts. As O'Reilly Herrera asserts, "The theme of maternal loss . . . thus functions as a metaphor for the losses that Cuba has sustained since the first colonial intervention. In some sense Celia's mastectomy—the removal of the maternal breast, the primal source of human nourishment—simultaneously suggests both the physical deprivation of the Cuban people as a result of severe food shortages and the maiming of Cuba as mother country" (86).[44] By centralizing the breast as the ultimate signifier of maternality, García illuminates its continued power to redefine mother-daughter relations across the sea. For the del Pino/Puente women, the bridge to reunification enables travel elsewhere, creating in-between spaces to tell the stories of their nation's history.

Bridges to Diasporan Elsewheres; or, Water's Way

Morrison and García create diasporic time within constricted space in homes haunted by memory and desire. Daughters who are mothers, Sethe and Lourdes, enter spaces that enable them to remember their maternal losses. Their attempts to reconstruct matrilineal bonds may seem frail, but their exposure to excruciating memories authorizes their daughters to take up maternal strands and continue interdependently on their own journeys. Despite the repetitive stasis that concludes the threnody section of *Beloved*—"You are mine / You are mine / You are mine" (217)—Morrison manages a ventriloquist's feat by establishing porous boundaries between mother and daughter that simultaneously embrace fusion, warn against seizing the other for one's exclusive desire, and, as Bhabha suggests, acknowledge a visible love, "where Sethe, Denver, and Beloved perform a fugue-like ceremony of claiming and naming through intersecting and interstitial subjectivities" (17). Together, they transform home space into a maternal community, thereby replacing the logic of slavery with the larger recovery project informing Morrison's novel: "the slave mother regaining through the presence of the child, the property of her own person" (Bhabha 17).[45] Through interstitial spaces, Morrison ultimately manages to link the incarnated ghost with the bridge that brought her to Ohioan shores, enlarging an examination of slavery beyond the failures of 1873, and, more generally, the era of Reconstruction.

In order to embrace complex intersections between mothers, mobility, and narrative, García situates the mother's return and daughter's return to Cuba during the 1980 Mariel exodus and the storming of the Peruvian embassy.[46] Lying on her back in her childhood bed, "in the little brick-and-cement house by the sea," Lourdes hears "old sentences lurk beneath the mattress" (237). Her father's "endless destinations" left Lourdes feeling completely unmoored as a child. Her return to Cuba allows Lourdes to formulate the thought that she cannot keep "her promise to her father," a nonstarter entreaty she carries with her from the Brooklyn Bridge to the parental home in Havana (237, 238). However, as she rolls and lights a cigar, Lourdes recognizes that the very idea of an apology refuses to form in her mouth, reflecting her nascent realization that she can neither offer an apology on behalf of another nor exact one from her mother, whose initial rejection of Lourdes is the primal wound from which she may never fully recover: "Like a brutal punishment, Lourdes feels the grip of her mother's hand on her bare infant leg, hears her mother's words before she left for the asylum: 'I will not remember her name'" (238). Unlike Morrison's Sethe, who pays dearly to have the word *Beloved* carved on her daughter's headstone, inscribing that name to suggest permanence, Celia's resistance to establishing permanence with her firstborn daughter needs the intervention of her granddaughter to bridge the gap in communication between Celia and Lordes, both of whom have suffered profoundly from abandonment by their mothers.

García's reclamation of the mother-daughter bond thus requires the intervention of another generation, represented by Pilar, who functions as the bridge between grandmother and mother. The larger recovery project working in *Dreaming in Cuban* enables further migration for the younger generation, represented by Celia's grandchild, Ivanito, whose passage out of Cuba not only recuperates the mother-daughter bond between Pilar and Lourdes but also ignites Pilar's realization that, in leaving Cuba, she is not abandoning her grandmother, whose cache of letters she takes back with her to New York. Pilar says, "I'd have to return to New York. I know now it's where I belong—not *instead* of here, but *more* than here" (236). The *more than here* is the extraordinary something Morrison and García incorporate in the final pages of their novels.

Bridges accommodate its avatars well in *Beloved* and *Dreaming in Cuban*. A diasporic entity, Beloved embodies water and can only describe her presence from the perspective of the interstitial space of the bridge: "The clearest memory she had, the one she repeated, was the bridge—standing on the bridge *looking down*" (119, emphasis added). Beloved emerges from the Ohio River, a major artery that flouts borders by flowing through or along the border of six states. But her ghostly presence extends beyond postbellum America and its waters. Readers nonetheless must recognize that Sethe approaches Beloved as the dead child she killed. Yet, as postmillennial readers living under different conditions, "we are reminded of what Morrison's characters cannot remember or digest in 1873: the more of Beloved's story as a slave-to-be who never arrived, a history of barely legible traces imagined or conjured" (Gordon 175). *Beloved's* epilogue recalls the epigraph of "Sixty Million and More," positioning Africa as the home space that frames a three-hundred-year-old history that, in Morrison's hands, is told through maternal relations previously repudiated and dis(re)membered under slavery.

Sethe and Celia recover their mothers through the sea. Like Morrison's *Beloved*, García's *Dreaming* is framed by water. No longer needing to defend herself from patriarchal cruelties employed to lessen her, Celia's days of being abused are over, but this mother will not choose to function maternally beyond caring finally for her own body's needs. Just as Sethe's response of incredulity and exhaustion to Paul D's disingenuous urging of Sethe to become pregnant again, so Celia's response to family division is met with neither anger nor powerlessness but rather with exhausted recognition of the consanguinity between family and nation: it is one and the same. She explains to her interlocutor, Pilar, "Families used to stay in one village reliving the same disillusions. . . . For me, the sea was a great comfort. . . . But it made my children restless. It exists now so we can call and wave from opposite shores. . . . *Ay, mi cielo*, what do all the years and the separation mean except a more significant betrayal?" (240) By 1959, Celia's stored treasure chest of letters is awaiting her granddaughter from the other shore, who not only will "remember everything"; she will also extend her grandmother's legacy with a similar understanding of its revolutionary potential.

Celia's decision to end her life in the Cuban sea is not self-denying but rather a return to the maternal.[47] A one-breasted woman warrior, Celia's death is no mere reflection of her inability to live as a free person. Rather, her death by water is an overtly gendered choice reflected in her artistry, which was facilitated by her othermother, Tía Alicia, who taught her great-niece how to play the piano—and—saved her life. Like her great-aunt, Celia claims a life of artistry, despite all obstacles thrown her way. Celia's life-long devotion to the music of Debussy and the poetry of García Lorca inevitably connects her to her first lover, Gustavo, but also increasingly weds her to an enlarged consciousness that is an admixture of Cuba's racial makeup, coming from Europe and Africa.[48] Throughout *Dreaming in Cuban*, García embraces a consciousness of *cubanidad*, from Felicia's immersion in Santería to Celia's final song with the duende, portrayed as a maternal voice of "throaty seduction." The duende is both alluring and calming, lover and mother.[49] Referenced in the novel as female, the duende calls out to Celia "through the poet" and generates Celia's final thoughts: "*Her black sounds charmed me, . . . Sing with me, . . . sing for the black sea that awaits your voice*" (243). In the sea, Celia is finally embraced by maternal arms. Racialized as a Black mother and a unique animating force, the spirit allows Celia to remember a history of subjugation that links her to Spanish folklore and Black American spirituals.[50] As her avant-garde granddaughter and mouthpiece iterates, "Art . . . is the ultimate revolution" as it refuses conquest and will not surrender its best thing: beauty. To paraphrase Morrison, *Beloved* and *Dreaming in Cuban* are stories to pass on (235).

For writers such as Morrison and García, who published their works during the late twentieth century, the influences of feminist and critical-race theories expanded their engagements with maternal representation. Nonetheless, all four writers discussed in chapters 1 and 2 were profoundly aware of reigning ideologies of motherhood, which allowed them simultaneously to engage those beliefs in a larger critique of egregious acts of violence against women, which severed bonds between mothers and daughters, sometimes forever. Employing confessional discourse in *Incidents* to illuminate the life-altering aftershocks of separation between mother and daughter, Jacobs reclaims the centrality of the maternal bond in her life's work with her daughter, Louisa, after her narrative ends. Cather's problematic move to autobiography in the epilogue of *Sapphira* is a miscarriage of justice. The shift falls flat and does not illuminate postbellum relations between mother and daughter, Till and Nancy, whose reunion must necessarily be kept between themselves. Kept stories are symbolized by Till's own treasure chest where she stows the "family" history of slavocracy: that is, the plantation history of her former enslavers. Quiet as it's kept, Till is the holder of this antimaternal family history. As Marilyn Mobley McKenzie explains, what Cather tries but fails to reveal through Till's spare modes of communication is "the racialized Africanist presence being used to reify the myth of domestic tranquility of the southern past," a domestic tranquility that never existed for Black women on plantation space (87).

For Morrison and García, maternal communication takes place without utterance, telepathically, and within letters never sent. Interventions through confessional scenes occur in private spaces between women as in the threnody section of *Beloved* and within an epistolary tradition in *Dreaming*. As we know, Morrison took the germ for her novel from the biographical story of Margaret Garner, whose daughter killing became briefly a *cause-célèbrè* in Cincinnati, especially for abolitionists.[51] García's novel has been read through the lens of autoethnography, a literary rhetorical method which examines zones of contact between cultures (and states) that exposes, as Mary Louise Pratt explains, "highly asymmetrical relations of power such as colonialism, slavery, or their aftermaths" (34).[52] Both Morrison and García recognize the fact that authorizing the self to speak truth to power during and within such aftermaths has also been part of women's narrative traditions, beginning with such early practitioners as Anne Bradstreet and Phillis Wheatley and including also powerful female memoirists and orators that followed, such as Susie King Taylor and Jarena Lee, to name just two.

Self-disclosures triggered by separation were not an uncommon topic narrated by confessional voices in American women's autobiographical traditions. Audre Lorde's and Kym Ragusa's narratives emerge from the generation(s) of Toni Morrison and Cristina García, respectively, but they choose instead to fashion nontraditional autobiographies in order to centralize hybridic selves in relation to the maternal. As a result of their narrative innovation, Lorde and Ragusa expand the perimeters of the crucial maternal bond through their exploration of the intersection between the erotic and the diasporic, which I examine in the next chapter.

Chapter 3

Matrilineal Desire and Geographies of Return in Lorde's *Zami: A New Spelling of My Name* and Ragusa's *The Skin Between Us: A Memoir of Race, Beauty, and Belonging*

Genre-Bending Daughters

For Audre Lorde and Kym Ragusa, the desire to belong, somewhere or elsewhere, is simultaneously a desire for the mother. Reclaimed reconstituted figures, mothers in *Zami* and *The Skin Between Us* transcend blood relations, permitting the authors to craft a maternal mythography that is at once a shared enterprise and an individual act of survival. Without ever denying their birth mothers, Lorde and Ragusa reckon with the a priori reality of ruptured maternal bonds by tracing their mothers' collective history back to a place and a time that has suffered dispersal. As a result of such loss, Lorde and Ragusa create narrating daughters who pose complex challenges to the experience of ruptured nurture, and, in the process, expose well-established systems of oppression that contributed to the fracturing of matrilineal bonds. While a generation separates these authors and their publications (Lorde was born in 1934; Ragusa, in 1966), a reader might at first glance struggle to determine which narrative came first as the authors' revelations and their organizational choices illuminate Lorde's bold innovations against Ragusa's quiet candor. Yet further advances made in feminist, critical race, and postcolonial studies in the intervening decades enabled a plethora of voices to emerge, Ragusa's among them. Such countervailing narratives published in the millennium continued to destabilize entrenched ideas about canonical writing within the genre of autobiography.

Situating their subjectivity within a mode of aesthetic and political representation that explores multivalent identities, Lorde and Ragusa disrupt their narrative chronologies in order to embrace more porous notions of time and place. In doing so, these writers reconceptualize maternity by centralizing the erotic in order to trace matrilineal bonds through stories of diaspora. Lorde's 1982 *Zami* exemplifies a form of genre boldness that forces readers to question if not challenge the entire function of the individual in a self-written account. Upon first blush, Ragusa's 2006 memoir, *The Skin Between Us*, seems timid by comparison, but such stylistic reserve is in fact a political strategy woven into her writing, which also offers an expansive notion of the self apropos to the creation of a narrative persona sharing experiences with a receptive audience. Lorde and Ragusa redefine the genre of life writing through their expansive narratives and their persistent seeking of home, through the malleable genre of autobiography and geography.[1] I argue in this chapter that both Lorde and Ragusa employ a multifaceted approach to home seeking to position the writing self as claiming a migratory subjectivity that addresses, as Susan Driver states, "marginalized genealogies of mother-daughter desire" ("Between Theories" 350). I draw on Lorde's description of the erotic in her oft-quoted essay "Uses of the Erotic: The Erotic as Power," to highlight an untapped resource to which Black women, including Lorde and Ragusa, must avail themselves to fight oppression. Wordsmith at heart, Lorde reclaims the etymological meaning of the "very word *erotic*," as it personifies "love in all its aspects—born of Chaos, and personifying creative power and harmony" (55).[2] Recalling the Greek myth to enlarge the definitional perimeters of the word *erotic*, Lorde encourages listeners and readers to celebrate work as a "conscious decision" ("Uses of the Erotic" 55). Both Lorde and Ragusa create hybrid narratives to elaborate conceptions of the self in relation to bonds of matern(al)ity; in doing so, they expand spatiotemporal dimensions in their works to retrieve the maternal.

Lorde and Ragusa are devoted to a form of life writing that recalls Jacobs's *Incidents in the Life of a Slave Girl* in their incorporation of constructed personae to tell mother-daughter stories.[3] While neither Lorde nor Ragusa adopts a pseudonym, like Jacobs's construction of a literary persona, Linda Brent, they distinguish between an autobiographical narrator and the author of their texts. This rhetorical standpoint is strategic in at least two ways: it allows the authors to place an autobiographical subject into a context of memory making, which at times feels both dislocating and destabilizing. By doing so, Lorde and Ragusa offer a modern rendition of a "memory theater," using mnemonic devices to recall specific spaces in Harlem, where their younger selves entered. This stance is then connected to a second strategy both authors adopt to fulfill their political objective of sharing memories in order to "reconstitute fragmented communities, or mark and mourn their loss" (Smith and Watson 26).[4] Neither *Zami* nor *The Skin Between Us* fits neatly into any category of autobiography, a decision for both authors that is equal parts necessity and strategy. The authors broaden conceptions of autobiography and perform multiple acts of narrative production inclusive of but not limited to their nods to the Black women's narrative of enslavement, the feminist confession, the immigrant autobiography, the coming-out story, and the autoethnography, each of which the authors deploy to varying degrees and in revisionary ways.

Both Lorde and Ragusa advance a politics of reparation on behalf of their mothers and the fractured communities whence they came. As hybrid texts, *Zami* and *The Skin Between Us* combine multiple registers of communication, including myth, migration history, and cultural practices, in order to claim marginalized genealogies of mother lines.[5] Alongside other scholars of autobiography, I continue to find Caren Kaplan's phrase *outlaw genre* constructive in describing a more fluid range of textual strategies, including oral, visual, and cultural practices, to expand notions of identity and self-representation in autobiographical narratives.[6] Kaplan explains that "outlaw genres renegotiate the relationship between personal identity and the world, between personal and social history" (130). Based on the titles of their works, Lorde and Ragusa are dedicated to expanding the borders of the genre itself, recognizing that this genre is not a "fixed form," but a "social action" that situates their self-representations within historically dynamic periods that marginalized their migrating ancestors but enlarged diasporic spaces for mobile daughters (Smith and Watson, 18). Lorde and Ragusa represent themselves as daughters whose movement is announced on the very covers of their books, which I discuss next.

Cover Stories: Lorde

The Crossing Press cover of Lorde's book highlights three words: "Zami. Biomythography. Audre." These three words comprise key elements in Lorde's construction of a migratory identity through a redefinition of the self as plural.⁷ These titular words also illuminate Lorde's project of reclamation through strategies of translation and neologism. The font for the first word in the title, **ZAMI,** employs large-scale typography and appears in bold upper case. Underneath the title and in smaller font, the subtitle also appears in upper case and in bold black color: **A NEW SPELLING OF MY NAME**. Lest readers despair at such an unusual title, all they need to do is flip the book to the back cover, in which a definition is proffered: "Zami, a carriacou name for women who work together as friends and lovers."⁸ Lorde's act of naming is an invitation to her readers to continue to engage in a defining feature of Black feminist praxis: reevaluating white heteronormative norms that overrate masculine thinking about individualism and the boot-strapping rubbish that supports it.

Lorde's nomenclatures are reclamations of alternative archives, what Smith and Watson refer to as "archives of remembering" (25). In fact, Lorde's authorial signatory is tripled on her title page with the appellations, *Zami* and *Audre Lorde*.⁹ As a child, Audrey Lorde dropped the *y* from her first name, centralizing two concurrent moments in a childhood marked by disability and silence: she finally speaks when she asks to learn to read.¹⁰ Learning to claim a new spelling of her name is not far behind. As Monica B. Pearl explains, "The very fact of claiming the power of speech over silence fulfills a coming out paradigm . . . a declaration of a struggle with language, and a central moment of naming" (306).¹¹ Pleased with the anagrammatic rearrangement of her name on the page, *AUDRELORDE* (*Zami* 24), Lorde's kindergarten creativity is met with punishment by her teacher for not following directions, which causes her mother to enroll her in a Catholic school and accelerate her to first grade, but she continues to be punished by nuns with straps. With or without the letter *y*, Lorde's first name etymologically means "noble strength," a quality that she connects with her mother, a "powerful woman," and, by extension, herself, an inchoate recognition of her own powerful difference, which was even less expressible in 1940 than the "'unexpressable' word combination of *woman* and *powerful*" (*Zami* 15).

The neologism *biomythography* continues to be noteworthy in its sui generis innovation. As Pearl explains, Lorde's use of the title, *Zami*, is a transliteration of her name: "By calling herself and her life story, *Zami*, Lorde finds an identity that embraces her lesbianism and her blackness as well as her matrilineal history" (306). Let us recall here that Harriet Jacobs was compelled by the slave narrative's authenticating measures to declare under her title a gesture of agency: "Written by Herself." However, more than a century passed before Jacobs's authorship of *Incidents in the Life of a Slave Girl* was biographically validated by the sleuthing archival work of Jean Fagan Yellin. Lorde's autobiographical gestures toward the liberation narrative and the coming-out story are some of the many tributes she simultaneously pays to her multiple identities, which she proudly reiterated throughout her life: "black, lesbian, mother, warrior poet," was a favorite incarnation; other lists included feminist, librarian, and cancer survivor (DeVeaux 367).[12] In a 1977 address, "The Transformation of Silence into Action and Language," she made to a largely white audience at the MLA (Modern Language Association), Lorde said, "Because I am a woman, because I am Black, because I am lesbian, because I am myself—a Black woman warrior poet doing my work—come to ask you are you doing yours?" (*Sister Outsider* 41–42). Lorde's *Zami* broadens these paramount considerations of race and sexuality by also incorporating diasporic stories and mythical histories that recall maternal lineage.

For Lorde, widening her vision constitutes a multipronged approach to embracing her matrilineal history, which is embodied in an act of translation illustrated by her title, *Zami*, reinforcing a plural identity. The daughter of Afro-Caribbean immigrant parents, Lorde's deliberate reference to *Zami* as a biomythography obliges her readers, as Heather Russell states, "to conceive her project in other than traditional autobiographical frames. We are asked to recognize her intended and purposeful resistance to Western discursive hegemony" (59). Lorde is a daughter of her parents' displacement in America, exacerbated by a racial hierarchy that refuses to recognize the value of the heritage cultures of Black immigrants, including her parents' Caribbean provenance.[13] In an interview with Claudia Tate, Lorde describes her coinage of the term *biomythography* as comprising "elements of biography and history of myth. In other words, it's fiction built from many sources. This is one way of expanding our vision" (*Black Women Writers* 115). In reference to the first word of her title, *Zami*, Chinosole explains, "'zami' is *patois* for 'lesbian,' based on the French expression, *les amies*. In Carriacou where the male population is small because they must leave this spice-growing island to find work, lesbianism is a known social phenomenon" (385). Among her many selves and stories, Lorde is both "telling the story of Zami" and "is Zami," as Claudine Raynaud has stated (221, 242). Lorde's project is as much mythography as it is mapping for she places her mother's country (Grenada) on the globe, a gesture of signifying that was geographically unavailable to her in the classroom and learned only through her mother's words (*Zami* 14).

The organizational structure of *Zami* reflects Lorde's devotion to enlarging ways of seeing, which includes enlarging an understanding of the maternal. While the thirty-one chapters loosely follow Lorde's biographical chronology from childhood to adulthood, the narrative gives equal credence to mythologizing aspects of time and carving out queer space that challenge strict notions of a teleological progress narrative. Lorde includes two unnumbered chapters, in fact, that function as revelatory interpolations inserted at the beginning and toward the end of *Zami*: "How I Became a Poet" and "The Last of My Childhood Nightmares" (31–34, 198–99). These seemingly nonlinear articulations, along with Lorde's before-prologue, prologue, and epilogue, all function to resituate her subject position to align with a matrilineal heritage that places her body in a physical and spiritual geography that exceeds normative history and contains the erotic maternal.[14]

In the second of her interpolations, for example, Lorde inserts a nightmarish dream sequence that portrays college-aged Audre "shrieking for exit" from her mother's house, in which she and her white roommate, Rhea, are sleeping in her parents' bed across a doorway exit barred by twice-described "hickory-skinned demons" and "hickory-faced devils" (*Zami* 198,199). Within the sequence, Lorde inserts maternal imagery to counter the hostile presence, dropping a bursting melon that splits open to reveal a "brilliant hunk of turquoise" (*Zami* 199). While I claim neither expertise in oneirology nor entomology, Lorde intimates a subtext here, ultimately suggesting that she will manage to survive the most baneful aspects of homophobia within her family and in the larger culture. Lorde's nightmare both recalls and anticipates her later discovery that her former roommate's sudden decision to leave their apartment was related to threats she received from work colleagues. Despite fear, Lorde's warrior status emerges in her nightmare as she enables Rhea's escape, taking her "white and milky" hand in the half dark to exit the family home one last time: "*This is no longer my home; it is only of a past time*" (*Zami* 199). Like the largest moth from the northern latitudes of Mexico, Lorde depicts Audre's maturation as a process as spectacular as the caterpillar's life cycle, expelling its larva to reveal a turquoise-colored adult regal moth.[15] That Lorde dates and spatializes this interpolation is no small matter. Irregularly inserting dates and years throughout *Zami*, the author's decision here is deliberately personal and formal as she inserts an inside address that includes the month-day-year format one would make on a formal business letter or memo to mark her independence from a place she already left three years before:

My Mother's House

July 5, 1954

As one of the most censorious and oppressive decades in twenty-century US history, Lorde manages to reference *Brown v. Board of Education* and the red-baiting hysteria that produced McCarthyism all within a couple of paragraphs describing the bus trip she makes to Washington, DC, to protest the execution of the Rosenbergs (*Zami* 148–49). These events in fact trigger Lorde's travel to Mexico in 1954, three years after leaving her mother's house. Make no mistake: Lorde feels that unsettled feeling of nonbelonging, which is similar to her mother's. Like first-generation Grenadian Linda Lorde, Audre shares her mother's exilic status but knows she must "fashion some different relationship to this country of *our* sojourn" (*Zami* 104, emphasis added). While she learns "other loving," and, I might add, "othermothering" from women outside her family, Lorde identifies all these women as warriors, including her mother, as *"they dance with swords in their hands"* (*Zami* 104).

While Lorde does not entirely flout traditional historical referents in *Zami*, she does not value those chronological markers unto themselves. For example, Lorde frames chapter 7 by referencing America's inevitable entrance into the Second World War after she and her family hear the radio announcement of the Pearl Harbor bombing. The six-page chapter concludes with Lorde's reference to the Harlem race riots, which the author introduces in a *subordinate clause*, "After the race riots of 1943," marking erased Black history *(Zami* 57). Lorde's focus here is also class based: her parents' upwardly mobile move away from the "'gutbucket' of Harlem" *(Zami* 58) was made possible by the capital available to Blacks in the war years, and Lorde's focus in this chapter is about her immigrant parents' lives during these years, which took them away from her, especially from her mother. "Bursting with pride that this important woman was my mother," third-grader Audre describes her mother's civic activities not only on behalf of the war effort—"watching for enemy planes from a roof culvert" and "giving out ration books from an official-looking table"—but also as a citizen, serving as a poll worker "every Election Day" (*Zami* 55). Linda Lorde's affiliative dedications increase during the war years, taking her into the community just as Celia's employment as a *guardia civil* in *Dreaming in Cuban* brought her into contact with members from the community. That the child, Audre, remarks upon this is noteworthy, for her child's eyes observe her mother's power before she fully understands the depth of her mother's triple oppressions inflected by race, gender, and immigrant status in the 1940s. Lorde recognizes that her parents' work lives were unrelenting and exhausting and demonstrates how her parents collaborated as a team to make ends meet, provide for their three children, and manage to move the family into a better neighborhood. All of Lorde's chapters are precisely detailed in this way, simultaneously legitimating the centrality of Audre's revelations and desires, which always leads her back to the mother and her mother's homeland.

Making the connection between the mother country and mythography permits Lorde to fuse a matrilineal homeland with her recuperative project of claiming the African goddess Afrekete as both mother and lover. *Zami's* cover design and illustration anticipate this focus. Positioned in the middle of the illustration stands a Black female, a figure bifurcated between two striking landscapes: one bucolic, one urban. We see the Caribbean Grenadines and their plantain trees with Mount Cinnamon in the background and New York City's high-rise buildings nearly blocking a recognizable icon, the art deco Empire State Building with its lightning rod antenna. The female figure gently extends an arm toward her mother's country: she is Zami, Kitty, and Audre Lorde. The bifurcation between countries is illuminated by racial codes in America that by the 1950s had succeeded in reducing color to black and white.[16]

The black-white color palette achieves its maximum intensity on the cover of *Zami* with the use of bright orange as border background (see figure 3.1). Orange is the color of mace, the delectable spice from the nutmeg tree, anticipating one of the most sensuous scenes in Lorde's narrative, the mortar-and-pestle passage in chapter 11, which also marks Audre's onset of menses.[17] Merging the mother country with the erotics of food, the menstruating Audre unites her memories of coming into womanhood at age fifteen with a culinary activity distinct to her mother's Carriacouan heritage, pounding garlic for souse with a mortar and pestle from native soil. This scene illuminates an Irigarayan form of "female autoeroticism" that is neither a compensatory pleasure nor an example of repressed female sexuality but, rather, as Irigaray states, "the geography

Figure 3.1 Cover design, *Zami: A New Spelling of My Name*, by Audre Lorde, Crossing, 1982. Photograph taken by Mary Jo Bona.

of her pleasure [which] is much more diversified" ("This Sex Which Is Not One" 26, 28). Even though Lorde learns to her dismay that there is only "one right way to do anything" in her mother's kitchen (after Linda criticizes her daughter for being dilatory), Audre's memory of her mother that day is profoundly sensual, ending with an olfactory description of her mother's hug: "I could smell the warm herness rising between her arm and her body, mixed with the smell of glycerine and rosewater, and the scent of her thick bun of hair" (*Zami* 80). The young Audre takes this elemental memory with her when she leaves her parents' house upon graduating from high school. "[S]haky and determined," Lorde's separation from her mother in fact deepens her relationship to her matrilineal ancestry, thereby increasing her compassion for her mother's migratory stories, which emerged out of longing and caused her mother's deep bitterness in America, the country of her "exile" (*Zami* 104). Second-generation daughter, in homage to her mother's own strength under adversity, will "fashion some different relationship to this country of our sojourn" (*Zami* 104), impelling a sustained and "mature appropriation" as Carol Boyce Davies explains, of her mother's Caribbean culture (93).

Equal parts dedicated to her race and her sexuality, Lorde's *Zami* anticipates if not reflects queer departures from Anglo-American lesbian narratives, or, from what Chinosole describes as "the closet of white decadence" (386).[18] Instead, Lorde insists on the ineluctable relationship between her mother's Grenadian homeland and Audre's lesbian sexuality, recognizing the intersection between, as Anne-Marie Fortier states, the diasporic home and queer migrations.[19] Arguing that *Zami* queers the ancestral homeland, Stella Bolaki extends Fortier's thesis by examining how "the ancestral homeland and the childhood home" undergo "a kind of translation" in Lorde's capable hands, demonstrating "the dynamic relation between race, ethnicity and sexuality" (779).[20] As in subsequent narratives in which queer daughters attribute their sexuality as emerging from the migratory home, Lorde's narrative provides an instance of queerness " 'exceed[ing] sexuality' (queerness emerging out of the fabric of a diasporic or 'queer' home), and, conversely, of fashioning a racial ethnic identity as a Caribbean American which 'exceeds ethnicity' " (Bolaki 784). Conveying a gravitas beyond consanguinity and birth giving, Lorde's *Zami* fuses life writing and theory, reconfiguring maternal bonds between mothers and daughters through a redefinition of the erotic as power.

Cover Stories: Ragusa

"Skin. Memoir. Kym." Ragusa's *The Skin Between Us* announces separation from and connection to its emphatic subtitle: *A Memoir of Race, Beauty, and Belonging*. Like Lorde's *Zami*, Ragusa's narrative advances a theory of race and ethnicity that exceeds traditional models of African American women's autobiography, immigrant autobiography, and feminist confession, genres upon which the author innovates. Ragusa's memoir comprises a protocol of reading that is centrifugal in its force, advancing a nimble response to the binary of race.[21] Thus, her memoir implicitly echoes African American women's autobiography from earlier centuries and, as McKay explains, in its challenge to "Western European discourses on freedom and race. . . . For race (which also implied class) was the crucial ground which relations of power developed between black and white people" (*The Narrative Self* 96). Ragusa extends this crucial ground through a nuanced analysis of both sides of her family, refusing the binary that continues to be ubiquitous in US-dominant discourse. In fact, Ragusa's skin is the contested topography upon which both sides of her family map their own sociocultural positioning on this racialized American terrain.

As Michela Baldo contends, Ragusa stages herself as the embodiment of Persephone, who must shift between the African American world of her mother's family and the Italian American one of her father's (9). A biracial child, Ragusa's mother is African American with a genealogy that can be traced back to the perils of the Middle Passage and its accompanying evils of slavocracy in America, which the author examines in the chapters dedicated to her maternal forbears. Ragusa's father is the son of immigrant parents whose families fled Mezzogiorno poverty in Calabria and Sicily, hazarding the transatlantic journey to enter an unwelcoming America on the brink of passing landmark restrictions on migratory movement from Europe and Asia.[22] In lieu of a genealogical tree, Ragusa documents family history through chapters organized in such a way as to narrate the structural metaphor that undergirds her life: the Black-white binary, which Ragusa both illuminates and deconstructs in *The Skin Between Us*. Ragusa conceptualizes this apartheid structure through chapter organization. Thus, readers are introduced in chapters 1 through 4 largely to Ragusa's maternal history centralized in West Harlem; chapters 5 through 8 then primarily shift to the author's paternal history, located originally in East Harlem and referenced as Italian Harlem in the early twentieth century. Within these chapters is the existential reality of Kym Ragusa, the mixed-race daughter of African and Italian forbears representing herself being shuttled back and forth between East and West and between maternal and paternal families. In the final chapter of *The Skin Between Us*, chapter 9, Ragusa seemingly runs roughshod over chronology and strictly binary ethnic constructions, but this is a strategy by which she unites both families through a form of mediation, culminating in a madcap scene in family court, to which I shall return.

By framing her memoir with a prologue and epilogue, moreover, Ragusa both compresses her complex upbringing in the racially segregated neighborhoods of East and West Harlem and enfolds those locations into a larger geography that links her racial and ethnic background to what I will call her Mediterranean consciousness, or, as Annarita Taronna describes as the author's "ethnography of Southernness" (110). Taronna argues that Ragusa's narrator "calls for a return to *the South*, not only as a geographical category, but also a state of mind, a horizon composed of histories, traditions, and values" (106). Ragusa thus encircles her family's diasporic history and spans the globe, beginning and ending in the land of her ancestors, Sicily: "Sicily is the crossroads between Europe and Africa, the continent from which my maternal ancestors were stolen and brought to slavery in Maryland, West Virginia, and North Carolina. Two sets of migrations, one forced, one barely voluntary. Two homelands left far behind. Two bloodlines meeting in me" (*Skin* 18). Ragusa's return to the South locates her at an intersection that links continents, illuminating two transecting world geographies to expose an admixture of cultural connections resulting from the multiple diasporas of her family. As in *Dreaming in Cuban*, where Cristina García contested the largely mythical claim of a purely white Cuban ancestral line, laying bare an amalgam of racial bonds within the formerly colonized Cuba, Ragusa fuses her maternal and paternal lineages, reclaiming a legibility borne of multiple legacies of color.

Unlike Lorde, whose parents experienced separation from their parents as a result of migrating to America in their twenties, Ragusa's subject position as a granddaughter largely influences how she organizes her approach to remembering. Similar to Lorde, Ragusa embraces multiple identity positions, including African American, Italian American, writer, documentarian, and granddaughter. As in many immigrant autobiographies, Ragusa interprets kin relations through the lens of migration, race, and class, highlighting in turn ongoing family patterns of material deprivation and limited upward mobility. Ragusa is the grandchild of grandmothers whose generational positioning and racial membership largely account for the choices the author makes in narrative construction. Any suggestion that Ragusa's nod to immigrant autobiography will reduce it to a "totalizing system in which autobiographers speak from a priori fixed positions" is thrown by the wayside as the author exposes a vexed immigrant status that continues to be one of the markers by which she interprets her family's historical trajectory (Wong 308).[23]

As the daughter of migrating women on both sides of her family, Ragusa represents different kinds of separation resulting from the migratory stories of both her grandmothers.[24] Such losses then often rearrange child-parent (and sibling) relationships, intensifying them as a consequence of movement and migration. Unlike traditional American generational rhetoric that borrows from biblical typology and spiritual crises in the colonies, Ragusa refuses to slough off the parental generation in favor of either a mythical ancestor or an actual grandmother. Mothers matter: they are also Demeter's daughters, suffering in this "man country," without institutional scaffolding to enable maternal support (Marshall 70).[25]

Ragusa confronts the consequences of maternal struggle emerging from systemic oppressions of racism, misogyny, and failed migration experiences. Through a category of women's autobiography called "feminist confession," Ragusa begins *The Skin Between Us* by portraying one of the rare occasions when both sides of her family share a meal. As Felski reminds us, "Given that women's lives have until now been largely defined by their location within the private sphere, this realm necessarily constitutes the starting point for critical reflection" (92).[26] This sphere constitutes one of the places that the author describes in her acknowledgments as a "woven . . . narrative out of many bits and pieces: fragments of my own memory" (*Skin* 7). Ragusa begins chapter 1 of her memoir on Thanksgiving Day, portraying a rare social gathering that momentarily ties the strands of her family, uniting grandmothers Gilda and Miriam one last time. The year is 1996, and Ragusa is a married adult woman who recalls the final time she will break bread with her maternal and paternal grandmothers, both of whom will die the next year from serious illnesses. Of import in this first chapter of her memoir is the "cover story" Ragusa shares with her readers, based on the only photograph the author has of herself *with* her two grandmothers, which happens also to be the only photograph that appears in *The Skin Between Us*, positioned strategically next to the title page on the front matter of the memoir.[27] The left to right juxtaposition of the photo and title invites an interpretation as the page is subtly highlighted by a graphic design that simulates a textile motif that combines quilting and openwork, aesthetic patterns traditional to African and Italian needlework (see figure 3.2).

The collective story Ragusa tells is about mother loss and motherlove, typical to feminist confession. From the outset, she informs her readers that this family story will include a kind of ekphrastic memory writing. In fact, the author invites the reader to interpret the photo before she examines it directly in her first chapter. Ragusa foregrounds this story about a longed-for intimacy by examining the fraught relationships between maternal and paternal families in alliance *with* her readers. Ragusa's choice to subject her feelings and frailties to readers' scrutiny permits "the erotic mutuality" she establishes between reader and narrator, allowing her to

Figure 3.2 Title page, *The Skin Between Us: A Memoir of Race, Beauty, and Belonging*, by Kym Ragusa, 2006. Photograph taken by Mary Jo Bona.

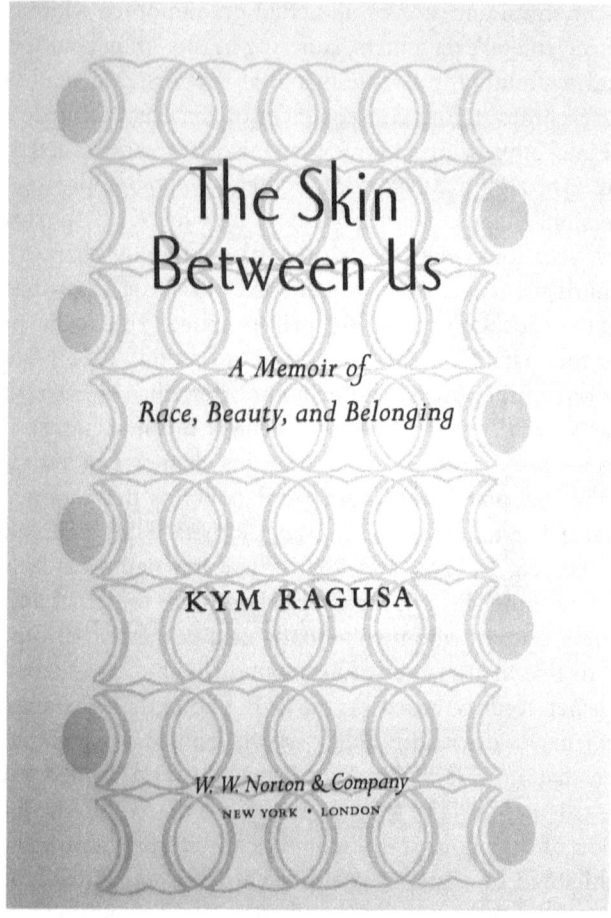

project a "community of female readers" who identify with her "emotions and experiences" (Felski 89). In trying to read the "unconscious emotions" behind the "unstaged" image of the photo, Ragusa first introduces readers to the candid moment captured by the photo: "Gilda to the left, Miriam next to her in the center, me a little off to the right. None of us look at the camera" (*Skin* 23). While notably the photo's inclusion appears in black and white, readers meet three figures whose race is clearly not the focus; rather, the triadic display suggests the iconography of three generations:

grandmother, mother, and daughter. Ragusa's photo performs a sleight of hand. We learn in chapter 1 that Gilda is a generation older than Miriam, and both women are grandmothers to Ragusa. We learn more importantly that both women are suffering the ill effects of cancer; Gilda's Alzheimer's disease confuses her ability to "sort the living from the dead" (*Skin* 23). Miriam's spreading cancer is camouflaged by her broad and generous smile, even toward Gilda, "who looks away. It's a look of hard-won love, of quiet victory. It took years of struggle, this tender gaze. It was work" (*Skin* 24). Mediator and "eternal daughter," Ragusa interprets her own image in the photo through a Mediterranean lens, or, as Evelyn Ferraro refers to it, through a kind of meridian thinking that permits her to share with her reader "a moment of peace between the three of us, a truce" (*Skin* 24, 23).[28] As Ragusa informs us, the truce was hard won, and the victory was borne by Miriam, her Black grandmother, who did the tough work.

Ragusa describes in transcendent terms the still-life aesthetic encapsulated by the photo, which she titles "Three variations on ivory, yellow, [and] olive" (*Skin* 25). Immediately juxtaposed to this "isn't-it-pretty-to-think-so" moment is the magnitude undergirding "the skin between us that kept us apart," which the author addresses fulsomely in her memoir (*Skin* 25). As Ferraro affirms, "The skin is the focus of her critical lens. . . . The physical reality of skin, with its troubling shades of color, is the ground where unstable boundaries are first drawn. . . . The shades of color may not be very different for the light-skinned Miriam and the southern Italian Gilda, but the awareness of the stakes enclosed in the US color line is a powerful source of opposition between them" (*Skin* 220, 221). Held at bay in this photograph is the underlying assumption inflicted on Ragusa at birth: that she does not belong—neither completely to her Italian family of origin nor to her natal country.

In the final paragraph of chapter 1, Ragusa extends the American grammar of Hortense Spillers's historically apt title, "Mama's Baby: Papa's Maybe," to include her parents. Documenting her birth, the author illuminates the difficulty of claiming her legitimacy as the child of differently raced parents as her mother was unwed, giving birth alone at the hospital, accusing Kym's father of abandoning her while she was pregnant. Italian Harlem might as well have been antebellum America for the way Ragusa's "barely white" father absented himself from her birth and thereafter concealed the truth from his family of his filial relationship to his daughter for the first three years of her life. As Ragusa explains, "My birth certificate has a line for my mother's name and her age, eighteen.

The line for my father's name has been left blank. Officially my father does not exist" (*Skin* 32). While Ragusa's father ultimately claims Kym as his daughter, and her surname bears testimony to this (*Skin* 231), Ragusa's relationship to both parents remains "bound by distance" throughout her growth into adulthood.[29]

Documentation equally illuminates the focus of Ragusa's visit to family court with her parents on the final pages of the memoir, the one flawlessly funny scene in the book. This time around, the issue concludes happily with the application of the author's passport, which awaits a hearing to determine whether Kym Ragusa's father was actually "her biological father, and whether he was contesting his paternity" (*Skin* 232). By spatializing her position before the family-court judge who adjudicates the matter, Ragusa reinforces her role as mediator and loving daughter, who continuously embraces her parents, warts and all: "We stood before him, my mother on the left, and my father on the right, me in between. I looked at them both, wondered what the judge thought of my hobbled little family" (*Skin* 232). When the judge asks, "'For the record, how old is the child now?' and my mother said, *Thirty-three*, the whole room erupted in laughter. . . . I laughed, too, at the absurdity of the situation, at how much it took to finally legitimize me. When the judge posed the final question, my father said he wouldn't contest the paternity: 'No, I'm her father—*just look at us*'" (*Skin* 232). This scene provides a momentary stay from the racial politics informing the skin between them, and, more largely, a testimony to Ragusa's profound desire to maintain intimacy with her parents (and get her passport renewed).

After the introductory interlude of intimacy between grandmothers in chapter 1, Ragusa uses italics to underscore the cruel history of racialized identity markers and those insidious tell-tale questions: "What are you?" and "Where are you from?" Such interrogatives underscore the assumption that a person like Ragusa does not belong, reifying her status as an outsider in the country of her birth. Before the narrator extends the borders and remaps locations, she offers her readers an unblinkered response to those questioners who have impugned her:

What are you?

Black and Italian. African American, Italian American. American.

Other. Biracial. Interracial. Mixed-blood, Half-Breed, High-Yellow, Redbone, Mulatta. N_____, Dago, Guinea.

Where are you from?

> I don't know where I was conceived, but I was made in Harlem. Its topography is mapped on my body: the borderlines between neighborhoods marked by streets that were forbidden to cross, the borderlines enforced by fear and anger, and transgressed by desire. The streets crossing east to west, north to south, like the web of veins beneath my skin. (*Skin* 25–26)[30]

Like Lorde, Ragusa embodies the bifurcation of racialized thinking in America; her racial in-betweenness is not only a reality of her daily life, but it will increasingly become a coveted state of mind. Skin, for Kym, *is* the liminal space, metaphorically both a mirror and a window. As she said in an interview with Livia Tenzer, Ragusa perceived her grandmothers as "mirror images of each other. Partially, this has to do with the ways in which both women were marginalized on the basis of race and ethnicity, and also in the ways that each story defies expectations" (215). In two award-winning shorts completed in 1997, *Passing* and *Fuori/Outside*, filmic precursors to *The Skin Between Us*, Ragusa tells stories about Miriam and Gilda. By filming *Fuori/Outside* as a visual "letter" to her Italian grandmother, Ragusa attempts to repair their relationship, using a narratorial voice-over to "examine the relationship between personal memory and 'official' history" (Tenzer 215).[31] Tenzer explains that Ragusa sought to share her film with "the person in her family who most resisted accepting the racially different Ragusa of belonging and of the same blood" (213–14). Just as Ragusa experiences a withholding from her paternal grandmother, so she equally experiences a sense of unbelonging in the larger American culture, both continuous events that "indirectly stress the tensions and ambiguities surrounding her own 'tenuous' position within the family" as Sabrina Vellucci explains (195).

In the opening sequence of *Fuori/Outside*, Ragusa spatializes this fragile position by filming from the outside looking into her Italian grandmother's window. As Vellucci explains, the "use of the window [is] a 'metaphor for the slippery notions of danger and safety of belonging and abjection' . . . [and] recalls the metaphor of skin in her memoir [as] 'the window functions as a membrane separating her from the rest of the family'" (196). Smith and Watson explain that Cherríe Moraga declares a social location that could also be Ragusa's: "Her skin [is] a source of her political consciousness," and it performs important tasks related to negotiating spatial barriers (50).

Ragusa's portrayal of Kym in *The Skin Between Us* introduces readers to an alert young girl who travels back and forth between families, bound by distance, a paradox Ragusa deconstructs through loving critique of the maternal women who raised her. In so many ways, Ragusa is both an eternal daughter and the always responsible middle child, whose role in her family as a mediator ultimately prepares her to embrace a matern(al)ity that has broad mythical and geographical implications. As though finding language for the first time to share what they are feeling and where they are going, Lorde and Ragusa formulate diasporic subjectivities for their younger selves that use erotic forms of power for movement elsewhere.

Made in Harlem: Daughters of Abduction and Migrating Backwards[32]

Lorde and Ragusa claim kinship with Harlem in ways their mothers and grandmothers could not. Products of sexual assault, violence, and radical unhousing, Lorde's and Ragusa's maternal forbears are fundamentally Demeter's daughters, ruptured from their mothers and their homelands. Cultural traditions, linguistic, culinary, and spiritual, to name just three, are maintained with enormous difficulty under assimilative pressures underwritten by American racism, nativism, and Progressive-era reforms of the late nineteenth and early twentieth centuries, the period in which the majority of first-generation African Caribbean and Italian immigrants landed on Ellis Island, many of whom made their way to Harlem. For many emigrants, Harlem was hardly a haven in a heartless world; rather, it felt more like Hades's realm, an underworld with no spring in sight. Describing the great migration of Italians in epic terms, Edvige Giunta explains: "America appeared a huge urban monster to those first-generation immigrants of not so long ago, peasants who had surrendered their ties to the land of Demeter and Persephone to enter what many describe as a hellish world" ("Persephone's Daughters" 776). Much the same might be said of Lorde's Grenadian immigrant mother, whose Harlem tenement space was, as the author learns, "some temporary abode," before she and her family would "arrive back in the sweet place, back *home*" (*Zami* 13). Informed by legacies of slavocracy and colonialism, Lorde's and Ragusa's maternal forbears display ongoing wariness toward America, never truly settled and never truly home. Extending their matrilineal subjectivity by incorporating maternal stories of migration, the authors present a counter-discourse to dominant narratives about upward mobility, assimilation into whiteness, and the efficacy of the nuclear family. Through inventions of mythography and translation, Lorde and Ragusa imagine and enact forms of return, migrating backwards to reclaim parts of their matrilineal legacies, inclusive of colonial and enslaved pasts.

Lorde's parents have no illusions about living in America. Of Grenadian and Barbadian heritage, her parents emigrated to New York in 1924 from Barbados and Grenada, respectively, countries that had been colonized under British-held domination (Watkins-Owens "Early Twentieth-Century-Caribbean Women" 25). Linda Lorde, the author's mother, was part of the first generation of African Caribbean women who migrated to New York in the first decades of the twentieth century. The peak year for women's migration from the Caribbean, 1924, was also a discernible year as it marked the passage of the Johnson-Reed Act, which effectually closed the golden doors. While Irma Watkins-Owens recognizes that these immigrant women migrated within "colonial and patriarchal structures that subordinated them on the basis of sex, class, and color," she equally notes that their status as Black immigrants differently affected their identities in New York as "they entered another arena of sex and race discrimination" ("Early Twentieth-Century-Caribbean Women" 26). Oswald Warner examines the saliency of race and ethnicity in relation to the social identities of immigrants such as Lorde's parents, distinguishing between ascribed or imposed racial identity and a selective ethnic identity many Caribbean immigrants embraced partially to distinguish themselves from Black Americans, a gesture of racializing "their ethnicity in order to socially separate and distance themselves from African Americans" (86).[33] African Caribbean immigrants like Lorde's parents were affected by a "US race and socioeconomic system," ascribed to them [as they] entered a country dominated by white society and unfamiliar racial dynamics that would emerge "between them and African Americans" (Warner 69). While not all immigrants uniformly disidentified with African Americans (who were at the same time migrating from southern states to the North), many emigrants from the African Caribbean sought to maintain cultural identifiers relating to their country's customs.

Lorde's family is no exception. While focusing on post-1965 second-generation Afro-Caribbean immigrants, Sherri-Ann Butterfield defines the terms *race* and *ethnicity* as continuously germane indicators of identity for descendants of first-generation immigrants, and this description is equally useful here in examining Lorde's position as a second-generation daughter: "'Race' is defined as a socially constructed distinction based in physical appearance, while 'ethnicity' is operationalized in distinctions based on national origin, language, religion, food, and other cultural markers" (Butterfield 308). Despite her parents' refusal to discuss American racism with their children, Lorde's schooling replaces their authority by teaching her hard lessons about the cruelties of public shaming and corporeal punishment, favorites of the Catholic nuns whose racism was as "unadorned" as the country's at large (*Zami* 30, 59). Though she responds differently from her parents with regard to her status as a descendant of African Caribbean heritage, the younger Audre, too, refuses to engage an oppositional model that bifurcates people either by race or ethnicity and also by sexuality or gender. Increasingly aware of fitting in nowhere, Lorde comes to realize that "*being black dykes was not enough. We were different*," addressing the process of becoming the ultimate outsider, which she and her sister outsiders must necessarily embrace as a place that is "the very house of difference" (*Zami* 226). For the author, this means that she will invent a mythography, uniting her personal story with a diasporan consciousness that exceeds categorical thinking.[34]

Ragusa similarly refuses to embrace binary thinking that has infected both her maternal and paternal families in *The Skin Between Us*. By using a paradigm of diaspora to examine both sides of her family, Ragusa manages also to critique white supremacy and compel a reexamination of how American racial politics has dealt its cheating hand to both paternal and maternal forbears, playing four-flusher for sheer divestment purposes. As James Baldwin remarked, in order to subjugate Blacks, European-descended peoples who emigrated to America to escape all manner of privations fearfully compromised their integrity, and by submitting to racism against Black people, "they divested themselves of the power to control and define themselves" (80). Italians were no exception.[35] Because the history of Italian immigrants' racialization in America was influenced by an "alchemy of race" that was much more variegated during the height of their migration period, the decades between 1880 and 1920, they were racially coded as the "white other" (Jacobson 52). Southern Italians likely emigrated to America with incipient sensibilities about race, having been pronounced inherently inferior by the Italian positivists of the day, but they just as likely arrived in the United States "without a consciousness of its color line" (J. Guglielmo 3).[36] Anti-Italianism in the new country was then reinforced by the Dillingham Commission's 1911 publication, a *Dictionary of Races or People*, "a taxonomic volume that enabled the Commission to create a hierarchy of colored races and place the new waves of immigration from Southern Europe in a category different from the Northern European ones, defined as 'darker'" (Lombardi-Diop 88). The racial line having been drawn before entry, Southern Italians extended their "southern problem" of racialized "inferiority" and "underdevelopment" to American shores (Roediger, *Working toward Whiteness* 112). As much as Italians were slotted into these "inbetween racial spaces . . . scrutinized, tried, examined, and ranked against other races," as David Roediger observes in *Working toward Whiteness* (58), they were also nonetheless "white on arrival," as Thomas Guglielmo asserts, though subject to racial codification, for example, in such documents as naturalization papers (31).[37]

Ragusa inherits this migration history from her Calabrese and Sicilian families. In her memoir, the author illuminates this history through the lens of a young Ragusa who is growing up during the 1970s. Despite the passage of the landmark Immigration Act of 1965, a year before her birth, which abolished national origins formulae and the "thirty-six European races enumerated by the Dillingham Commission," the bill also discriminated against "'would-be immigrants from . . . colonies of the West Indies,'" reducing discussions of race and immigration to Black and white (Jacobson 117). Thus, the author explores how her younger self negotiated her multivalent racial and ethnic culture against this backdrop, refusing America's reduction of her story *only* to racial opposition, which was indeed a paramount issue for her, literalized by the titular metaphor, *the skin between us*. As Maucione argues, Ragusa's memoir is both a "mixed-race" and "post-neighborhood" narrative, recognizing how the "organization of identities and neighborhoods around ethnic, racial, or any other category of homogeneity" invites forms of violence "to expel, according to the logic of homogeneity, that which does not belong" (Maucione 239, 229). Out of such logic, Ragusa can never belong to either family without sacrificing the other and is always in imminent danger. She righteously asserts, "Safety in my father's world was always provisional" (*Skin* 131). While to some degree Ragusa portrays Kym as remaining "steeped in . . . mythologies" about, for example, Italian Harlem as safe place, a paradise to which she longs to return, Maucione notes that the memoir also works to "complicate forms of dualistic thinking aligned with a black/white binary" (*Post-Neighborhood* 234). Ragusa accomplishes her goal to complicate intersections between race and ethnicity in two interrelated ways, moving toward a new definition of "her name," which signifies her belonging to spaces she will embody in New York and Sicily with a Mediterranean consciousness that embraces paternal and maternal families.

Ragusa first accomplishes this feat by introducing an alternative archive that centralizes the "intense marginalization" of her grandmothers based on race and ethnicity (Tenzer 215). To reiterate, Tenzer asked Ragusa if the earlier documentaries she made about her paternal and maternal grandmothers speak to each other, even though highlighting opposite sides of the experience of race. Ragusa's response: "Yes. I see them as mirror images of each other. Partially, this has to do with the ways both women were marginalized on the basis of race and ethnicity, and also in the ways each film defies expectations: a light-skinned mixed-race woman who doesn't choose to pass, even though her life may depend on it, and an Italian American woman whose life does not follow the familiar narrative of the American Dream" (Tenzer 215). The narrator interprets her family's genealogy through the movements of her grandmothers, whether it is her Italian family's oceanic journey on a packed immigrant ship, traveling in steerage, or her grandmother Miriam's terrestrial encounters in dangerous space beset by a Jim Crow South.

Second, Ragusa extends these movements to larger diasporic trajectories, which will lead her narrator eventually to Sicily. As Teresa Fiore states, through emigration, Ragusa "knots her family's historical ties to Africa through slavery and to Southern Europe through emigration, two demographic movements that despite some profound differences the reader is asked to read in parallel ways through the forced or semi-forced deracination that they impose and the economic struggles and forms of discrimination that they both entailed" (58).[38] Ragusa ultimately ruptures dichotomous thinking by submitting the idea of race to historically fluid interpretations. Referencing both waterway (Strait of Messina) and crossroads (Sicily), Ragusa identifies an ancestral passageway for both maternal and paternal forbears, and, by implication, also invites readers to consider focusing on the homelands of both ancestral groups through the lens of colonial memory, which allows for a deepened understanding of how, as Lombardi-Diop argues, an "Italian colonial racial discourse [might] shed light on the process of racial identity in other diasporic contexts such as the building of Italian communities in the New World" (85).

Both Lorde and Ragusa inflect their life narratives by focusing on maternal movements, thereby reinterpreting their own geographical dislocations, which will eventually lead them to embrace an Anzaldúan borderland consciousness that supports "perpetual transition" (Anzaldúa 100). In their life writings, Lorde and Ragusa portray their younger narrators developing a deepened recognition about their own locations, especially when they enter what I call queer diasporic spaces closer to home. Those Harlem spaces simultaneously invoke the maternal and unite the authors to matrilineal and mythological pasts.

Carving Out Queer Spaces: The Lesbian Bar and the Religious Procession

Throughout their autobiographical narratives, Lorde and Ragusa retrospectively engage histories specific to their young adult experiences, each author migrating backward to the space she was made: Harlem. As such, these narrators record for readers an archive of remembering on both hallowed and insurgent grounds, designating specific spaces as possessing personal significance for their political objectives. To reiterate Smith and Watson, for such life narrators, "public, shared memories can reconstitute fragmented communities, or mark and mourn their loss" (26). Both Lorde and Ragusa acknowledge the casualties of their respective communities, young people not dissimilar to them, defeated by racism, homophobia, misogyny, or class oppression. That Lorde reiterates the word *hostile* like a litany throughout *Zami* signifies her early awareness that she will have to fight to survive. Similarly, Ragusa's experience of ongoing precarity in segregated neighborhoods of the 1970s and 1980s intensifies her feelings of unbelonging, and yet she establishes close connections with her Aunt Angela and cousin Marie, wedding tenacity and vulnerability simultaneously.

The lesbian bar scene of the 1950s deftly portrayed by Lorde in *Zami* may have inspired writers of the 1980s (and beyond) to portray Black lesbians creating and inhabiting gay spaces during denunciatory decades beyond the mid-twentieth century. Lorde performs a calculated shift in her final chapter of *Zami*, moving back from and forth to lesbian bars in the Village to recall private parties elsewhere, elucidating the author's commitment also to carving out a queer space for Black lesbians. Illuminating separate space for Black lesbians is both a strategy of protection and a political position known to second-wave feminism. In this paradoxical way, Lorde retrospectively anticipates and critiques an era dominated by white feminist voices. Lorde merges two time periods in her personal life spatialized in the private home and the lesbian bar to introduce Kitty, a woman whom Audre had met two years earlier at a house party in Queens. In her final chapter, Lorde underscores the necessity of Black lesbian space for "exotic sister outsiders," who, in fact, band together privately but also enter the "gay-girl" bars where lesbians from both races meet (*Zami* 241). Lorde clarifies that despite the presence of Black and white lesbians in Greenwich Village bars, Black lesbians still faced hostility in those queer spaces like the Bagatelle, but their existential presence helped the young Audre survive and grow stronger: "Every Black woman I ever met in the Village in those years had some part in my survival, large or small" (*Zami* 225).[39] Of the 1950s racially mixed bar scene, Lorde explains, "Lesbians were probably the only Black and white women in New York City in the fifties who were making any real attempt to communicate with each other; we learned lessons from each other, the values of which were not lessened by what we did not learn" (*Zami* 179). While this claim may be difficult to substantiate, Lorde is not being nostalgic. Rather, her own experience corroborates a pedagogy of liberation, validating cross-racial communication between women whose sexual differences invited border crossing well before the 1964 Civil Rights Act (which nominally ended legal segregation). Lorde's expansive understanding of lesbian sexuality includes not only cross-racial liaisons but also her mother's maternal genealogy in Grenada.

As Driver explains, "*Zami* brings her lesbian sexuality into alliance with her mother's history" ("Between Theories" 367), refusing ruptured maternal lines by reimagining and enacting matrilineage through a brief, but life-altering relationship with Kitty, a single mother from Georgia. Lorde takes us back in her final chapter as though in a dream, reinforcing an authentic experience grounded in historical and mythographic time. Here in this dreamscape of reverie she introduces the woman who will take her to the crossroads by the conclusion of the narrative. "One of the women I met at one of these parties was Kitty" is Lorde's carefully chosen semantic introduction to this foremost figure (*Zami* 241), compelling readers to experience this meeting alongside her persona, Audre. Lorde's reference to the word *crossroads* later in the chapter strategically unites African symbology with Black queer lesbian feminism.[40] Doing this allows Lorde to accomplish one of her central aims in *Zami*, that is, to secure an erotic maternal epistemology through an African Caribbean lesbian identity. Ball describes Lorde's focus on Audre's meeting with Kitty as *Zami*'s crowning achievement as the narrator "receives the gift of knowledge of herself and learns a way to live on the borders of her multiple identities" (61). One of those always-shifting borders includes the lesbian world of love and ritual in 1950s Greenwich Village.

What follows in chapter 31 is Lorde's minihistory of Black lesbian subjectivity as inflected by a variety of cultural markers, including clothing, food, and dance, upon which Audre comments in luxuriating detail.[41] Here, I briefly focus on dress codes. As I examined in chapter 1, Willa Cather, herself a youthful cross-dresser, portrayed Nancy's escape from slavery in *Sapphira and the Slave Girl* through what Halberstam calls an "epistemology of the wardrobe," donning clothes that signify her status as a waiting maid to her white employer, Rachel, whose own gestures of clandestine dressing enable Nancy's escape. Both women employ dress codes in *Sapphira* to seek liberation, Rachel from her mother's plantation-"mistress" domination and Nancy, more trenchantly, under disguise to protect herself during her escape on the underground railroad. The underground quality of queer space is not *overtly* highlighted in Lorde's narration, as though she takes a cue from her mother, who shuns what she cannot control: racism and Jim Crow. Lorde's own references to clothing choices among Black lesbians suggest nonetheless the underground nature of queer space as these women must demonstrate guile to work against existing regimes of racism and homophobia.

Lorde blurs the boundaries between butches and femmes in her description of the Black lesbian underground, anticipating if not recognizing the fluidity of gender as a transgender category; she also anticipates Judith Butler's destabilization of the distinction between imitation and original in her resistance to the homophobic charge "that queens and butches and femmes are imitations of the heterosexual real" (21). Lorde portrays the guise of costuming without seeming to do so, depicting Black lesbians who reify and challenge homonormative femme-butch practices. While mentioning role playing through choice of clothing and partner dancing, Lorde does not strictly commit to butch-femme gender roles, and Kitty seems to fit both categories and neither category simultaneously. As Judy Grahn has argued, butches were saying, "'Here is another way of being a woman' and . . . what lesbians learned in the lesbian subculture was to 'imitate dykes, not men'" (as qtd. in Faderman, *Odd Girls* 169). When responding defensively to Kitty's nonchalant question, asking if Lorde's first name was an abbreviation, Audre questions back, 'What's Kitty short for?' 'A cool cat,' Kitty responds, snapping her fingers to the music, 'Afrekete. . . . That's me. The Black pussycat'" (243).[42] In its revelatory praxis, feminist confessional memoir strives to "encode an audience" (Felski 86). Revealing Kitty's formal name at the same time for her reader as for her youthful narrator packs a punch and prepares us for the intensely erotic relationship that will quickly ensue. Chinosole explains, "Through Afrekete/Kitty, Lorde circles back to a racial and sexual identity begun with her foremothers of Carriacou," demonstrating her "need to mesh a collective racial identity and an individual sexual one" (384).

When Audre and Kitty first dance, an emphasis on attire and roles gets set aside in the author's recollection (though zippers are highly prized by butch and femme alike), replaced by an olfactory identification closer to home: "Kitty smelled of soap and Jean Naté, and I kept thinking she was bigger than she actually was, because there was a comfortable smell about her that I always associated with large women" (*Zami* 243). The comfort Lorde feels originates from her mother, and, of course, the maternal erotic woman who is mythologized in *Zami* through African myth. Two years elapse before Audre and Kitty meet again, this time on the dance floor of the Page Three bar.

Audre's attraction to Kitty is once again both erotic and maternal. The author's "carapace" (245) softens during their dance, ultimately leading to a return to Afrekete's top-floor kitchenette apartment in Morningside Heights, a West Harlem neighborhood Audre knows well. Shifting between italicized sections composed of lesbian erotica and recalled discussions about each woman's racial and sexual histories, Lorde attributes to Kitty some of the most important lessons she will carry with her into a future woven with maternal resonance: "Afrekete taught me roots, new definitions of our women's bodies" (*Zami* 250), which together they display *in public* during summer solstice in West Harlem on a "sweltering midnight," where folks are sitting on stoops (*Zami* 252). Recalling her mother's Carriacouan homeland, Lorde does not replace her mother's memories, but, as a second-generation daughter, she noticeably embraces a Harlem homecoming on 113th Street, stating that "the mothers and fathers smiled at us in greeting as *we* strolled down to Eighth Avenue *hand in hand*" (*Zami* 253, my emphasis). Of the manifold ways in which to approach Lorde's final chapter of *Zami*, this gesture between women is galvanizing. Imagine such intimacy displayed in 1957, Lorde seems to say, imagine and remember.

A half century after the heyday of immigrant communal life in Italian Harlem between 1880 and 1950,[43] Ragusa enters women's space in East Harlem for the Feast of the Madonna of Mount Carmel to recount and update a ritualized performance across racial and ethnic groups. The *festa*, which culminates in the Procession of the Madonna of 115th Street, was popularized by Italian immigrants who recognized a mother figure in their patron saint, a sister outsider who migrated with them to America, sharing "the poverty and ostracism of their early days" (Orsi, *The Madonna* 50). In chapter 6 of *The Skin*, Ragusa recounts the migration history of her Italian ancestors. Using archival materials such as census records and urban histories, Ragusa fleshes out the stories she hears from her Italian family, the untold violence suffered by married women whose lives in America continued to look more like a disastrous fallout than a dream fulfilled.

Ragusa furnishes revelatory information about her paternal grandmother, Gilda, the mother who bore her father in 1944 when Italy was an Axis Power during World War II. This time period was made especially difficult for many Italians, including Gilda, whose brothers fought overseas, and though deployed to Pacific skies as combat fliers, they resultantly fought against their ancestral homeland. Utilizing memoir as a form of piecework, Ragusa skillfully weaves a persuasive narrative about her Italian grandmother's life during childhood, tying bits and pieces from family lore and archival documents.[44] The story she unearths isn't pretty. It reveals an ugly fact of patriarchy: how maternal abandonment occurs close to home with no movement involved. Gilda's mother, Luisa, upholds Calabrese customs to ensure her own maintenance of power, submitting her daughter to the same suffering Luisa endured but transcended in an unhappy marriage with an abusive man. Not so her daughter. Abruptly ending Gilda's girlhood in tenth grade, Luisa arranges her marriage to a "man from the village back home," though Luisa and her parents had migrated to the United States a generation before (*Skin* 122). A dominating presence with nearly mythological import, Luisa's reputation as the legendary matriarch of the extended family is all but guaranteed by the time of Ragusa's father's generation, but the author discovers that Luisa was an abused wife who fought back, took in boarders to pay the rent, and changed the locks on her doors when her husband abandoned her and the children (*Skin* 141).

Refusing to afford the same power to her daughter, Luisa forces Gilda into a premature marriage at sixteen. Luisa's gesture of trafficking her daughter as a "deal made between two families, a custom in southern Italy that was imported to Italian Harlem" (*Skin* 124) is interpreted by Ragusa through an intersectional lens, giving the lie to the mythology of

Italian Harlem as a safe place: "It was 'our' place, the family was together, everybody looked out for each other" (*Skin* 119). Ragusa writes, "It must have seemed like a dream to Gilda, watching Luisa sign away the rest of my teenage grandmother's life to a greenhorn she didn't know, who was ten years older and spoke no English" (*Skin* 127). After filling in the silences about Gilda's experience of being taken out of high school in her sophomore year and apprenticed in youth into participating in the other kind of homework—piecework from the garment factory—Ragusa revises the "collective disparagement" toward Gilda that became accepted family lore regarding her grandmother. Correcting the record, Ragusa recognizes *her* grandmother to be a highly skilled domestic artisan, and, as "she was the first person in her family to read and write in English," Gilda works in the larger public sector as a wage-earning hotel maid who hands "over her weekly wages to her parents," working poor Italians who do piecework and bootblacking (*Skin* 123). Ragusa concludes, at sixteen, her grandmother's "girlhood was over—she said goodbye to her textbooks and her notebooks and her pencils and prepared to become a wife" (*Skin* 125).[45] Utilizing the rhetorical trope of polysyndeton ensures Ragusa's emphasis on the gravity of this topic, that education is essential to a woman's liberation, recalling those autobiographical narrators such as Linda Brent, whose literacy enabled her escape from slavery.

Ragusa also critiques her Italian family's disregard for schooling, which is demonstrated by Gilda's loss of literacy in both languages, providing a contrast to her African American grandmother, Miriam, high school educated, with "a desperate love of books [who] found a way to put the story of Persephone and Demeter, an ancient story of the troubled ties between mothers and daughters, into my hands" (*Skin* 107). Mindfully merging African and European heritages, Ragusa continues to integrate the complicated cultures of both sides of her family, informing her readers that Miriam read Kym bedtime stories from Greek mythology, and her grandmother grew up in a neighborhood and family "where African American and European immigrant cultures coexisted, indeed bled into each other" (*Skin* 107–8). Ragusa's desire to understand her Italian grandmother's past is also a desire to dismantle the seduction of Italian Harlem as safe *because* it is "their own perfect little world," a haven from dangerous outsiders. Nothing could be further from the truth, Ragusa explains, as the peril begins in the home (*Skin* 120). To encapsulate this point further, Ragusa concludes her chapter outside and at night, demonstrating the strength of shared customs when women gather in numbers to share their faith.

It is no exaggeration to say that "Italian popular faith in both Italy and America sought the streets to express itself" (Orsi, *The Madonna* 2). Italian popular Catholicism enacted in the festa not only served to reinforce Southern Italian devotional practices (so opposed by the official Church) but also to assert "ethnic hegemony of the area as well as extending popular notions of a religious moral imperative to the city streets" (Sciorra 330). It is in this context that Ragusa inserts revisionary thinking about the Feast of the Madonna, underlining the fact that Little Italys throughout the country were always multiracial in composition. In addition, the procession is fundamentally a story about movement outdoors "to affirm sacred membership in community" (Turner 6), despite enmity from the ecclesiastical hierarchy in the United States. Southern Italian immigrants, like Ragusa's ancestors, partook in a religious culture "characterized by lay-led, communal rituals, the annual feast day celebrations of town patron saints, and a folk culture of anti-clericalism" (Brown 558). Though it was Great-grandmother Luisa in *The Skin Between Us* who devoted her life to the Madonna of Mount Carmel, collapsing and dying on the steps of the church on her way to morning mass, it is for Gilda that Kym takes back the night on the final day of the celebration (*Skin* 143).

Returning to Italian Harlem in midsummer to partake in the procession led by women, Ragusa portrays Kym retracing the steps of Italian women of yore, carrying "huge tiers of lighted candles on their heads as they walked in the procession" (*Skin* 143); Ragusa links the idea of a return home with African imagery: "a woman carrying what is most precious to her on her head: water, grain, fire" (*Skin* 143). Skillfully weaving pieces of a literary quilt, Ragusa also links this African image of women with her earlier reference to a famous photograph of an Italian immigrant woman with "a towering bundle of clothes on her head, walking down a New York street" (*Skin* 122) (see figure 3.3).

Like other city folk, Italian Americans "create a sense of moral order for themselves," mapping onto the landscape of the city streets a narrative that makes sense: "it is safe here, our kind of people live here, we understand the codes in force here but not there. Conversation becomes cartography" (Orsi, "The Religious Boundaries" 336).[46] By the year 2000, the streets of East Harlem are filled, as Ragusa describes, with "skins of every color," including "Italian Americans, and Puerto Ricans, Mexicans, and Haitians, all moving together like an exhalation of breath" (*Skin* 144).

Figure 3.3 Italian woman carrying heavy bundle of clothing on her head near Astor Place, New York City. She will sew the garments at home for low wages. February 1912. Photograph by Lewis Hine. Stock photo. Public domain.

Ragusa relays songs of devotion emerging from multiple traditions and languages, engendering a heightened sense of belonging as boundaries between sacred and secular soften.

Sharing feelings of shame with her readers for her inability to sing any of the devotional hymns does not prevent Ragusa from walking by the side of the Madonna, exclaiming her regality in terms that transcend maternity, superimposing sacred power onto Harlem streets: "The Madonna glides by on a cloud of white and gold, underneath a canopy topped with a huge, glittering crown. . . . [S]he's rising up from the flowers . . . as Aphrodite rose from the waves. . . . Not an image of selfless maternity, but one of absolute sovereignty and limitless power. She is the center here, not Christ, not the Father. All around her now the women are praying, crying out: *Maman! Santa Maria!*" (*Skin* 145). Ragusa accomplishes several aims here. She prepares the reader for her trip to Sicily in the epilogue; unites women across racial groups; and fuses the veneration of the Madonna with Aphrodite, linking her both to the erotic and to movement, capturing Lorde's description in "Uses of the Erotic" as a power that is a "personification of love in all its aspects, . . . an assertion of the lifeforce of women; which we are now reclaiming in our language, our history, our dancing, our loving, our work" (*Sister Outsider* 55).[47] Ragusa and Lorde envisage the erotic maternal in their life writings by engaging expansively in border-crossing mythologies that centralize women who exemplify maternality in imaginative and powerful ways. The maternal erotic leads both authors to experience mobility by formulating seascapes while they discover the matrilineal sources of their power. In doing so, Lorde and Ragusa redefine a homeplace through a porous acceptance of their multiple identities.

Geographies of Return

In *Zami*, Lorde invokes both West African and European mythologies, including the water deity, Aphrodite, who, as Ball explains, is interpreted as a sexual not a maternal archetype (68).[48] By deploying a water divinity, a protector of the seas, Lorde posits both Aphrodite and Afrekete as transoceanic deities who will protect and enable her own movements as she continues to explore her Afro-Caribbean roots, revolutionizing an intersectional identity that merges the maternal and the erotic. In this way, Lorde claims for herself the lesbian maternal, which she saw encapsulated by her powerful mother, Linda Lorde, and by her lesbian lover, Afrekete/Kitty.[49] Both divine and erotic, Aphrodite and Afrekete invite Lorde to redefine diasporic space as movements toward many homes, enabling her queer survival. Likewise, Ragusa also references the love goddess in her capacity as a sea deity, an equally bold maneuver to abrogate divisions and return this mobile daughter to diasporic spaces. When Ragusa returns in the epilogue to Sicilian shores, she thereby recapitulates the mother-daughter plot through veneration of Demeter and her daughter, Persephone, mythological figures, Lucia Chiavola Birnbaum argues, who "may have come to Magna Graecia (southern Italy and the islands) from

Africa" (37). In choosing Persephone as one of her selves, Ragusa deftly chooses the Ovidian version of the story. Refusing vulnerability, she opts for the radical alterity fundamental to Ovid's *Metamorphosis* in which Persephone steals the pomegranate, "breaks open the rough red skin of the fruit, and puts the seven seeds into her mouth . . . choosing her own fate" (*Skin* 238). Ragusa's choice is as delectable and empowering as Lorde's discovery of "nutmeg nestled inside its covering of mace" (*Zami* 33). Both autobiographers recall material culture to invoke the place names of their matrilineal ancestors, Carriacou and Sicily, respectively, and thereby reassemble parts of themselves in order to reclaim the blood of the(ir) mothers:

> There it is said that the desire to lie with other women is a drive from the mother's blood. (*Zami* 256)

> She asked . . . solemnly, *Is this child really of your blood?* . . . *Then she is sangu du sangu meu,* she pronounced. *Blood of my blood.* (*Skin* 152)

For Lorde, discovering the potentialities intrinsic to a diasporan consciousness is coeval with her process of becoming. She prepares the reader for such a trajectory, writing in her before-prologue: "*To the journeywoman pieces of myself/ Becoming/Afrekete*" (*Zami* 5). Ragusa's path has always been about belonging, the present perfect progressive that graces her subtitle, and continues to be about locating a homeplace she finds by way of Palermo: "My Italian ancestors, those who came from this island and those who came from the mountains of Calabria, were a mingled people, whose disrupted bloodlines had found their way to me" (*Skin* 234). Both narrators, Audre and Kym, offer revisionary readings of mythological figures with particular reverence for Afrekete and Persephone, enabling their own renewals borne of hard-won survival, withstanding multiple losses and inevitable separations.

Lorde writes that in that place of separation is "where work begins" (*Zami* 255). *Zami* and *The Skin Between Us* continue the recovery work of maternal stories excluded from official discourses. By embracing an epistemology that names the maternal erotic along a continuum that includes women loving women, Lorde and Ragusa compel a generous revision of maternal bonds across race, class, and place. In chapter 4, I suggest a different revision and extension of maternal bonds through an analysis of women's caretaking during the AIDS epidemic of the 1980s and 1990s in the United States, specifically located in New York City and Chicago. Extending an embrace of maternal epistemology to illuminate queer kinship, I focus on how maternal bonds extend beyond affiliative borders to examine how othermothers, lesbian friends and sisters, attend to dying men from their own generation.

Chapter 4

Queer Maternality in Maso's *The Art Lover* and Makkai's *The Great Believers*

Carole Maso and Rebecca Makkai embrace a maternal epistemology in their novels that identifies queer kinship as coterminous with caretaking.[1] By identifying the queer maternal as a space to enact intimate bonds across sexuality and ethnicity, Maso and Makkai represent motherless daughters crossing borders to redefine the meanings of nurturance as they attend to dying men from their own generation. For the white ethnic daughters[2] of *The Art Lover* and *The Great Believers*, border crossings enable their courageous movements on behalf of dying friends just as Lorde's and Ragusa's journeys overseas generated an expanded understanding of matrilineal heritage and female desire. Lesbians and sisters function as reparative[3] figures in *The Art Lover* and *The Great Believers*, respectively, serving not merely as surrogates or replacements for family members but as maternal figures whose daughterhood has been transformed by the AIDS pandemic.[4]

In the first section of this chapter, I outline how Maso and Makkai deploy the genre of historiographic metafiction to tell stories about reparenting maternal figures whose lives have been utterly transformed by the fatal illnesses of their loved ones. In particular, I argue that the principal maternal characters adopt and enact various forms of queer kinship with their loved ones, mirroring an empathy that simulates couvade syndrome, also called sympathetic pregnancy, as these women experience somatic responses to pain that exceeds their own physical and emotional limits.[5] In fact, Makkai portrays her principal maternal character, Fiona, literally going into labor while sitting at the bedside of her dying friend. Such responses paradoxically enable these maternal characters in Maso's and Makkai's novels to struggle in pain alongside their loved ones, simulating a queer form of kinship as their bodies respond to incomprehensible suffering.

Overlaying each novel is a recurring story about ruptured mother-daughter bonds, exacerbated by the AIDS crisis but not defined by it. To examine this intersection, I argue that both authors engage in specific critiques of modernism to expose its brutal influence on relations between mothers and daughters, largely determining the daughters' emotional trajectories in adulthood. In particular, I examine how Maso's protagonist, Caroline, challenges the modernist belief in the salutary effects of art, which proves disastrous for Caroline's mother, to which I shall return. In addition, throughout the second and third sections of this chapter, I examine two intersecting narratives to show how the authors portray the female-identified characters, Caroline of *The Art Lover* and Fiona of *The Great Believers*, supporting the artistic ambitions of their suffering friends by engaging visual artforms to memorialize the era of AIDS.

Throughout this chapter and more specifically in my final section, I show how the authors engage a specific form of historiographic metafiction by gesturing toward a post-Holocaust literature to establish a metonymic relationship between AIDS and Holocaust victims. Both authors echo the atrocities of the Holocaust to reinforce the continuing trauma of the past on the present. By doing so, they reclaim the unsung histories of men who died catastrophic deaths and shape narratives of grief through the lens of women who loved them. Caroline and Fiona assume maternal roles as a result of the AIDS crisis and simultaneously reveal themselves to be the daughters of mothers who are absented too soon from their young lives, their mothers abducted by patriarchal norms that delimited their mother's maternal development. The daughters' embrace of othermothering challenges and expands the readers' understanding of true mothering[6] and ultimately permits the authors to examine the multidimensional ways in which maternal care is portrayed under times of extremity.

Mourning the Body Electric: Metafiction and Maternality

The purpose of this section is to highlight the fact that Maso and Makkai incorporate metafictional devices such as visual iconography and nonlinear conceptions of time to compel readers to question mainstream and often invidious discourse surrounding the AIDS crisis. Simultaneously, both authors centralize maternality as the means by which these stories of extremity are retold through the lens of women's experiences of caretaking.

Maso and Makkai challenge normative conceptions of storytelling through narrative experimentation. They do this through what Linda Hutcheon has identified as historiographical metafiction, a category of postmodern fiction in which authors display "a theoretical self-awareness of history and fiction as human constructs" (*A Poetics of Postmodernism* 5).[7] The authors simultaneously engage feminist projects by reclaiming not only silent or erased histories—women's artistic contributions in particular—but also histories "narrated from the hegemonic center" (McCormack 39), by which I mean white, mainstream, and canonical, fundamentally contesting how those histories have too often dominated the discourse, ignoring "narratives of witness" (Hutcheon, *Politics* 36). Because they are engaged in "rethinking and reworking the forms and contents of the past" (Hutcheon, *Poetics* 5), Maso and Makkai incorporate intertexts and paratexts within their novels, borrowing from other nonfictional forms, including letter writing, newspaper reports, epigraphs, illustrations, footnotes, and photographs. Incorporating and referencing such features in their novels "complicates rather than precludes their evidential value, highlighting the fictive quality of all narratives (be they literary or historical), while retaining their 'aura' as artifacts" (McCormack 38).[8] By using such nonfictional forms, both authors infuse their novels with "a documentary impulse,"[9] aligning their stories about the AIDS era with specific cities—New York and Chicago—and deploying constant references to art, challenging normative interpretations of its value in the face of other stories of loss narrated in these works.

Maso and Makkai also reconfigure maternal plots in their novels. They do this by centralizing the intersection between mothers, mobility, and narrative during the AIDS epidemic of the 1980s. Both authors experimented in ways that reflect the period about which they wrote and the decade in which they published their novels. A generation separates the publications of these books with Maso publishing *The Art Lover* in 1990 during the height of the AIDS epidemic, after having personally witnessed the death of her childhood friend, Gary Falk.[10] In contrast, Makkai published *The Great Believers* in 2018 after life-saving antiretroviral therapies emerged, compelling her archival researches into Chicago's leading LGBT newspaper, the *Windy City Times*. Maso, who writes within the contemporary AIDS crisis, decreases the distance between the AIDS pandemic and her narrator's response to it: temporal and spatial distance are recalibrated through the author's lyricism, her visual iconography, and her language of lamentation. By contrast, Makkai's novel was published during a post-AIDS era, and it is written by neither a survivor nor a first-person witness. Instead, Makkai invested in Chicago's AIDS history through her archival research, attempting to strike the right balance between "allyship and appropriation" as she writes in her acknowledgements (*The Great Believers* 420). Although her characters' lives are entirely fictional, Makkai admitted to thinking about her central character, Yale Tishman, as a friend she just lost.[11] The intimacy each author establishes between their female protagonists and the men for whom they care requires a devout intensity that changes the characters' narrative trajectory, transforming their conceptions of time and enlarging their understanding of maternal love.

The daughters in *The Art Lover* and *The Great Believers* engage in a style of maternal caregiving simultaneously excessive and reiterative, perhaps a response to having lost their mothers in different ways. Maso and Makkai reinforce this maternal approach through character development and postmodern narrative structures, employing historiographic modes of metafiction to convey the undertows of maternality and memory during the AIDS crisis. While Caroline and Fiona refuse to reify the AIDS crisis through moralizing discourses that quickly emerged in the 1980s, one of which linked homosexuality with sinful behavior leading to death, both are aware of the vitriolic language used against AIDS victims during this time. To wit: both authors reference the political conservatism of the 1980s, attributing President Reagan's refusal to use the word AIDS or to recognize a national health emergency as being complicit with those whose agendas were overtly homophobic.[12] Maso and Makkai disrupt any kind of totalizing narrative about homosexuality and AIDS in favor of portraying central characters devoted to their dying friends, broadening knowledge of maternal love during this era.

Maso and Makkai deploy narrative strategies of reparenting and sister-brother bonds, terms I have borrowed from Blau du Plessis's *Writing beyond the Ending*, to examine depictions of nonaffiliative bonding between maternal protagonists and the men they love.[13] In queer kinship terms, the authors illuminate the concept of what Bradway and Freeman call "kincoherence," that is, demonstrating "the simultaneous unbinding and multiplying of relational forms; it understands these forms as emerging within and through the social and the historical (understood as embedded and embodied) while stressing that they are not fully determined by them" (11). By reinvesting in the dynamics of maternal love through depictions of caregiving by young women who embrace the ruthlessness of the AIDS epidemic, Maso and Makkai emphasize the fact that this illness exceeds their ability to process their own mourning.[14] Yet in trying to express the inexpressible these protagonists continue to meditate upon the relationship between private emotion and public awareness of the crisis. As Sara Ahmed explains, the role of emotion conveys "feminist alliances and identifications"; this description exemplifies the primary characters' commitment to ensuring their roles as memory keepers individually and collectively.[15] As a result of their efforts, these caregivers assume multiple roles, including primary supportive care for their loved ones. The authors gesture toward the necessity of public outreach to highlight the AIDS emergency in America that beset a generation of whom a high percentage were gay men in the 1980s. For example, Caroline in *The Art Lover* retrospectively questions (and ultimately judges) the seeming indifference of her father, Max, to the catastrophic number of deaths in New York City of young men while her own closest friend, Steven, is dying.[16] In *The Great Believers*, Fiona attends an ACT UP protest with an ill Yale in Chicago, risking the consequences of police brutality.[17] Memory keepers both, Caroline and Fiona inchoately recognize that despite having no framework for understanding what is happening to their loved ones, they will function as the scaffolding to support them.

Maso's and Makkai's authorial investment in the othermother clarifies the complementary dimensions of motherhood portrayed in both works. Blau du Plessis's articulation of reparenting permits me to connect this form of othermothering to the activity of repairing, which includes keeping memories, in which the protagonists are intensively invested. A question posed throughout this chapter is: How do these reparenting othermothers respond to the radical unhousing of ill men who for all intents and purposes become their sons? Maso portrays Caroline's daily visits to Steven at St. Vincent's, the hospital that opened the first and largest AIDS ward on the East Coast.[18] A young Fiona filches food for her brother, Nico, who has been cast out from their parental home well before contracting AIDS; she thereafter nurtures Nico's friend, Yale, whose unhousing occurs before his final illness in *The Great Believers*. These young men are subject to a form of deportation traditionally ascribed to daughters in narrative discourse; they are largely abandoned by parents, requiring maternal nurturance from others.

After these men become ill, they are regularly segregated and placed in epidemic space: they embark on nightmarish journeys marked by pain and separation. Some of the symptoms of their illness also mimic those experienced by pregnant women (especially morning sickness) and Holocaust victims (particularly wasting syndrome). Such examples highlight the authors' investment in historiographic metafiction to illuminate macrosocial sicknesses shared across cultural periods. I reiterate here Linda Hutcheon's point that historiographic metafiction lays claim to "historical events and personages" (*Poetics* 5), to observe that both authors crystallize the intersection between reparenting othermothers of AIDS victims and other historical tragedies, including contemporary events (e.g., the 1986 *Challenger* space-shuttle explosion; the 2015 Paris terrorist attacks), and earth-shattering events of the past, including world wars and the Holocaust. In doing so, they enlarge the historical bandwidth to include the role of maternality during one such period of extremity.[19]

Maso and Makkai centralize lesbians and sisters as caregivers[20] while simultaneously incorporating and critiquing traditional mother-daughter plots within their postmodern narratives. Both authors structure their novels to intensify the connections between the primary plot that focuses on illness and various mother-daughter plots interlaced throughout both works. What's more, in their depictions of traditional marriage and motherhood, Maso and Makkai expose the stakes held in sustaining the phallocentric family structure. By redefining caretaking that includes a border crossing between life and death, these authors centralize a mothering praxis that embraces mourning and mending—reparenting through repairing—using distinctive incorporations of visual artforms, which I examine more below. Suffice to say here that both authors represent a transformational shift in their protagonists' understanding of mother-daughter relations as a result of their maternal work during the AIDS epidemic.

Maso and Makkai represent their female protagonists as central to reappraising their own understandings of maternality, focusing on the use of art as a vehicle to consolidate their reparenting activities as caregivers. Both authors employ references to art in order to centralize the relationship between female othermothers and men dying in the prime of their lives, unable fully to engage in their artistic enterprises. The roles that these female caretakers assume in both novels suggest the reparative nature of their love as they shepherd through and/or exhibit the artistic contributions of men too ill to do so themselves. Alongside canonical and postmodern artists, Maso showcases Gary Falk's artwork seven times in *The Art Lover*, acting herself as an art lover, a museum curator, and a queer mother. Makkai portrays Fiona's intercession on behalf of Yale to enable his curation of her Great-Aunt Nora's art collection from the first World War, framing tragedies of loss at the beginning and end of the twentieth century.

Maternal surfeit and final-stage AIDS illness adjoin in the authors' portrayals of death vigils in *The Art Lover* and *The Great Believers*. As principal caregivers, Caroline and Fiona, respectively, exhibit maternal profusion, repeatedly referencing excessive suffering and apostrophizing the beloved. Desperately longing to support their dying, these women emphatically witness the unimaginable, "events in excess of [their] frames of reference," as Shoshana Felman and Dori Laub explain of those traumatized by Holocaust witnessing (qtd. in Gilbert 98).[21] They also willfully align their maternal bodies with the dying bodies of their loved ones, mirroring empathy during the death vigil and enacting shared kinship through practices of couvade syndrome.[22] As a result, Caroline and Fiona claim a queer maternal and filial relationship with their dying, insisting on a connection that not only embraces and exceeds these bonds but also fundamentally redefines them.

As memory keepers, the maternal protagonists of *The Art Lover* and *The Great Believers* engage in documenting the era of the AIDS epidemic in conjunction with twentieth-century historical calamities, including the Holocaust, referencing it as a mediated memory.[23] Maso and Makkai allude to the Holocaust not to rehearse historical fact or present personal lineage but to suggest a historical parallel between incomprehensible occurrences.[24] *The Art Lover*'s Caroline manages to process her mourning as a form of lament, while Fiona's grieving in *The Great Believers* is repeatedly melancholic, her grief a timeless present, stifling her ability to heal.[25] Both authors reshape their fictional accounting of the AIDS crisis to fit the demands of their metafictional historiographies, and, in doing so, their works arguably function as post-Holocaust novels through intertwining tropes and references to bodies in extremis. I examine this connection more fully in the final section of this chapter.

I mean no condescension when I say that both authors commit their novels to the distinct possibility of failure, an authorial decision of no small achievement. This in contrast to Cather's deliberative shift into autobiography at the conclusion of *Sapphira and the Slave Girl*, an ending that paradoxically disclosed her need to camouflage antebellum history, thus erasing mother-daughter bonds between Black women. Maso and Makkai explicitly risk failure on formal and theoretical grounds, engaging in antinarrative approaches in response to the catastrophe of AIDS.[26] Both authors also refuse tidy resolutions to the disastrous consequences of traditional marriage and motherhood for women. Maso uses metafictional devices to elucidate the failures of modernism to succor marginalized others, including abandoned mothers and men dying of AIDS. Makkai shows how failure is inscribed into the structure of the heteronarrative, to use Judith Roof's term, which proscribes empathy between women.[27] Finally, in subscribing to theories of memory promulgated by Hirsch and others,[28] both authors refuse to distinguish between memory and imagination in their homages to a generation of lost men, laying bare the parallels between historical events and literary reconstruction. In doing so, Maso and Makkai fashion living archives of the AIDS era, discussed below.

Caroline's Hieroglyphs of Hope

In *The Art Lover*, Maso represents queer maternality through narrators and characters engaged in resisting regulatory cultural narratives about the traditional nuclear family. Introducing intersecting stories about families in crisis (father abandonment, mother death), Maso deploys these stories to enable her to reinstall the maternal plot through a critique of narrative discourse that represents late twentieth-century traditional American families dismantled in recognizable ways: a father abandons his wife and two daughters; a mother dies tragically young, leaving her daughter to put the pieces together. These overlapping stories enable the protagonist, Caroline, to assume characteristics of both Persephone's abduction and Demeter's ongoing desire for her daughter. Like Persephone, she is raised without a mother by a father who influences her view of the world through a dispassionate response to loss. As the passionate daughter of a mother who committed suicide when she was only six years old, Caroline adopts a Demeter and Persephone-like approach to maternal nurturance: she cannot bear her daughter's absence, and she cannot bear being absent from her mother. Caroline's own maternal approach borders on the unbearable. Her modus operandi could not be more apposite to the times.

Working on her novel when her friend became ill, Maso explains in an interview with Nicole Cooley that during this period, "the book completely changed" (Cooley 34). While she tried to write *The Art Lover* in the mornings before visiting Gary in the hospital, Maso shelved her novel about a fictive family that her protagonist, Caroline, narrates, and "stopped writing for a year" (Cooley 33). After her friend became ill, Maso began collecting images, as "a defense against chaos, . . . collecting things to keep the world in place" (Cooley 35). Cooley explains that all the focus on "listing and documentation in *The Art Lover*" is reflective of Caroline's desire to "order her world, saving things. Assemblage becomes a way of recuperating the self" (33). Maso affirmed that she did not have "any language for this," so she managed to collect things in place of storytelling (Cooley 35). After Maso's year-long writing hiatus, she admitted she "didn't know what the book would be, or if it would be" (Cooley 35), which, as Patricia Waugh notes, is a tendency of metafiction: to question the viability of the novel, which is "characteristic of the exhaustion of any artistic form or genre" (9). The desire to fulfill the "harrowing task" of writing about AIDS became "the real test of faith" and Maso's artistic goal in trying to approximate a calamity for which she had no language. The result is *The Art Lover*, which was published after Gary Falk's death, to whom her second novel is dedicated (Cooley 35).

The Art Lover comprises three intersecting narratives, which overlap and merge at times throughout the novel. The first narrative functions as the overplot as it intersects across all others, including Maso's autobiographical fifth section "More Winter." The overplot is narrated by Caroline Chrysler, a thirty-year-old novelist whose bestseller, *Delirium*, has been adapted into a "major motion picture" (*Art Lover* 66). Carolyn returns from a writer's colony to attend to the estate of her father, Max, a renowned art historian, who recently died from a brain aneurysm. Caroline's father subscribes to a modernist belief in the salvific and transcendent role of art, which she begins to challenge not only in the novel on which she is working, but in her reexamination of the untimely death of her mother, Veronica, who died by suicide when Caroline and her brothers were small children. At the same time that she is trying to compose a new novel, Caroline's childhood friend Steven is dying from AIDS. In Caroline's novel-in-progress, which functions as the "novel-within-the-novel," Maso incorporates a second maternal narrative, featuring a traditional nuclear family (Maggie, Henry, and their two daughters, Candace and Alison), which is dismantled by father abandonment and Henry's marital infidelity, losses that ultimately refocus mother-daughter relations in mutually interdependent ways, especially as mother and daughters reconsider maternal relations through women's art, rejecting the detachment of transcendence as a proper response to loss. Candace implores her mother, "Fuck Poussin, Mother. Your husband left you for a twenty-nine-year-old. Let's show a little emotion. Stop looking for the perfect order, reason, symmetry. There's no such thing" (*Art Lover* 96).

Described by one critic as "the harrowing—and remarkably transgressive fifth section"[29] of *The Art Lover*, Maso's third narrative shifts into autobiography. In this section, Maso uses her own body as an example of incorporation, that is, a demonstration of how the author incorporates the death of her friend Gary (fictionalized as Steven in the overplot) into a multidimensional text revolving around mother loss, separation, and abandonment. Fictionalizing heterosexual romance, marriage, and motherhood as subject to long-term suffering and grief in the overplot permits the author to integrate the queer love story between Carole and Gary alongside rather than apart from the other narratives. Juxtaposing nuclear family stories that parallel rather than contrast the narrative of gay desire and queer friendships, Maso refuses a hierarchy of grief. She also assumes traditional roles of mother, sister, and lover in response to her deep-boned grief over the death of Gary Falk. As Maso explains in an interview with Joyce Hackett, she moved into the autobiographical section of *The Art Lover* because she "came up against the limits of fiction: it was clear that I would never be able to save my friend Gary's life, no matter what I wrote. . . . All the way through writing the book, I thought that, quite possibly, I'm not going to be able to believe in writing enough anymore to do it. And only at the very end was it clear that this was going to be okay, that the *effort* is beautiful as much as the final product" (Hackett 66). Maso's effort in *The Art Lover* is equally reflected in her decision to include dozens of images.

As a result of Gary Falk's fatal illness, Maso explained to interviewer Victoria Frenkel Harris that she "began to write a different book" (106), refusing her editor's request to "take out the graphics," as she told Cooley, "and to make the non-fiction section fictional, integrate it into the fiction" (33). Charles B. Harris infers that Maso "must have realized . . . that to make that choice would have constituted a kind of betrayal, not only of her artistic integrity, but of Gary Falk as well" (170). Maso includes some sixty-five images in her revisioning of the novel, making the graphics a textual strategy that is part and parcel of the novel. As a result of Maso's inclusion of embedded photographs and the autobiographical section, the overplot that features Maso's protagonist also undergoes radical revision, including Caroline's novel-in-progress about the Maggie-Henry-Candace-Alison fictive family to which she returns a year after her father's death.

Unsurprisingly, "Winter" comprises the longest section of *The Art Lover* (131–92). In it, Maso depicts Caroline revising her novel-in-progress to portray a transformed mother-daughter relation that echoes the final scene of Virginia Woolf's *To the Lighthouse*, in which Lily Briscoe invokes Mrs. Ramsay to inspire the completion of her painting.[30] Caroline thereafter inserts a memory of night fishing with Veronica during the last summer of her mother's life, merging Lily Briscoe's maternal-erotic invocation with the deferred boat trip the adult Ramsay children take with their father to the lighthouse (*Art Lover* 80). Coming to some resolution about Veronica's suicide permits Caroline to accept the ongoing effects of mother loss in her own life, inviting her to reconsider maternal nurturance in her manuscript as Maggie learns how to nurture her daughters differently as a result of Henry's fortuitous desertion. Henry's absence, while shockingly painful to mother and daughters, paradoxically enables each to search and find in their overwhelming outrage a new way of being and of belonging, reducing their feelings of disorder and anger. A relevant instance: in the final section of the novel, "Spring, 1986," Caroline returns to her book, juxtaposing a lovely recursion to and revision of Woolf's rowboat scene in *To the Lighthouse* with a final dinner she prepares for Steven, who is briefly out of the hospital. Juxtaposing the rowboat scene between Maggie and Alison with a celebratory dinner Caroline prepares for Steven is both contrapuntal and monophonic as Maso manages to merge the intersecting plots with a maternal through line, to which I shall return.

Caroline's revision of her novel-in-progress also reflects a paradoxical decision to reject her art historian father's belief in the transcendent nature of art as she finally gives herself permission to grieve her mother's death. By portraying Caroline addressing Max directly through apostrophe in *The Art Lover*, a form of posthumous address employed throughout the novel, Maso reinforces the immediacy of her protagonist's challenge to her father's credo about art's "consoling nature . . . its ability to help distance," accusing Max of objectifying her mother by painting her (*Art Lover* 185). Each of the scenes works as a palimpsest, layering loss upon loss. Maso includes the following passage in the longest section of the novel, "Winter," which occurs about midway through *The Art Lover*. This section is framed by Steven's announcement to Caroline of his illness and Caroline's rejection of her father's distancing measures in showing love to his wife and children. The interactive response below conveys both Caroline's astronomic sorrow and her proclivity for ordering things:

Chaos

Despite my penchant for order. This is the world. We name it.
And what good does it do? We arrange it on a page.
You were here and now you're gone.
You were well and now you're sick.
You were a painting by Matisse, but you took sleeping pills. (138)

Apostrophizing Max, Steven, and her mother, Caroline ironically achieves her own measure of distance, but she continues to reckon with desire, a libidinal economy that anticipates, as Maso said, "the end of certain kinds of possibility" (Cooley 33). For Caroline, the dynamic of desire has subjected a generation of men to an unanticipated doom; mourning her losses, feeling the body's uncertainty, Carole and Caroline nonetheless attempt to embrace the body in all its corporeality, including fatal illness.

In the final section of the novel, Maso juxtaposes scenes of harmony that portray Caroline's novel-in-progress, "The Sky at Night," with Maso's overplot, "Hieroglyphs of Hope," in which Caroline prepares a birthday dinner for Steven, who briefly recuperates and is out of the hospital. Both scenes are scaffolded by two intersecting stories: the mater dolorosa and the Passion. It's no wonder that Maso gives the name of *Veronica* to her protagonist's mother; legend has it that Veronica wiped Christ's brow on his way to Golgotha,. a maternal figure of empathy who is honored at the sixth Station of the Cross. During their mother-daughter boat ride, Maggie "cries out in the night," moving from anger to sorrow to succor while rocking "back and forth, back and forth in this small boat in the middle of the night," a mater dolorosa and Christ figure who holds her daughter (*Art Lover* 235). Unlike Veronica, Maggie will not "hold still and then die" (*Art Lover* 234), a potent example of Caroline's revision of her mother's tragically foreshortened life. Unlike Veronica, Caroline will not stop too long at one sorrowful station: movement matters. In revising her novel-in-progress, Caroline comes to terms with an existential fact: the daughter's sorrow, including her own, is always about the mother's originary abduction; as Alison comes to realize about her mother Maggie, so Caroline comes to accept about her mother: "she has been missing her mother her whole life" (*Art Lover* 232).

It is no coincidence that "Hieroglyphs of Hope," the epigraph to one of the final sections of the book, portrays Caroline and Steven united outside the hospital one last time. In this scene, Maso reimagines a delectable

Last Supper, including the recipe for the butterflied leg of lamb (at least the marinade) along with the music of *Der Rosenkavalier* (thankfully, a comic opera, the prologue Steven wants played at his funeral) (*Art Lover* 134). Maso clarifies this crucial point: joy and desire are still alive when Caroline prepares herself to miss Steven the rest of her life: "When I close my eyes he is still there. When I look away he is still there" (*Art Lover* 237): "Probably he will hurt me more than I can possibly imagine. Certainly we will never be the same again. . . . Of this I am sure. I will love him even more than I do now. He is my brother, and looking at him and knowing all of this, I realize that it is as perfect a moment on earth as I can expect" (*Art Lover* 238). In response to Steven's imminent death, Caroline accepts multiple roles of mother, sister, lover, and widow, but she refuses the role of grief inside the perimeters of patriarchy: she will be the lesbian widow who embraces the fact that her beloved is dying from an incurable disease and from state indifference. Unlike the traditional widow's response: "I was not ready. I'm a widow" (Gilbert 22), Maso writes in contrast: "I can't believe this happened to *you* (*Art Lover* 206, emphasis added).[31] As an observing witness, Caroline is also learning how to be with Steven through his illness, paradoxically turning illness into an exhilarating story about what Frank calls "other-relatedness": "*this other has to do with me as I with it*" (35). Understanding Caroline's/Carole's role is also part of a collective experience. Maso largely engages the defining mantra of ACT UP through her epigraph "Because Silence Has Always Equaled Death," alluding not only to the iconic poster made by the collective but also to demonstrate Caroline's and Steven's marriage of true minds: "We are singing for our lives. [. . .] We are fighting for our lives. [. . .] We are speaking for our lives" (*Art Lover* 163–64) (see figure 4.1).[32]

The ineluctable bond between Caroline and Steven is presented as hieroglyphic hope, comprehensible to neither but framed by the protagonist's devotion to Steven and the overwhelming fact of his dying. Maso brackets off this section with stacked images inserted between Caroline's prose: an **AZT S friend** in bold font, an illustration of the arrival of Haley's comet, a sign language card, a fourth detail of Giotto's *Noli Me Tangere*, and a reproduction of Matisse's *Virgin and Child on Starry Background*.

Suffice to say that Maso's inclusion of Matisse illuminates the author's focus on the three recurring narratives in *The Art Lover*, ascribing Matisse's revisionism to an ethos of maternality. Surrounded by the simplicity of stars, Matisse's lithograph *Virgin and Child* releases the mother-child bond

Figure 4.1. SILENCE = DEATH, © 1987 ACT UP, designed by the SILENCE = DEATH collective (Avram Finkelstein, Brian Howard, Oliver Johnston, Charles Kreloff, Chris Li). Reprinted with permission.

from its strictly biblical story, displaying a youthful Mary surrounding her child with heart-shaped arms and stars surrounding both. In a one-sentence conclusion before Maso inserts the Matisse reproduction, Caroline moves her hand toward Steven across the dinner table, declaring to herself: "It is not nearly over," a radical revision of the final words of Jesus on the cross, "It is finished" (John 19:30). When Caroline declares that "the dream of resurrection breaks in my heart," she simultaneously rejects finality, neither affirming nor denying her belief but, rather, accepting that her desire to love has intensified as a result of Steven's illness (*Art Lover* 163).[33] While Caroline willingly entertains the thought of reuniting in the afterlife with Steven, who is Jewish, she also knows it might be an illusory dream. Adopting instead the traditional lexicon of kinship, Caroline both inhabits and, as Freeman explains, "exceeds the matrix of couplehood and reproduction" ("Queer Belongings" 297), and in her relationship with Steven, she embraces a queer belonging that claims filial, widowed, and maternal status: "He is my brother"; "you have become my child" (*Art Lover* 238, 202). Unlike the formality of funeral rites, Caroline's mourning rituals are "intimate, private, oral and informal," permitting her to express fear, anger, and grief as a form of lamentation (Gilbert 33). As I said previously, Maso modeled the character Steven on Gary Falk, reproducing several of his artworks throughout the novel, thereby reinforcing the semiautobiographical nature of Caroline's story. In so doing, Maso composes a memorial to Gary Falk *and* completes her novel dedicated to him.

By inserting and thereby juxtaposing the Matisse reproduction with Gary Falk's *Red Dawn*, Maso highlights flight as Falk's graphic art portrays a Pegasus-like figure flying away from a sickbed and toward a star. Falk's use of chiaroscuro includes a bifurcated background of charcoal for the white-framed bed; and black background for the winged horse shown in flight crossing from charcoal to black. Maso recognizes Falk's willingness to probe the unknown and to continue questioning the uses of art to assure a continuity and movement that might not exist. By refusing to submit to nihilism as any final response to loss, Caroline recalls even if she cannot reclaim her father's modernist aesthetic. By embedding nonfictional documents from newspaper clippings to reproductions of paintings, Maso offers her own testimony to the epidemic even though she knows that "to write it down is always to get it wrong" (*Art Lover* 199). In this way, she is in agreement with modernist poet W. H. Auden, who famously wrote, "For poetry makes nothing happen" ("In Memory of W. B. Yeats" part 2, line 5) but, in a later poem, also wrote: "Words are for those with promises to keep" ("Their Lonely Betters" line 16). That last Auden passage was used as an epigraph by Timothy F. Murphy, who published one of the earliest coedited collections on AIDS. Murphy insists that "it is better to write something than to say nothing and thereby let death, in its extinguishing finality, arrogate to itself all privilege in deciding the fate and worth of human life" (307).[34] Maso commits to representing finality through actions taken by maternal figures such as Caroline, whose othermothering practices redefine a maternal epistemology that embraces the desiring body. In contrast, for Fiona of Makkai's *The Great Believers*, *maternality* becomes another word for mourning without reprieve.

Mourning Becomes Fiona

As I said earlier, a generation intervenes between the publication of Maso's *The Art Lover* and Makkai's *The Great Believers*, permitting Maso to portray drastically altered relationships within the gay community as a result of experiencing firsthand the virus's effects. Makkai, in contrast, partly depends on archival materials, differently persuasive in illuminating the harrowing effects of the epidemic during and after its occurrence in the United States. In preparation for writing the novel, Makkai engaged in extensive research, including archival and one-on-one interviews with survivors, both of which influenced her approach to writing about illness during an era that destroyed the lives of so many young men. As typical of historiographic metafiction, Makkai alternates chapters, toggling between two periods of social history—1985 through 1992 and 2015—to trace the fallout of this historical period, to examine maternal bonds beyond normative conceptions of motherhood, and to interweave the mother-daughter conflict between Fiona and her estranged daughter, Claire. In the 2015 chapters, Makkai portrays Fiona's maternal failure with her daughter as a reverberated trauma, emerging from her brother's death during the AIDS era that, as Makkai said, "stole a generation" (Fahle). *The Great Believers* goes to great length to examine the ongoing aftereffects of that mourning, which becomes a version of never-ending remembrance for Fiona, positioning her into an unsettling temporality that is recursive rather than linear, affecting her ability to mother her own child.

Makkai's representation of queer life through the second decade of the millennium can be described as *repronormative*, to use Freeman's term, and resultantly, as I wrote in the introduction, characters are portrayed as "living aslant to dominant forms of object choice, coupledom, family, marriage, sociability, and self-presentation, and thus out of synch with state-sponsored narratives of belonging and becoming" (*Time Binds* xv). Makkai chiefly elucidates the repronormative through Fiona's story, whose brother Nico dies of AIDS before the narrative begins and whose memorial comprises the first chapter of *The Great Believers*. Fiona's unending sorrow over the loss of her brother enables her to undertake a queer maternality for Yale Tishman, one of her brother's friends who falls ill with AIDS during the novel. Serving as an othermother for Yale while also pregnant with her daughter, Fiona must navigate multiple demands of pregnancy under the retraumatizing event of Yale's illness. Like Maso, Makkai implements representations of art as a reparative tool as Fiona spearheads and ensures the success of Yale's exhibit curated for an art gallery at Northwestern University. Makkai's implementation of two periods of social history in *The Great Believers* shows time fluctuating recursively, subverting normative notions of time by presenting a queer maternality and temporality that reached a kind of apotheosis in 2015, when a complicated reunion transpires between the gay survivors of Yale's generation and between Fiona and her daughter. Uniting the two periods of social history within a diasporan context, Makkai reprises the queer community of friends of Yale's and Fiona's pasts, American artists and friends in Paris.[35]

Alternating two chronicles of social history allows Makkai to expose her readers to archival Chicago history during and after the AIDS epidemic. Shifting between two periods permits Makkai not only to interlace and but also to expand the stories of the two principals, Yale and Fiona, whose interior thoughts are focalized throughout *The Great Believers*. Enveloping the entire novel is Makkai's focus on art, with the first and final chapters bookended by interconnected visual exhibits. As Makkai said of her novel in an interview with Jennifer Solheim, "It really always was a story about art, from the beginning." Makkai enlarges her fictional canvas through references to the 1920s art scene in Paris (through the character of Fiona's Great-Aunt Nora, an artist's model and unheralded artist herself) and contemporary art from both the 1980s and 2015 (through the character Richard Campo, a now famous photographer whose retrospective of the Chicago pandemic previews at the Pompidou toward the end of the novel). Despite Makkai's initial focus on the 1920s Paris art world, the thrust of *The Great Believers* focuses on the epidemic. Refusing to reduce the enormity of the AIDS crisis to a "subplot," the author explains that, after being drawn into extensive research on AIDS in Chicago, her focus "migrate[d] over" (Williams). By alternating the time periods, Makkai is able to explore the permanent effects of loss for survivors like Fiona and the gay community to which she has devoted her life.

Within both Yale's and Fiona's chronicles, Makkai makes references to traditional motherhood through an ensemble cast of characters, including mothers, sisters, and friends. Of particular relevance to my analysis are Yale's and Fiona's mothers as they are minoritized in the novel. Yale's mother early rejected the maternal role, a far-reaching choice that left

Yale unmothered at a very young age, partly spurring his migration later from small-town Michigan to Chicago, where he finds love and a chosen community in Boystown, one of the oldest LGBTQ* inclusive neighborhoods in the Midwest. There, Yale becomes partners with Charlie Keene, editor and founder of the gay newspaper *Out Loud*, a minimally concealed reference to the *Windy City Times*.³⁶ As though in response (and homage) to those first-generation survivors of the AIDS epidemic, Makkai portrays Yale as an abandoned child, echoing Michael Cunningham's *The Hours*, which itself recasts Virginia Woolf's *Mrs. Dalloway* and *To the Lighthouse*, novels that incorporate mother-daughter plots alongside the atrocities of war. That Yale's partner is of English heritage is playfully deferential on Makkai's part; that Charlie's mother moves into his Chicago apartment to assume the role of primary caretaker during his final illness (after he and Yale have separated) suggests the author's refusal to categorize maternal care by any one vector. Makkai's maternal through line echoes Maso's in its incorporation of queer desire and its disruption of normative genealogies in favor of nonaffiliative relations. One such relation is captured in the Yale-Fiona plot that overlays the entire novel.

Excommunicated from the family home when he was fifteen, Fiona's brother, Nico, later dies of AIDS in 1985, a newly identified virus with no cure. Beginning the novel with a memorial to Nico at Richard Campo's house in Lincoln Park (Richard is married and living a closeted life at this point), Makkai installs the Fiona and Yale plot, ensuring their intersection throughout the remainder of this novel through a maternal plotting that explores the effects of what Makkai calls in an interview with Emily Eakin the "long arm of grief" for survivors ("Rebecca Makkai: 2019 National Book Festival"). Fiona maintained communication with her older brother after their parents' denunciation of his sexuality, which initiated an irreparable falling-out with both parents. Fiona cannot reconcile her parents' rejection of their son; as a result, Fiona's judgment toward them is equal parts ferocious and unforgiving, profoundly affecting her ability to heal from the death of her brother. Decades elapse before Fiona allows herself to wonder if her mother knew that she had taken over the maternal role on Niko's behalf; as Niko would say to his roommates of his sister, "This is the lady that raised me" (*Great* 4). In order to extend her role as memory keeper for her brother, Fiona plays a pivotal role in helping Yale curate her Great-Aunt Nora's art collection, which initiates a kinship between Nora and Yale and indirectly embraces art as a way to connect generations that have endured excruciating loss. For Nora, the atrocities of the first

World War left her lover, artist Ranko Novak, disabled and suicidal; for Yale, the epidemic of AIDS killed many of his friends, including Charlie, obliterating an entire generation of young men. As a result of chronicling loss over and across alternating periods of social history, Makkai expands the reach of time, resisting any narrative of progress. Pulling "generations backward transforms notions of generational succession and progress" (*Time Binds* 65).[37] Consider two passages I juxtapose from *The Great Believers* from the perspectives of Nora and Fiona, respectively. Each represents a disparate historical era but sound eerily similar, even interchangeable:

> We'd been through something our parents hadn't. The war made us older than our parents.
>
> [. . .]
>
> How could she explain that this city was a graveyard? That they were walking every day through streets where there had been a holocaust, a mass murder of neglect and antipathy[.] (*Great* 311, 184)

Extending the focus on loss across a century, Makkai is able to accomplish several goals: situate the AIDS crisis within a larger historical canvas, linking the "Lost Generation" cohort[38] of World War I with the first generation of AIDS victims, many of whom did not survive; place the onus of survivorship on the keepers of memory, in this case, Nora and Fiona, whose devotion to Nico extends to Yale, centralizing his desire to curate Nora's 1920s paintings on behalf of the art gallery at Northwestern and establish a permanent collection where he is the development director on campus. Makkai is also able to examine a subject to which she often returns in her writing and refers to as the experience of the "one generation removed" (Schneiderman). Authoring *The Great Believers*, Makkai accurately describes herself as one generation removed from the AIDS era (she was seven years old in 1985).[39] Moreover, the temporal potential of "one generation removed" permits Makkai to explore the concept of "inherited memory," which she mines, like Maso, through references to the Holocaust ("Other Types of Poison") on behalf of the men killed by the 1980s epidemic and on behalf of the central Demeter-Persephone plot advanced in the 2015 chapters. I will reprise both of these points later in this chapter.

The first chapter, "1985," exposes the intersection between Yale's and Fiona's plots, which continues throughout the novel and is marked by extraordinary loss. To offer an early example: an eleven-year-old Fiona manages via public transportation to wend her way to Nico's apartment on Broadway (a gay-friendly neighborhood in Chicago), ensuring his care by bringing food, money, and allergy medication to him (*Great* 4). That a sister like Fiona served as an othermother for her brother who suffered the effects of family rupture may not be unusual. That this sister was aged eleven at the time is remarkable. Makkai represents Fiona's childhood as ineffably marked by struggle; her surname, *Marcus*, a patronymic name of Latin origin, also means in ancient Rome marked by war. Having lost the fight with her parents over Niko's care, Fiona remains all vim and vigor, triggered by rage and sorrow, preparing for the long-haul war as she succors Yale before and after he tests positive for HIV, his illness narrative taking precedence over her own bodily needs. Makkai encapsulates the paradoxical realities involved in mothering when she portrays Fiona's testimonial of going into labor while sitting vigil at Yale's deathbed, shunting aside her labor pains and simultaneously mirroring empathy, stroking "the skin between Yale's eyebrows," the only spot on his body not in mortal pain (*Great* 406). Each is only concerned with the other's pain. Yale and Fiona mirror the body in pain as each struggles to breathe. Fiona is finally escorted to the maternity ward by Debbie, the night nurse, permitting Yale to agree with Dr. Cheng to discontinue the AIDS drugs and start hospice on morphine. Fiona's inability to accept Yale's death without her ministrations reflects a guilty conscience she stores in her heart for thirty years, dramatizing the haunting power of trauma for this othermother.

Fiona can say along with Yale, "We are fighting for our lives," and observe a "whole neighborhood . . . dying," as Caroline says in *The Art Lover* as she watches Steven die alongside an entire community (Maso 164, 48). More than midway through the novel, Makkai elucidates how Fiona and Yale establish a close relationship intensified by Yale's precarity. During this section of the 1986 narrative, Yale finds himself unhoused (having broken up with Charlie), staying at the upscale Marina Towers in the apartment of donors of the Northwestern art gallery, whose presence in Yale's life is supportively consistent until the end. Before the catastrophe of testing positive, Yale must decide whether or not to pursue getting tested, making the refrain "to test or not to test" one of a plethora of unsettling questions men in this era had to ask. Fiona's intervention on behalf of Yale instrumentally enables him to secure the doctor who ultimately does preside over his final days (Yale's interior thought anticipates this). Fiona's intervention on behalf of Yale is both a surfeit and a reprisal of maternal service: she saves the dying cat Roscoe from her brother's former apartment, where his lover, Terrence, has recently died; and she becomes the best friend and sister to Yale even though such othermothering exceeds her own physical, emotional, and financial capacities. Yet Fiona's care work illuminates the extremity of the crisis, and she remains astonishingly effective. Working as a nanny to remain financially independent from her parents, Fiona's maternal praxis does not go unnoticed by Yale when she bundles up the two children she is minding to meet Yale at the zoo. There, Yale remarks to the twenty-year-old Fiona, "You'll make a great mom" (*Great* 269), praise that clanks hard against the reality of the 2015 chapters, but the reach of maternality in this novel is fluid and requires the crossing of boundaries and a collective undertaking of the work of mothering, which we see in the AIDS ward from nurses, especially.[40]

It's worth reiterating here that metafiction "self-consciously and systematically draws attention to its status as an artefact in order to pose questions about the relationship between fiction and reality" (Waugh 2). The metafictional quality of a mid-to-late chapter, "1986," is highlighted by Yale's concern regarding Fiona's well-being, as he anticipates the 2019 chapters as though having already lived through them himself: "Here's what I don't want. I don't want you to adopt me next, and then whoever else gets sick, and then the next guy, and before you know it you're fifty and you're living in a ghost town surrounded by all our old clothes and books" (*Great* 275). Of course, this is pretty much on the mark as, after her divorce, Fiona runs a resale shop to benefit housing for AIDS patients in Chicago. At fifty, Fiona's living with her "stack of ghosts," wishing, as Yale thinks to himself after he is ill, that "it was forever 1985" (*Great* 184, 379). To maintain the gravity of the central narrative arc—the AIDS crisis—Makkai exposes the relationship between fiction and reality through her deployment of extraliterary materials culled from her own interviews, issues from the *Windy City Times*, and repeated references to and inspiration from visual culture, writing fiction to reinvent the story and to "honor lived history" (Eakin).[41] Fiona's stack of ghosts continue to haunt her well into the millennium.

Fiona's perpetual mourning enabled her to perform maternal care that demonstrated enormous love for her brother and Yale, but it also continuously reveals an adulthood marked by melancholic trauma stopped in time, troubling the mother-daughter relationship. Fiona's struggle with loss is the same in 2015 as it was in 1985. For Fiona, the unending experience of loss "rather than heterosexual desire," as Robin Silbergleid says of Maso's *The Art Lover*, sponsors this narrative production (*Narratives of Loss* 55). Similar to Sethe in *Beloved*, Fiona lives her present as an ongoing trauma of the past, undeterred by a post-AIDS era. Within this temporality, Makkai depicts Fiona's response to her daughter's abduction, which launches the 2015 chapters as a pregnant Claire had already disappeared with her boyfriend into a cultish commune in Colorado; she has already survived a potentially lethal childbirth, and, with her daughter in tow, has left the states and is living as a single mother in Paris when Makkai recommences the plot. Desperately seeking Claire, Fiona's perambulations abroad intensify her melancholic feelings of loss. Before arriving in Paris, Fiona employs a private investigator ("A private investigator! How was this her life?") (*Great* 37) to help locate her daughter, which successfully occurs but does not resolve this mother-daughter rift.

Late in the novel, Fiona acknowledges her moral failure in a key confessional scene, which she shares with another mother, Cecily, who worked closely with Yale at Northwestern in the 1980s and is the paternal grandmother of Nicolette, Claire's daughter. In this pivotal scene, Makkai manages to merge maternal mourning across plotlines and generations, highlighting the sacrifices made by women during the AIDS epidemic, which Yale himself compares to "living in the trenches for seven years," applying Nora's World War I imagery to Fiona's "shell-shock," which, on his own deathbed, he believes she will suffer (*Great* 405). In her desperate need to claim Yale as her charge during his dying, Fiona's maternal identification becomes possession. Inundated by trauma, Fiona's emotional life as a survivor is punctuated by traumatic memory in this scene with Cecily, grandmothers permitted to babysit Nicolette at the park while Claire is working. Traumatic memory seizes Fiona's body before she can verbalize her shame and humiliation to Cecily. Fiona's confession unveils her reactionary response to seeing Yale's mother at the hospital where he lay dying in 1992. Displaying unexamined heternormativity, Fiona's behavior discloses her own uncharted misogyny toward another woman, proscribing empathy between them as a result of Fiona's surfeit of grief for Yale and undealt rage toward her own mother. Fiona's woundedness, as J. Brooks Bouson says of Sethe in *Beloved*, "defies all healing" (134). This is also dramatized by Fiona's plight as she continues to suffer from the reiterative power of trauma as trauma is wont to intrude upon the present as " 'fragmented sensory or motoric experiences' " (Bouson 134).[42]

Case in point: Makkai portrays Fiona "doubling over crying" at the park when Cecily declares that their granddaughter is "just so beautiful" (*Great* 387). Verbalizing her shame for the first time in twenty-three years to an accommodating witness in Cecily, Fiona finally utters what she recognizes is her greatest maternal failing:

> Fiona said, "I sent away his mom."
>
> I don't understand.
>
> "Yale's mom. [. . . .]
>
> Four days before he died, his mother showed up at the hospital."
>
> Cecily's face went still. [. . . .]
>
> "It was the biggest mistake of my life, Cecily. I think I'm being punished for it now. I shut my own mother out and I sent Yale's mother away, and it all boomeranged and hit me in the face." (*Great* 387, 388, 391)

Despite all her resistance to normative discourses of gender, family, and sexuality, Fiona submits to behavior that Marilyn Farwell explains is typical to "traditional narrative structure," in which "narrative is everything but lesbian" and "posits an oppositional and hierarchical relationship of male and female as the foundation of both heterosexual and male homosocial or homosexual plots, and as a condition of those structural alignments, disrupts or prevents female bonding" (15). Under the auspices of the heteronarrative, Fiona resorts to straight form, despite her exceptional self.

Fiona's confession to Cecily enables movement beyond the boomerang. Literally speaking, the word *boomerang* means to return to the originator. Fiona's admission of this shameful action is no more original than the trauma from which she suffers, but it is *hers*, and, as it pertains to beginnings, it will allow her to move forward thirty years after Nico's death in 1985. For Fiona to survive emotionally outside her role as the sister survivor during the AIDS era, she must move beyond her melancholy and into a process of mourning that enables her to embrace her dead and her living together, which includes her daughter, Claire, whom she is perpetually seeking, even after she is found. As for Alison in *The Art*

Lover, so for Claire in *The Great Believers*: their mothers were abducted before they were born. Unbeknownst to them until adulthood, each can say: "She had been missing her mother her whole life" (*Art Lover* 232). Like Maso, Makkai commits to representing finality and restoration through actions taken by the principal maternal figures in their novels, who support their beloved during and after their deaths. To suggest the recursive nature of their mourning, both authors shift the focus in their narratives to document the lived realities of those dying from this unforgiving disease. As a result, both authors implement antinarrative stances to acknowledge their own inability to contain the wreckage within their fictional frameworks, which I discuss next.

After Such Knowledge, What Forgiveness?

Elaine Scarry notes that "whatever pain achieves, it achieves in part through its unshareability, and it ensures this unshareability through its resistance to language" (4). To convey the simultaneity and unreality of time during the AIDS epidemic, Maso and Makkai portray their othermothers relying on a synesthetic experience to encapsulate their communication with dying men. From the Greek, *synesthesia* means "together" (synth) with "perception" (esethsia). Blending sensory modalities enables the conveyance of pain through overlapping sensations, bringing sound and color to bear on what these witnesses see. In Maso's author's note, part addendum, part unwillingness to depart from a devastation that just keeps getting worse, Maso describes Gary Falk toward the end of his life, having lost his sight, hearing in his left ear, and feeling in his left hand: "In the end, I was only hands to him," but Gary, like Carole, shares this synesthetic perception: "What the light looks like is hoops of gold wrapped around your body" (*Art Lover* 143, 243, 242). In *The Great Believers*, Yale's pain is so unbearable that he cannot be touched anywhere except "that one spot"; Fiona scoots closer to his deathbed to "stroke the skin between [his] eyebrows," intimately aware of his bodily needs (*Great* 406).

While the authors must paradoxically engage in language to describe the indescribable, they also showcase narrative breakdown in their shift into antinarrative techniques. I apply Robert Scholes's placement of postmodern antinarratives in a metafictional context because such narratives "frustrate our automatic application of these codes [chronology, causality] to all our event-texts[,] ... ultimately forc[ing] us to draw our attention away from diegesis according to our habitual interpretive processes.... The function of anti-narrative is to problematize the entire process of narration and interpretation for us" ("Language, Narrative" 211). Maso's autobiographical fifth section, "More Winter," and Makkai's chapter "July 15, 1986" represent each author's recognition that fictional narrative has exceeded its ability to get the story of loss right. The fictive curtain falls as both authors delay fictional movement to problematize the stories they tell. I suggest the authors do this out of respect for the men whose stories they are telling, but the stories they are telling are inadequate no matter their well-meaning intent. But each author tries anyway, even though "nothing makes it stop.... Nothing. Not the writing of this. Not the writing of *The Art Lover*" (*Art Lover* 206). And let me add: not the writing of *The Great Believers*, a generation later.[43]

Maso's move into autobiography more than halfway through *The Art Lover* exemplifies her continued disbelief that AIDS happened to Gary, her childhood friend and fellow artist whose understanding of desire is her own. At the beginning and ending of this section, Maso frames her autobiographical shift linguistically, intensifying her disbelief through refrain: "Whoever is responsible for this is not forgiven.... How could this be allowed to happen?"; "It means I miss you. It means: I can't believe this happened to you" (*Art Lover* 195, 206). Maso's incredulity is shaped by an awareness of the complicity of silence underlying the nation's slow response to this health emergency. To suggest an everlasting present, Makkai accedes to pausing the narrative; like Maso, she puts on the breaks late in *The Great Believers* in an attempt to narrate the inenarrable. Neither survivor nor othermother, Makkai steps aside to imagine what the unspeakable might feel like for Yale in "July 15, 1986." The author's shift into antinarrative represents an entrée into a queer time in the 1980s. The only chapter in a novel of 418 pages that's given an actual day, month, year, Makkai knows that her survivor audience understands this anniversary as sui generis: domesday for gay men; historical marker and anniversary date of when they tested positive for the virus. Makkai imagines Yale's ruminations, offering a list of things that he will miss: Lake Michigan, hot bread from the oven, the Cubs winning the World Series, Chagall, Picasso, and more. His thoughts are a mixture of profound and quotidian, all of the sundry "o taste and sees" he will not be able to experience. Juxtaposed in italics between the spaces of Yale's four-page list is

Dr. Cheng's mindful ministrations, offering informational and emotional support, literally catching Yale when he falls, "*Whoa, there, let's lie down. Let's get you lying down*" (*Great* 337).

In the interstice between fiction and life, Maso and Makkai represent the AIDS body in extremis, part of both authors' engagement in post-Holocaust narratives as they historicize the 1980s epidemic through tropes related to a destructive and violent past. Juxtaposing historical tragedies with the 1980s era of AIDS in no way undermines their dedication to exposing the realities of bodily carnage for its victims. Silbergleid's explanation of *The Art Lover*'s use of Holocaust imagery can also be applied to *The Great Believers*: "Invoking the Holocaust in this way elevates the politics of AIDS in the novel, not merely its sorrow. . . . [T]he novel itself situates the AIDS epidemic within a century of loss motivated by difference (sexual, racial, religious)" (*Narratives of Loss* 112). Such differences are also highlighted by the fact that the central male characters in each novel are not only homosexual, but Jews as well; not only intellectual, but artists as well. While I do not suggest that Maso or Makkai solely focus their narratives on delineating a post-Holocaust genre, I do argue that the authors engage in post-Holocaust narratives in order to accomplish the following:

- Illuminate the bodily connections between Jewish characters dying of AIDS and victims of the Holocaust;
- Examine the concept of "post memory" for daughters like Caroline and Claire with no direct memories from their mother's generation, but who suffer as a result of maternal melancholy;
- Recuperate the mother-daughter relation after the tragedy of separation.

In the section "Winter," Maso leads into a direct reference to the Holocaust in relation to the AIDS era, acknowledging the genocidal history by advocating for the existential necessity of remembering it in the present. Maso first begins this section with the epigraph "Not Steven." Caroline's denial is repeated three times in this short section, the news of Steven's diagnosis propelling her simultaneously backward and forward in time: "Death is not only a big-breasted woman whispering over a man whose brain, whose whole body will explode so stupendously; it is also a beautiful man, muscular, faceless, lying on a pier, years ago in the bright sun" (*Art Lover* 134). Juxtaposed to Caroline's response to Steven's illness is the recurring reference to the *Challenger* explosion, which Caroline quickly connects to Steven's diagnosis: "an explosion in the sky" (*Art Lover* 134). Before invoking the Holocaust, Maso inserts epigraphical sections to the shuttle explosion, which occurred the same year Gary Falk died: 1986. She carefully calibrates an interconnection between the countdown of the main engine of the shuttle and the decreasing T-cells which will ultimately kill her childhood friend. While Maso honors the first civilian on board the shuttle, Christa McAuliffe, she damns the political administration whose benign silence on the topic of AIDS is unforgivable. In her autobiographical section, Maso furiously writes, "They say they are not surprised, are not sorry. They tell us we deserve it" (*Art Lover* 203).

Thirty years after Maso published *The Art Lover*, Makkai recalls the space-shuttle explosion in *The Great Believers* with Yale thinking, "A handful of dead astronauts and Reagan weeps with the nation. Thirteen thousand [as of 1986] dead gay men and Reagan's too busy" (*Great* 246). Implicitly, both authors also make a connection between the present and the past: the 1980 AIDS victims in America and a genocide in midtwentieth century. Maso writes:

> Steven, forty years before this, in another country, would have received a death sentence as well.
>
> Intellectual.
>
> Homosexual.
>
> Jew. (*Art Lover* 157)

Employed as a refrain in *The Great Believers*, Makkai's references to the Holocaust are made for political and phenomenological reasons: without the complicity of the government, the initial costs of AZT might not have been $10,000 a year, ensuring the deaths of thousands of mostly uninsured men. In addition, Makkai explores the unreality of seeing the devastated AIDS body, which Yale witnesses when he meets Charlie's mother at Masonic Illinois Hospital to say goodbye to his former partner. Charlie has been ravished by the disease: "He was an alien, an Auschwitz skeleton, a baby bird fallen from its nest. Yale's mind kept searching for metaphors, because the simple fact of it—that this was Charlie—was too much" (*Great* 354). Individual sorrow and collective consciousness combine in this scene as Yale, who feeds Charlie water, "drop by drop," recognizes the ubiquity of the disease: "He could feel it all around him. How down the corridor, and down other hallways and other hospitals around Chicago and the other godforsaken cities of the globe, a thousand other men did the same" (*Great* 355).

When Maso shifts into autobiography in "More Winter," she reiterates the Holocaust reference, this time referencing the ovens as she addresses Gary: "Gary, I am trying to talk to you. You were put in an oven and cremated. I don't know where your ashes went" (*Art Lover* 200). Gary's eyes "bulge in [his] bony head" when submitting to blue dye screening tests. Carole bears witness to his "small shrunken genitals. Your nearly transparent hands. . . . I am told that there are certain bones that burn slower than others. They can be fished from the ash and crumbled by hand" (*Art Lover* 204). There is no more time for denial as Carole daily witnesses Gary's excruciatingly slow death. Let us remember: these were young men. As witness and othermother, Carole accepts that Gary "has become my child" (*Art Lover* 202). In this autobiographical section, Maso reveals important details about Gary Falk's commitment to art and his supportive interest in Carole's novel, *Ghost Dance*, which he read in galleys just before going blind. As well, Maso shares her love of the nurses on the fourteenth-floor AIDS ward: "How beautiful they were . . . unflagging, attentive, diligent," spurring memories of her mother, a nurse: "And I love her so much in this instant, once a twenty-year-old woman like these women, in a white uniform, thinking she could save anyone" (*Art Lover* 198). Fiona Marcus *is* the twenty-year-old woman in *The Great Believers* whose unflagging devotion to Nico and Yale is beautiful and attentive, though neither can be saved.

While there might be no forgiveness in *The Art Lover* and *The Great Believers*, both authors gesture toward recuperation. They do this through what I am calling "queer maternal reunions." Such gatherings I interpret through the context of Freeman's queer belonging as a practice of renewal: "it simply makes people more possible. . . . to endure in corporeal form over time, beyond procreation. . . . To want to belong, . . . to 'hold out' a hand across time and touch the dead or those not born yet, to offer oneself beyond one's own time" (299).[44] If this sounds utopic, it is.[45] Such queer gatherings are presented at the conclusions of *The Art Lover* and *The Great Believers* as recuperative and consoling gestures, reprising the maternal plots as well. Caroline's fanciful dream of being reunited with "Max and Mom, David and Grey, Steven" is actualized by a final photograph Maso includes at the end of her novel: a photograph of Gary Falk with the author, a memento mori, perhaps, but also furnished evidence[46] of their filial bond (*Art Lover* 227, 243).

Yale's end-of life fever dream in which he becomes Fiona and then Fiona gives birth to her brother, Nico, is nestled next to the final chapter in which Richard Campo's retrospective at the Pompidou has its preview. That Claire attends Richard's show, *Strata*, is a sign for Fiona to declare her desire to stay in France to be near her daughter and granddaughter despite Claire's understandable lack of forgiveness for her mother's emotional abandonment during childhood in favor of serving as "Saint Fiona of Boystown" (*Great* 399). Claire is profoundly her mother's daughter. Her barbed comment signifies a postmemory response to her mother's traumatic experiences during the AIDS era. Yet Claire remains at the Parisian exhibit and listens to survivor Julian, who serves as an unjudging witness of Fiona's story, reminding Claire about this: "I know she did her best. . . . You two are on the same planet at the same time. You're in the same place now. That's a miracle. I just want to say that" (*Great* 400–1). Like Maso, Makkai commits her novel to subverting traditional ideas of linear time and generational progress. Richard Campo's show epitomizes queer love exceeding its own time: Richard installs a glowing light box of photo strips entitled *1983* (which includes a photo of Fiona with Terrence, Nico's partner) and a video installation that loops around again and again, reminding viewers and survivors alike that maybe it "was forever 1985" as Yale thinks earlier in the novel (*Great* 379). The final lines of the novel, especially for those of us who survived, including me, are heartbreaking: "Then the whole film looped again. There they all stood. . . . Boys with hands in pockets waiting for everything to begin" (*Great* 418). Everything to begin: not begin again. Just begin.

By attempting to memorialize a generation of men whose lives were cut short by an epidemic, Maso and Makkai embrace a queer temporality that honors their suffering by narrating their unbecoming, that is, narrating their shift into debilitation *and* honoring their remains by which I mean their artistic legacies. Maso and Makkai develop a maternal epistemology that embraces queer kinship as a practice in an era in which a generation of men died horrible deaths. Maternal figures—othermothers, nurses, mothers—found ways to forge ahead by loving their dying in all their vulnerability. Reparative figures, Caroline and Fiona demonstrate the staying power undergirding their courageous journeys as sister-mothers. However haltingly they may have moved, these maternal women mobilized their resources to take care of the bodies of ill men they loved, staying time a little to remember their beauty.

Coda

During the time period in which I was writing this book, the following assaults on American democracy took place: the Dobbs decision stripped away women's right to an abortion; a record number of states passed anti-LGBTQ* legislation, in particular, antitrans legislation; books by and about BIPOC and LGBTQ* people were increasingly targeted by school boards for banning; anti-immigration laws continued to stymie progressive reforms; and educational gag orders restricted how teachers discuss slavery and race. Bolstering these attacks is a right-wing ultranationalist movement bent on suppressing others, using fascistic tropes to promote antisemitic, anti-Muslim, white supremacist discourse. *Washington Post* opinion columnist Jennifer Rubin could have been describing many states across the country when she wrote that such retributive behavior reinforces an environment where "empathy, decency and kindness go to die." The increasing rise in antidemocratic practices has been lamentably ingrained into the wax and wane of American life. Although these phases are neither natural nor inevitable, the most baneful effects of such nihilism are all too familiar to the authors examined in these pages.

Motherhood studies—across multiple disciplines—continues to be a resurgent praxis that responds to such crucial social issues; from the Latin *resurgere*, to rise again, my study of American literary narratives marks a comparative, multiethnic return to maternality, illustrating the care work that was accomplished under appalling circumstances. Returning to those foundational studies on motherhood enabled me to illuminate narrative voices of assertion and survival embodied by the authors who theorized capaciously about maternity across a century and a half of literary expression in the United States. In addition, these authors' works exposed the fundamentally intersectional nature of social categorization, compelling redefinitions of mothering across a swath of urgent social circumstances. The authors battled against egregious forms of institutional oppressions, deftly responding to signs of tyranny in repressive eras of slavocracy, dictatorship, pandemic, and virulent right-wing despotism. As authoritarianism is once again on the rise, movements for social change such as Black Lives Matter and #MeToo (to name just two) have responded valiantly to racism and sexual violence. By constructing counternarratives about maternal care, the authors explored in *Mothers, Mobility, Narrative* utilize, as Grace McEntee said of Jacobs's vision of racial equality, an ethos of motherhood to stimulate change in "a national culture," forming friendships "across racial lines . . . inspired and fueled by the power of mother love" (200). Expanding the definitional perimeters of maternality, the authors tap into the meanings of motherlove's inventive power to expose a radical alterity inhering in maternal work, inclusive of othermothering practices by friends, sisters, siblings, and lovers.

As Audre Lorde reminds her readers in "Uses of the Erotic," love is born of chaos, which in ancient Greek cosmology refers to the abyss before order was established. Of its many uses, love personifies "creative power and harmony" and serves as a guidepost beyond an underworld of disorder (*Sister Outsider* 55). The authors I explore ignite a necessary recognition that such maternal praxis is produced through ongoing negotiations outside normative discourse and powered by creative uses of the erotic. Refusing to fall prey to a nostalgic conception of home, for example, the authors portray Demeter and her daughters forcibly removed from maternal support and unhoused. Such extremes compel these writers to generate new conceptual and material spaces in the lives of their personae and characters, disrupting traditional expectations of the genres that undergird their narratives. The authors claim multifaceted conceptions of kin in their varying uses of othermothering as a gesture of "literary and cultural emergence, assertion and survival" as Edvige Giunta explains ("Persephone's Daughters" 769). As a result, these authors generate new narrative directions in their works through their innovative adaptions of maternality, claiming nonaffiliative kin as their own and calling new places home. Despite barriers to their movements exacerbated by oppressions of slavocracy and racism, coerced migration and anti-immigration legislation, and institutional hegemonies threatening women-identified people whose bodily protections are under attack, these authors unrepentantly refuse a path that would direct them into erasure.

Having been removed from maternal support, sometimes forcibly, the narrators and protagonists of these stories discover ways to survive through a form of reconnaissance calibrated through a vigilant manipulation of time and space. A modern Penelope, Harriet Jacobs manages time through the proficiency of her hands, projecting a future of freedom through letter writing while in the present sewing warm clothing for her children. Text and textile merge in Jacobs's autobiography, but her classic freedom-fighting tale is marred by many factors, including the tomb-like shed in which she hid for seven years and the institutional persecutions she met up North after escaping, unable to reunite with her grandmother before her death and unable to provide a home for her children.

In postbellum America, Harriet and her daughter, Louisa Jacobs, continued their efforts to establish free schools for Black children, though neither woman achieved economic independence from white patronage. Despite the failures of Reconstruction, mother and daughter continued their efforts to increase educational opportunities for Black children in Northern and Southern states, warily persisting when "seeds of violence" sprouted in the former Confederacy (*Harriet Jacobs* 200). As her biographer, Jean Fagin Yellin writes of Jacobs's long life, she "had outlived her generation," dying in 1897 at the age of eighty-four, with Louisa Jacobs, "the devoted daughter of an extraordinary mother" by her side (*Harriet Jacobs* 259, 265). Mother and daughter managed time carefully, responding to racist insults with activism, Louisa fulfilling her mother's "old dream of becoming a public lecturer," inherited from a mother who knew how to measure time to control her destiny (*Harriet Jacobs* 202).

Goddess of the underworld, Beloved is Sethe's Persephone, her haunted girl come home. But it is Denver who is the new-world daughter who ensures her extraordinary mother's survival in *Beloved* as Toni Morrison extends the Margaret Garner story to include a postbellum future for Black women in America. An escapee who goes into labor during her flight from the plantation Sweet Home, Sethe pays nomenclatural homage to Amy Denver, a white girl on the run, who helps Sethe birth her child. By naming her daughter Denver, a place name, which in Old English connotes movement such as crossing and passing, Sethe also inchoately ensures her own survival. Despite a nearly paralyzing agoraphobia, Denver heeds her deceased grandmother's advice and steps off her mother's porch to enlist aid from the community of othermothers to help her dying mother. Baby Suggs refuses to whitewash racial realities in telling her granddaughter there is no defense against the wrath of white people, but she must nevertheless "go on out the yard. Go on" (*Beloved* 244). Denver's movement emerges as a form of othermothering for her traumatized mother and a new cultural emergence for both women despite postreconstruction failures. Denver's mobility enables her mother's survival. This is reinforced by Morrison's temporal shift into the present at the conclusion of *Beloved*. As such, Denver's presence in the town spurs the presence of community othermothers, all of whom assemble in front of 124 Bluestone Road, a reconnaissance of reckoning, which interrupts Sethe's rememory and ensures her survival.

When daughters themselves suffer from the trauma of survivorship as Fiona does in *The Great Believers*, mothering a child incredulously takes second place to the metamorphic experience of othermothering dying men. Rebecca Makkai compels a reinterpretation of mothering under the exigencies of a pandemic in which epidemic space becomes coeval with maternal work. The global dimensions of AIDS in the twenty-first century continues to illustrate the racism inherent in continued benign silence in response to this disease. Fiona's motherlove for Yale is remarkable in its effectiveness and intensity, transforming her conception of motherhood and enabling her efforts to reunite with her estranged daughter. While Fiona's narrative trajectory is ostensibly about a mother's movements toward reconciliation with her daughter, it is also simultaneously about her failed relationship with her own mother, who had rejected her gay brother. Such rejections in families continue with another pandemic, Covid-19, which hovered over the writing of this book. The effects of misinformation about the life-saving necessity of vaccines regarding the Covid-19 pandemic has caused long-lasting estrangements between people, often polarizing families irreparably. In her effort to repair relations with her daughter, Fiona travels across the Atlantic to initiate a reunion with Claire and perhaps clear a space should her daughter wish to mend ruptured bonds. Travel often effects a form of reversal that has the capacity to revitalize female networking across generations and gaps of time.

Carole Maso represents female networking in *The Art Lover* through her interlocutor, Caroline, who recovers a new maternality during the throes of a virulently deadly virus. To respond to this health catastrophe, Maso represents gendered time through unconventional narrative modes that disrupt traditional genres of autobiography and fiction, enlarging ideas about maternal genealogy and storytelling. Implicitly recalling Woolf's famous declaration in *A Room of One's Own* that women think back through their mothers, Maso inscribes new affiliations that reimagine maternity detached from family trees and official routes, portraying other-mothering ministrations from a lesbian on behalf of her childhood friend. By revising and extending Lily Briscoe's incantatory call to Mrs. Ramsay at the end of Woolf's *To the Lighthouse*, Maso ushers in a Lordian house of difference for the catastrophically suffering figure in *The Art Lover*. Maso's form of reconnaissance compels a scrutinizing of the effectiveness of the novel as a genre capable of telling an unspeakable story. More than midway through the novel, Maso shifts into autobiography, stopping all the fictional narratives of *The Art Lover*. Doing this enables her to emphasize the impossibility of fictionalizing her loss. Instead, Maso travels to a space and time that is an immediate and searing present, repeating her disbelief that this cruel suffering and death happened to Gary, her beautiful friend.

Travel as a form of reversal of space and time informs several of the works here. García represents Lourdes's ghostly encounters with her deceased father on the Brooklyn Bridge, a borderland space that ultimately, like Sethe's mental meanderings, takes her over the sea to the homeland she rejected. Lourdes's surname (del Pino/of the pine) and married name (Puente/bridge) anticipate her return to Cuba but ensure her mobility to leave again, rooted and winged. In very different ways, Cather, Lorde, and Ragusa, all make returns South by engaging in maternal mobilities that expand their perceptions of home. Cather's Southern connections were as much influenced by memories of a homeplace from which she was wrested at nine years old as they were about her own anti-Blackness. In contrast, several of the authors examined in *Mothers, Mobility, Narrative* have crafted what Annarita Taronna calls "ethnographies of Southernness" for expansive purposes, including travel to other countries (108). For Lorde and Ragusa, for example, Southern peregrinations take them to Mexico and Sicily, respectively, expanding diasporic spaces that embrace larger notions of maternal genealogies, linking them intimately to home spaces and maternal figures that are simultaneously nonaffiliative and otherworldly. Unlike representations of some maternal figures from earlier generations, whose migrations were often coerced, whose bodies were separated from kith and kin and immobilized by the extremities of slavery and poverty, writers such as Lorde, Ragusa, and García, for example, extend commentary on the maternal that posits a form of caretaking that is fluid, fluctuating between stasis and movement.

In *Dreaming in Cuban*, for example, Celia willingly embraces a maternal water spirit, the Duende of the Cuban sea. Lorde's Afrekete is a daughter to "the great mother of us all," emerging from a place called Carriacou, which becomes an expansive definition of othermothering for "woman who work together as friends and lovers" (*Zami* 255). Ragusa's daughterly searches take her to Sicily, which she identifies in *The Skin Between Us* as the crossroads "between Europe and Africa" (18). A traveling Persephone, Ragusa's liminal position "forms and reforms identity, shaping a sense of self characterized by in-betweenness" (Vellucci 192). Whether this in-betweenness is racial or spatial, for mobile daughters, it compels them to redefine for themselves what it means to claim a home and be comforted by it.

Figure C.1. Christine Perri, *Detail, Shipwreck in a Tree, Figurehead with Cloth*, 2016. Wood and Embroidered Canvas Series. Photograph and loan of image by kind permission of Christine Perri.

I have been thinking about mothers a long time. Like these writers, I recognize the necessity of thinking back through the mothers in ways that enlarge the terrain upon which maternality lives, including my own nurturing and othermothering. For mothering occurs in a myriad of ways, despite life-denying circumstances and confined spaces, including the kind of harrowing caregiving that occurs in a coffin-sized shed located at the interstices of house and roof or in a hospital ward where othermothers show fierce love for abandoned sons. What's more, in thinking back through the mother—Demeter, Afrekete, the Madonna, the Duende—these authors examine how doing maternal work is always also playing the role of negotiator and trickster. To inspire an enlarged ethic of motherhood, then, these authors seek a language of love that refuses a restrictive narrowing that tells people whom and how to love; by doing so, they simultaneously refuse normative definitions about mothering and care work. Othermothers all, the daughters' movements in these works enabled them to create narratives of resistance about maternality in order to illuminate the fact that caretaking is as fluid as the sea, and, as such, it reveals a place of origin that differs from a homeland long gone. No wonder that the authors reference the sea: it is as much a "disquieting space" that recalls unknown ancestors as it is a "liquid materiality" that reconnects women to the maternal (as qtd. in Ferraro 224). The writers in these pages offer daughters of abduction a way to find home, or, as Morrison writes in *Beloved*, all the daughters are looking for "the join, . . . a place to be" (213). Finding a place to be may usher in a redefined ethic of maternal care in our fraught twenty-first century. These authors show us how they did it under outrageous conditions.

Notes

Introduction

1. Throughout this study, I use the terms *maternality* and *maternity* interchangeably, to examine how the authors represent their complexity beyond what Wesley N. Barker describes as a "care-driven, natality-centered discourse of maternality itself" (203), nonetheless recognizing how several of the authors centralize giving birth as a core feature of a person's autonomy. The *OED* defines maternality through an ontological framework, the "quality or condition of being maternal;" its secondary definition, "motherly remarks or discourse," invites a broader analysis of discursive formations that represent maternal desire disconnected from fecundity (*OED* 1743).

2. See *Canons and Contexts*, especially "Teaching Nineteenth-Century Women Writers" (114–32).

3. I take the term *reparenting* from Rachel Blau Du Plessis's *Writing beyond the Ending: Narrative Strategies of Twentieth-Century Women Writers*. My use of the term slightly diverges from Du Plessis's focus on the Oedipal crisis within a heterosexual paradigm, but the narrative strategy remains the same as it aims to "forge an alternative fictional resolution [in order to end] sexual polarization . . . to construct from available male and female roles, sibling and parent-child ties, some set of relationships that would be less emotionally damaging" (83). Generally speaking, Du Plessis examines the "transgressive invention of narrative strategies, strategies that express critical dissent from dominant narrative. These tactics, among them reparenting, woman-to-woman and brother-to-sister bonds, and forms of the communal protagonist, take issue with the mainstays of the social and ideological organization of gender" (5).

4. While it is beyond the purview of this study, I want to recognize the actual cases of abduction of children from their mothers, especially in Indigenous communities throughout North America, and institutionalized in the early nineteenth century by church-operated boarding schools. For a superb discussion of

the period of assimilation (1879–1934) in which children were forcibly separated from parents and sent to boarding schools, see Beth H. Piatote's *Domestic Subjects: Gender, Citizenship, and Law in Native American Literature*. I thank Liza Black for discussing this with me via email correspondence on February 29, 2024.

5. For an explanatory gloss on Cavarero's use of the phrase *birth-no-more*, see Tuhin Bhattacharjee's "Antigone/Mother: Second Death and the Maternal in Lacan and Cavarero." Bhattacharjee explains:

> In Cavarero's interpretation, the power of Demeter as mother lies in her agency both to generate and not to generate, to perpetuate life and to freeze it into nothingness, or what she calls "birth-no-more," the symbolic equivalent of the end of the world. This sterility, however, is not the death implied in the masculine symbolic order, not the nothingness of death, but rather "the *nothingness* of birth, a mute petrification of *phyein*: the desolate land where even death dies of unmourned immobility." Unlike in death, where the decomposition of life is only a stage for the beginning of a new differentiation, of new permutations and combinations of matter and form, "the nothingness of birth" refers to a withdrawal of this movement altogether. It implies a stiffening stasis where the very cycle of death-bearing life and life-bearing death comes to an abrupt halt. (198–99)

6. Cavarero is influenced here by Irigaray's earlier argument that an "act of matricide" is the founding gesture of Western thought. See also Margaret Whitford, *Luce Irigaray: Philosophy in the Feminine*.

7. See also Collins's *Black Feminist Thought: Knowledge, Consciousness, and the Politics of Empowerment*. For recent approaches to motherhood through the lens of Collins's conception of othermothering and mothering of mind, see Kaila Adia Story's edition *Patricia Hill Collins: Reconceiving Motherhood*.

8. Though beyond the purview of my study, I do want to mention that Collins raises a serious concern about the concept and activity of othermothering applied to Black women within the context of the academy, stating, "If the institution can find a way to exploit African American women's inclinations toward othermothering, and remix it within those particular traditions [such as mentoring] why wouldn't it do that?" (Story 181).

9. For a historical overview of the phrase *the cult of true womanhood*, see Barbara Welter's *Dimity Convictions: The American Woman in the Nineteenth Century*.

10. Since her 1990 release of *Black Feminist Thought: Knowledge, Consciousness, and the Politics of Empowerment*, Collins has articulated, as Kaila Adia Story argues, an "epistemological specificity," illuminating "the non-complacement and

resistant traditions of Black and Female scholarship, activism, and research. [. . .] By connecting motherhood as an institution to manifestations of empire, racism, classism, and heteronormativity, Collins has been articulating an alternative view of black womanhood within the academy and beyond" (1). Interdependent dimensions of motherhood are generously reflected in the narratives I study and regularly challenge ideologies of motherhood traditionally represented by the (white, middle-class) nuclear family.

11. Gallop's *The Daughter's Seduction: Feminism and Psychoanalysis* pays homage to Juliet Mitchell's *Psychology and Feminism* but moves away from largely Anglophone feminism and toward Lacanian psychoanalysis in order to stage dialectical tensions between psychoanalysis and feminism. While Gallop focuses on the father-daughter relationship through the lens of psychoanalysis, she reframes the encounter through the activity of feminist writing, which has the potential of shifting the dyad away from the parent-child model.

12. While not primarily focused in literary motherhood studies, see Claudia Tate's *Psychoanalysis and Black Novels: Desire and Protocols of Race* for her use of psychoanalysis to articulate the "complicated conflicts of narrative desire in African American literary texts," including writers from the late nineteenth through mid-twentieth centuries such as Emma Dunham Kelley, W. E. B. Du Bois, Richard Wright, Nella Larsen, and Zora Neale Hurston (15).

13. See Hirsch's "Mother and Daughters," in *Signs: Journal of Women in Culture and Society*.

14. See *Inside/Out: Lesbian Theories, Gay Theories*, ed. Diana Fuss.

15. Deep gratitude must be extended to Andrea O'Reilly, who has striven to institutionalize motherhood studies in academia and continues to revitalize theoretical analyses of motherhood studies across disciplines and in a variety of publications, of which I include only a selection: *Toni Morrison and Motherhood: A Politics of the Heart*; *From Motherhood to Mothering: The Legacy of Adrienne Rich's "Of Woman Born,"* ed. Andrea O'Reilly; *Rocking the Cradle: Thoughts on Feminism, Motherhood, and the Possibility of Empowered Motherhood*; *Maternal Theory: Essential Readings*, ed. Andrea O'Reilly; a second edition of *Maternal Theory*, published in 2021, includes thirty new chapters; and *Encyclopedia of Motherhood*, ed. Andrea O'Reilly.

16. Chodorow's references include middle- and working-class women-identified white writers. In the essay that set the groundwork for her longer study, Chodorow exclaims that the "embeddedness in relationships to others" is "described particularly acutely by [white] women writers" ("Family Structure" 58, 59), a cross-disciplinary comment she (unfortunately) does not include or develop in *The Reproduction of Mothering*.

17. According to Brenda Silver, Rich's statement on the relationship between mothers and daughters is "one of the most widely cited statements to come out

of the women's movement" (265). For example, see Cristina Herrera's 2014 monograph, *Contemporary Chicana Literature: (Re)Writing the Maternal Script*, which includes Rich's statement as an epigraph.

18. The relationship between Lorde and Rich cannot be underestimated. In addition, both writers are experiencing yet another resurgence in feminist literary scholarship. A brief list follows: *Audre Lorde: The Berlin Years, 1984–1992*, a 2012 documentary directed by Dagmar Schultz; *I am Your Sister: Collected and Unpublished Writings of Audre Lorde*, coedited by Rudolph P. Byrd, Johnnetta Betsch Cole, and Beverly Guy-Sheftall; Suryia Nayak's monograph, *Race, Gender and the Activism of Black Feminist Theory: Working with Audre Lorde*; *The Selected Works of Audre Lorde*, edited and with an introduction by Roxane Gay; Alexis Pauline Gumbs's *Survival Is a Promise: The Eternal Life of Audre Lorde*; Claudia Rankine's "Adrienne Rich's Poetic Transformations"; *Adrienne Rich's Collected Poems: 1950–2012* with an introduction by Claudia Rankine; Hilary Holladay, *The Power of Adrienne Rich: A Biography*. See also the special issue on Adrienne Rich, edited by Cynthia R. Wallace, in *Arizona Quarterly*.

19. See O'Reilly's "Politics of the Heart: African American Womanist Thought on Mothering;" Arlene E. Edwards's "Community Mothering: The Relationship between Mothering and the Community Work of Black Women" and Njoki Nathani Wane's "Reflections on the Mutuality of Mothering: Women, Children, and Othermothering" in O'Reilly's edition of *Mother Outlaws*.

20. On the classical origins in African American literature, see also Tracey L. Walters's *African American Literature and the Classicist Tradition: Black Women Writers from Wheatley to Morrison*.

21. I am referencing Luce Irigaray's lyrical prose piece, "And the One Doesn't Stir without the Other." Irigaray employs a psycho-linguistic approach to maternal theories further providing me a perspective on the nuances of desire vis-à-vis the maternal. Turning to an experimental mode of writing in recalling the classic figures of Demeter/Persephone through their immanent mutuality, Irigaray writes: "And the one doesn't stir without the other. But we do not move together. When the one of us comes into the world, the other goes underground. When one carries life, the other dies. And what I wanted from you, Mother, was this: that in giving life to me, you still remain alive" (67). Translator Hélène Vivienne Wenzel explains the English does not entirely convey Irigaray's sentence in French, "Mais ce n'est ensemble que nous nous mouvons," which imparts "a sense of ambiguity since it suggests as well that 'it is only together that we (can) move'" (67).

22. I borrow the description *radically unhoused* from Heather Love's essay on Radcliffe Hall's *The Well of Loneliness* to describe Stephen's exile in the "no-man's land of sex" as a result of her "gender transgressions" (500, 501). Unlike Stephen, whose upper-class status authorizes her to set up a home in another location (or at least move to Paris with that option), the biographical and literary women I examine in contrast are socially located in homes that are certainly not theirs to

inherit. I use the word *inherit* probatively, aware of its Middle English usage as early as 1304, when it meant then, as now, "to "receive as a right" (*OED* 1437). Whether related to the inheritance of property, a right, or a privilege, women have neither by natural descent nor through transmission from parents or ancestry traditionally been inheritors of anything—property, rank, or title—as they historically had no legal or officially authorized rights. However, like the literary meaning of *coverture*, a protective covering, the legal doctrine of coverture also conceals vital facts about white women's strategies to overcome the custom of marriage wherein all property and legal rights are putatively ceded to husbands. The truth about such women's lives lay somewhere else as otherwise documented by historians who expose the lie that has claimed that all women were in a subordinate position of legal dependence. For my purposes, I will expose the malice of Southern white women in antebellum culture, many of whom maximized their power through participating in slave-owning culture. As Stephanie E. Jones-Rogers explains in *They Were Her Property: White Women as Slave-Owners in the American South*, slave-owning Southern white women were directly engaged in the economic benefits of the system. Both Jacobs's and Cather's narratives bear this out, which I discuss further in chapter 1.

23. See Adalgisa Giorgio, Anastasia Christou, and Gill Rye's "Mothering and Migration: Interdisciplinary Dialogues, European Perspectives, and International Contexts."

24. As Pinto explains, "Diaspora . . . can challenge the order of things—the way we come to recognize and interpret our specific historical and social realities—its difficult play between the known and the unknown, between recognizable forms of being, knowing, belonging, and acting in the world and the new forms that emerge as we try to understand its shifts" (5). For an excellent overview of the term *diaspora* as a concept and a dynamic method of study, see Kim D. Butler, "Defining Diaspora, Refining a Discourse."

25. As McKittrick explains in *Black Women and the Cartographies of Struggle*, "we make concealment happen; it is not natural but rather names and organizes where racial-sexual differentiation occurs" (xvii). See also Jenny Sharpe, *Ghosts of Slavery: A Literary Archaeology of Black Women's Lives*.

26. In using the term *interstitial*, I am specifically referencing Miranda A. Green-Barteet's essay "The Loophole of Retreat: Interstitial Spaces in Harriet Jacobs' *Incidents in the Life of a Slave Girl*." Deploying an architectural term, *interstitial*, to analyze the garret space that Jacobs inhabited for seven years, Green-Barteet offers a persuasive reading of space in relation to Jacobs's narrative, as garret space is positioned as "a border space, one that exists betwixt and between other more clearly defined spaces" (53).

27. Drawing on Lefebvre's conceptual model that posits social space as neither an abstraction nor a container, "but a social production," Gwin further explains that "making space mean only what we want it to mean blinds us to 'the social

construction of affective geographies' and to the ways in which social relations are concretized and embedded in space" (15). Citing feminist geographer Gillian Rose, who expresses a yearning for an "elsewhere," Gwin writes that "imagining this elsewhere would allow women to feel safe and powerful, 'somewhere beyond capture'" (15).

28. See Nora Doyle's *Maternal Bodies: Redefining Motherhood in Early America*.

29. For the foundational book on women's domestic fiction (or what has been derogatorily termed the *sentimental novel*), see Nina Baym's *Women's Fiction: A Guide to Novels by and about Women in America: 1820–1870*. See also Saidiya V. Hartman's *Scenes of Subjection: Terror, Slavery, and Self-Making in Nineteenth Century America*, especially chapter 3, "Seduction and the Ruses of Power," for an analysis of Jacobs's virtuoso rhetorical performance portraying the narrator exerting agency when recounting Linda's "fall from virtue" while simultaneously sustaining the "reader's empathic identification" (106).

30. In "Edna O'Brien and Narrative Diaspora Space," Tony Murray draws upon the work of Avtar Brah to argue that letters represent a "'narrative diaspora space' which illuminate[s] the relationship between mothers, daughters and writing in Irish migrant experience" (85). While I am not specifically analyzing migrant fiction here, I find useful Murray's critical framework based on the work of Brah's notion of diaspora space applied to literature.

31. From Collins's "Shifting the Center: Race, Class, and Feminist Theorizing about Motherhood." See also "The Meaning of Motherhood in Black Culture and Mother-Daughter Relationships." Both of these articles are reprinted in *Maternal Theory: Essential Readings*, edited by Andrea O'Reilly. All references to "Shifting the Center," are taken from the O'Reilly edition. See also *Mothering, Ideology, Experience, Agency*, edited by Evelyn Nakano Glenn, Grace Chang, and Linda Rennie.

32. Hirsch uses the term *postmemory* to describe the relationship that the "generation after" bears to "the personal, collective, and cultural trauma of those who came before—to experiences they 'remember' only by means of stories, images, and behaviors among which they grew up. But these experiences were transmitted to them so deeply and affectively as to *seem* to constitute memories in their own right. Postmemory's connection to the past is thus actually mediated not by recall but by imaginative investment, projection, and creation. [. . .] These events happened in the past, but their effects continue into the present" (*Generation* 5).

33. In the first sentence of his review of Sandra Cisneros's *Caramelo*, Stavans asserts, "Genealogy rules Latino literature tyrannically," as seen in a "battalion of novels" published in the late twentieth century and into the millennium (30).

34. Anzaldúa writes, "Now let us shift . . . the path of conocimiento . . . inner works, public acts" (*Gloria Anzaldúa Reader* 578). Grateful acknowledgment to Andrea J. Pitts for her reference to this essay in "Gloria E. Anzaldúa's Autohistoria-teoría as an Epistemology of Self-Knowledge/Ignorance" (361).

35. A mother of two when she first published this narrative, Lorde views maternality from a distinctly lesbian perspective, which, for Lorde, centers on the maternal erotic, which I argue is a mode of othermothering the author embraces. See Smith's "The Truth That Never Hurts: Black Lesbians in Fiction in the 1980s."

36. From Shoshana Felman as quoted in Arthur W. Frank, *The Wounded Storyteller: Body, Illness and Ethics*. I return to Felman's idea about the overwhelmed body in chapter 4.

37. In "The Laugh of the Medusa" (887). As Cixous explains,

> Flying is a woman's gesture—flying in language and making it fly. We have all learned the art of flying and its numerous techniques; for centures we've been able to possess anything only by flying; we've lived in flight, stealing away, finding, when desired, narrow passageways, hidden crossovers. It's no accident that voler has a double meaning, that it plays on each of them and thus throws off the agents of sense. It's no accident that women take after birds and robbers just as robbers take after women and birds. They (illes) go by, fly the coop, take pleasure in jumbling the order of space, in disorienting it, in changing around the furniture, disclocating things and values, breaking them all up, emptying structures, and turning propriety upside down. (887)

As Cixous's translator notes, *flying* also means "to steal. Both definitions of the verb *voler* are played on, as the text itself explains in the following paragraph" (887).

Chapter 1

1. For an analysis of republican motherhood, see V. Lynn Kennedy, *Born Southern: Childbirth, Motherhood, and Social Networks*.

2. This largely unread and untaught final novel of Cather has nonetheless been buttressed into canonical distinction by Cather scholars and infrastructural support mechanisms such as scholarly editions of the author's entire oeuvre. See the scholarly edition of *Sapphira and the Slave Girl*, which includes a historical essay and explanatory notes by Ann Romines.

3. On white writers discussing the largely underexplored topic of slavery, Cynthia Griffin Wolff explains that it has been a story "intrinsically bounded by silence . . . a story whose fundamental elements remain entombed in the not-utterable chaos of not-memory and not-recognition. . . . For Cather, the process of *withholding* information was purposive and pervasive. . . . Cather's last completed

effort *Sapphira and the Slave Girl* explores the oldest, deepest things: Virginia, slavery, the untellable story" ("Time and Memory" 212, 213, 221).

4. Scholars on *Incidents* are mixed in their approach to Jacobs's use of the pseudonym, *Linda Brent*. They either reference Harriet Jacobs as synonymous with the fictionalized name of Linda Brent, or they distinguish between Jacobs as author of her narrative and the persona she creates, Linda Brent. I am taking the latter approach and will make reference to Jacobs when referring to her authorship of *Incidents* and to Linda when referring to Jacobs's creation of a literary persona. In this way, I am in agreement with Stephanie Li, who views Linda "as a constructed character in the text (rather than the author of the text) . . . adopted as a strategic rhetorical stance that would fulfill her political objectives" ("Motherhood as Resistance" 27). Let us recall that Jacobs had been living in the North for eleven years before she made the agonizing decision to write *Incidents in the Life of a Slave Girl*. As Jacobs's biographer, Jean Fagan Yellin explains, "She could not write the book. But neither could she not write it" (*Harriet Jacobs: A Life* 119).

5. In this regard, I agree with Traci B. Abbott, who takes to task critics who too readily conflate "mistress/slave with mother/daughter," as such false parallels risk "repeating the pattern of paternalism that white Americans have so often used to oppress other races" (28).

6. See Romayne Smith Fullerton and M. J. Patterson for an examination of popular media's proscriptive portrayals of motherhood, "Procrustean Motherhood: The Good Mother during Depression (1930s), War (1940s) and Prosperity (1950s)." In *Maternal Thinking: Toward a Politics of Peace*, Sara Ruddick argues that ideas about motherhood are regulated by a binary between an idealized Good Mother and her shameful other, the Bad Mother whose "evils are specific, avoidable, and worse than her own" (31–32).

7. Angelyn Mitchell describes Jacobs's *Incidents* as "The Ur-Narrative of Black Womanhood" (22).

8. While Jacobs's activist work with her daughter, Louisa, is beyond the scope of this project, I do want to make reference to Louisa Jacobs's correspondence with a circle of family, friends, and elders, including her mother, Harriet Jacobs. See Mary Maillard, *Whispers of Cruel Wrongs: The Correspondence of Louisa Jacobs and Her Circle, 1879-1911*. See also Jean Fagan Yellin's biography, *Harriet Jacobs: A Life*.

9. In describing the tensions between the lived maternal (white) body and the ideal body created by the discursive literature of the early nineteenth century, Nora Doyle explains, "As the maternal body began to vanish from cultural representations of motherhood, so too did the perception that motherhood involved (re)productive labor. [. . .] [A]s the concept of physical labor vanished from cultural depictions of motherhood, it also became clear that sentimental motherhood was profoundly defined by notions of class and race. Physical labor was associated in American society with the lower classes and the enslaved" (7).

10. See Barbara Welter's seminal article "The Cult of True Womanhood: 1820–1860," in *American Quarterly*, and her book-length study *Dimity Convictions: The American Woman in the Nineteenth Century*.

11. See Jean Fagan Yellin's *Harriet Jacobs: A Life*, especially part 3, "Mrs. Jacobs: Public Demands for Freedom and Homes," for detailed information on the decades of work Jacobs devoted after the publication of *Incidents* to liberating others in her abolitionist efforts and educational work. The second half of Yellin's biography particularly emphasizes how Jacobs and her daughter struggled to earn their livelihoods in postreconstruction America.

12. All references to Harriet A. Jacobs's *Incidents in the Life of a Slave Girl: Written by Herself* are taken from Jean Fagan Yellin's edition and will be cited parenthetically within the chapter.

13. Jacobs's grandmother, Molly Horniblow, earned her freedom through a brilliant sleight of hand. Refusing to be privately sold, Jacobs's grandmother publicly enacts what Dr. Norcom wants to privatize: her sale to the highest bidder. Jacobs details this event in chapter 2 of *Incidents*: "Her long and faithful service in the family was also well known, and the intention of her mistress to leave her free. When the day of sale came, she took her place among the chattels, and at the first call she sprang upon the auction-block. . . . No one bid for her. At last, a feeble voice said, 'Fifty dollars.' It came from a maiden lady, seventy years old, the sister of my grandmother's deceased mistress" (*Incidents* 11–12, 262n6). See further details in Yellin's biography on Molly's refusal to be privately sold (20–22). According to the 1830 Census for Chowan County, after this incident, Molly Horniblow bought a "house and lot on King Street" and lists "six persons inhabiting the residence of Marey Horniblow" (*Incidents* 263n1).

14. Yellin explains, "Samuel Tredwell Sawyer was young, personable, and single. The oldest son of Margaret Blair and Dr. Mathias Sawyer—a descendant of a colonial governor of North Carolina and a relative of the current governor—he was the scion of the family that wielded both wealth and power. . . . Sawyer was Grandmother Molly's [Harriet's grandmother] neighbor, and interested himself in the family, offering help and finding occasions to talk with her attractive granddaughter" (*Harriet Jacobs* 26–27).

15. In "Losing and Finding 'Race': Old Jezebel's African Story," Ann Romines references scholarship in African diaspora studies to examine Cather's treatment of race in African-born Jezebel's origin story, beginning with her capture on the Gold Coast of Africa, "detailing her experience of the Middle Passage, and ending with her death" (398). (Nancy is Jezebel's great-grandchild.) I appreciate the fact, as Romines explains, that Cather did "significant research" in the 1930s at the New York Society Library to tell Jezebel's story (398), but clearly the author did not have access to an understanding of the complexity of slave communities in antebellum culture. Cather's depiction of Jezebel is of an isolated woman of unusual strength, used as a sexual commodity and portrayed stereotypically, which

I read less as Cather's "mocking" critique of white Americans' fears as Romines contends than as a submission to handy stereotypes and racial bias, for example, about Africans "and cannibalism" (398). I agree with Naomi E. Morgenstern that Cather's narration of Jezebel's history is "remarkably dispassionate" and, I might add, racist (187). Salas explains regarding Till's reticence in asking after her daughter, "A byproduct of Sapphira's plot will be the long-lasting feelings of alienation that Sapphira's campaign against Nancy will engender among the slaves, as seen when Till . . . must [e]ffect an uncaring appearance about Nancy's disappearance" (100).

16. This endorsement appears on the paperback edition of Vintage Books (a Division of Random House), 1970. Cather herself contributed to this interpretation, writing the jacket copy on the front-cover flap of *Sapphira and the Slave Girl*, which reads that her novel is about "the subtle persecution of a beautiful mulatto by her jealous mistress" (Romines, "Historical Essay" 365). See also David H. Porter's "Cather on Cather III: Dust Jacket Copy on Willa Cather's Books," in *Willa Cather's Newsletter and Review*.

17. For readings that use critical-race theories to approach Cather's final novel, see Roseanne V. Camacho, "Whites Playing in the Dark: Southern Conversation in Willa Cather's *Sapphira and the Slave Girl*; Marilyn Mobley McKenzie, " 'The Dangerous Journey': Toni Morrison's Reading of *Sapphira and the Slave Girl*"; and Lisa Marcus, " 'The Pull of Race and Blood and Kindred': Willa Cather's Southern Inheritance."

18. Romines continues, "*Sapphira* makes it very clear that a rending conflict is coming and that the issue of slavery, grounded in race, will be at its center. The war is not 'drained of evil;' instead, the 'Terrible' presence of evils grounded in slavery blights, at least partially, almost every relationship in the book" ("Willa Cather's Civil War" 14–15).

19. For a brilliant examination of the artificial codes of conduct undergirding Sapphira's community, a contaminated system of empty gestures, see Arnold's essay " 'Of Human Bondage': Cather's Subnarrative in *Sapphira and the Slave Girl*."

20. Explaining their choice to settle in the remote, westernmost edge of the Virginia backwoods, John C. Inscoe speculates that Sapphira and Henry

> had retreated to this remote mountain community, it seems, so that the aristocratic Sapphira could avoid the humiliation of facing judgmental family and neighbors for having married a mere miller. . . . Back Creek was certainly remote. . . . Sparsely settled by small farmers growing corn, wheat, and oats, there was little demand for slaves. In Frederick County, slavery was on the decline in 1860; about 11 percent of the populace were slaves, and those were owned by a mere 2 percent of white households, and most of those owned five slaves or fewer . . . The Colberts arrival there with some 20 bondsmen and women in tow made them social anomalies. (128–29)

21. The Grimm brothers completed their final version of the "Snow White" story in 1854, two years before Cather sets her tale in 1856. *The Grimms' German Folk Tales*, trans. Magoun and Krappe, 1960. Cather referred to this fairy tale overtly in *My Antonia* (215). The Disney animated film, *Snow White and the Seven Dwarfs*, was released in 1937, three years before *Sapphira* was published.

22. See Giambattista Basile's *Il Pentamerone*.

23. Nancy of Cather's *Sapphira* also parallels the "difficult miracle" of June Jordan's essay on the poet, Phillis Wheatley, as both girls are "tortured by rupture" by the absence of their mothers (22). Nancy's mother, Till, is represented by Cather as minimally involved in protecting her daughter from her mistress and the trap Sapphira sets, represented by "the master's visiting nephew" (*Sapphira* 22). While Jordan focuses on Phillis Wheatley's forced migration and enslavement in early America (1761), her focus on girl children and slavocracy parallel Cather's novel as well.

24. For a visual portrayal of the utter lack of privacy for Blacks in plantation spaces, see Avery F. Gordon's reference to an 1859 painting *Old Kentucky Home—Life in the South* by Eastman Johnson, which portrays a white woman coming into the yard of enslaved persons unannounced in *Ghostly Matters* (137).

25. For analyses of how African American discourse in the early twentieth century counteracted antebellum depictions of Black women's racialized sexuality, see Beverly Guy-Sheftall, *Daughters of Sorrow: Attitudes toward Black Women, 1880–1920*.

26. In *Demonic Grounds*, McKittrick explains, "Geography is not, however, secure and unwavering; we produce space, we produce its meanings and we work very hard to make geography what it is" (xi). McKittrick's analysis "reveals that the interplay between domination and black women's geographies is underscored by the social production of space. Concealment, marginalization, boundaries are important social processes. We make concealment happen. It is not natural but rather names and organizes where racial-sexual differentiation occurs" (xi–xii).

27. According to William Gleason's "I Dwell Now in a Neat, Little Cottage," while cottage space was not a recognizable feature of American architectural vocabulary in 1800, by the 1850s, "cottage structures were one of the most popular topics in American architectural treatises and pattern books. No longer chiefly suggestive of inadequate means, cottages had become respectable, even desirable, rural housing" (150). Writing her narrative during the 1850s, Jacobs would no doubt have known that her northern reading audience would be familiar with cottage residences and perhaps also be familiar with the name of the famous landscape architect Andrew Jackson Downing, who popularized the "the new cottage ideal" for Americans (Gleason 150).

28. In her chronology of Harriet Jacobs's life, Yellin explains that in 1835 "through a trader, Sawyer [Sands] buys Jacobs's brother and the children, whom he permits to live with her grandmother" (*Incidents* 223).

29. As Stephanie Li explains, "Linda frees her children by posing as a bad mother" (24). See also Carolyn Sorisio's comment: "As a mother, Linda understands how much pain her grandmother would experience at their separation. However, she is not willing to sacrifice her children's future for her grandmother or for herself. . . . As her readers are made to understand, it is not a lack, but rather a surplus, of motherly love that motivates her flight. Repeatedly, Linda portrays all slave mothers, regardless of racial classification, as caring deeply and permanently for the fate of their children" (207).

30. The Dismal Swamp is "ten miles wide and thirty miles broad, begins in Virginia and extends into North Carolina to a point thirty miles north of Carbarrus Pocosin" (*Incidents* 282 n.1). For a twenty-first century reflection on Black crisis during the Covid-19 pandemic, Sarah Stefana Smith revisits the history of the Great Dismal Swamp through an analysis of the petit-maroon communities that resided in the marshy region during the period of 1763 up through 1856, in "Keeping Time: Maroon Assemblages and Black Life in Crisis," *South Atlantic Quarterly*.

31. Green-Barteet explains, "It is the garret's in-between status, its very interstiality that renders the space useful when she finally determines to escape slavery." Her grandmother and uncle "choose the garret because its structure makes it uninhabitable" (54).

32. Yellin explains, "In this cramped space, Hatty [Harriet] began experiencing classic symptoms of sensory deprivation. Experts write that when people lack an environment with normal stimulation to the senses—sight, seeing, touch, taste, smell—they experience 'massive free-floating anxiety . . . perceptual distortions and hallucinations, illusions in multiple spheres (auditory, visual, olfactory).' These are accompanied by acute confusion, sometimes by 'mutism [which Harriet experiences], and subsequent partial amnesia'" (*Harriet Jacobs* 50). In chapter 29 of *Incidents*, "Preparations for Escape," Jacobs's mask of utilizing the literary persona of "Linda" falls off, shifting into autobiography when she writes: "I hardly expect the reader will credit me, when I affirm that I lived in that little dismal hole, almost deprived of light and air, and with no space to move my limbs, for nearly seven years. But it is a fact; and to me, a sad one, even now; for my body still suffers from the effects of that long imprisonment, to say nothing of my soul" (148).

33. Jacobs's daughter, Louisa Matilda, was "sent to James Iredell Tredwell (1799–1846), a Brooklyn merchant. Tredwell and Sawyer were first cousins" (*Incidents* 281n2).

34. According to Mary Maillard, who discovered and collected the letters of Louisa M. Jacobs, "Louisa never forgot that night and never betrayed her mother. Long after they were reunited in New York—and throughout the rest of her life—she remained silent on their shared history. She was so intensely private that she did not divulge the details of her life even to her closest, oldest friend until

1905, when she was over seventy years old" (3). See also Jean Fagin Yellin, Joseph M. Thomas, Kate Culkin, and Scott Korb, eds., *The Harriet Jacobs Family Papers*.

35. In "The Novel Démeublé," Cather writes, "Whatever is felt upon the page without specifically being named there—that, one might say, is created. It is the inexplicable presence of the thing not named, of the overtone divined by the ear but not heard by it, the verbal mood, the emotional aura of the fact of the thing or the deed that gives high quality to the novel or to the drama, as well as to poetry itself" (50).

36. Rachel's class and gender status would limit her mobility and autonomy, separating her from enslaved Blacks and poor whites from the Appalachian Mountain areas close by. By refusing to abide by standard customs, Rachel "indicates her rejection of plantation proprieties, as 'Traveling alone was absolutely forbidden to white plantation women. Chaperonage was necessary, and the price for this protection was high, in isolation and limited mobility'" (Romines, explanatory notes, *Sapphira and the Slave Girl* 419).

37. Cather's obduracy in including the double § in the epilogue chapters may be her way of claiming her Southern affiliation to Sapphira, and, as such, to white racism. Lisa Marcus argues, "Cather literally writes herself into the end of the novel, making Sapphira a genealogy of her own American subjectivity" (113).

38. In "Race, Labor, and Domesticity in *Sapphira and the Slave Girl*," Gayle Wald situates her comments in the context of Hortense Spillers's examination of Black women's gender and sexuality and the "grammar" of American slavery, arguing that Cather's novel imagines "black women's labor to be the site . . . in which it is naturalized—that is, imagined outside of the coercive context of slavery, and thereby paradoxically figured as the product of their [Sapphira and Henry Colbert] *own* desire and volition. . . . One of the effects of interpreting Sapphira primarily through the lens of Sapphira's sexual jealousy and vindictiveness is to render black women's labor invisible within the critical discourse as well" (92).

39. See Janis P. Stout's "The Observant Eye, the Art of Illustration, and Willa Cather's *My Antonia*," p. 3.

40. Morrison writes, "Unable to please Sapphira, plagued by the jealousy of the darker-skinned slaves, [Nancy] is also barred from help, instruction, or consolation from her own mother, Till. That condition could only prevail in a slave society where the mistress can count on . . . the complicity of a mother in the seduction and rape of her own daughter" (*Playing in the Dark* 21).

41. I was particularly struck by Patricia Yaeger's observation of Nancy as "cartilaginous," without any bones, suggestive of a "bodyscape of female abjection" ("White Dirt" 138). Though I do not read Cather's novel through the lens of homoeroticism (as many critics have), I find Naomi Morgenstern's discussion of the nostalgic with the erotic quite useful to my reading of Cather's use of obfuscation and indirection to tell a brutal story through distancing and disguising measures

("Love Is Home-sickness" 187). See also Merrill Maguire Skaggs's chapter, "The Return of the Native: *Sapphira and the Slave Girl*," for an interpretation of the novel's evasion of facts about moral iniquity: "We may have to classify the novel as a guilt-without-sin fiction for the malevolence is real enough, but it achieves nothing. In fact, ex-Southerner Cather seems guiltlessly to reject the slave system and the economy it supports, while also guiltlessly loving the land that developed both" (167).

42. This is Traci B. Abbott's argument in "'A Good Girl Like Nancy': Willa Cather's *Sapphira and the Slave Girl*." Abbott explains, "Sapphira's rape plot disquiets the novel's nostalgic tone and, more significantly, discredits its historical authenticity" (27). Abbott asserts that Nancy's relevance is central to Cather's exploration of "gender, race, and sexuality *from a modern perspective*, denying her victim status and asserting her place as a prescient example of black female sexual autonomy" (26, emphasis added).

43. Romines explains, "The mother of Willa Cather's maternal grandfather, William Lee Boak, was Eleanor Lee, a member of a prominent Quaker family and Boak himself may have been a Quaker . . . , as were several of Cather's relatives. No major character of *Sapphira* is a Quaker, but the Quaker presence is evident in the book" ("Historical Essay" 306–7).

44. A widow of thirty-six or thirty-seven, Rachel Blake returns from Washington, DC, where she lived with her husband, a congressman, and three children. Her husband and son die from yellow fever in New Orleans. Michael Blake leaves his wife and children in debt which Henry Colbert pays off. Rachel Blake moves back to Virginia but lives in a separate house, "by the road," from the Mill farm. Rachel is skilled at nursing and cares for prosperous and poor families alike. Sapphira thinks to herself, "Rachel was poor, and it was not much use to give her things. Whatever she had she took where it was needed most" (38). Perhaps Cather is paying homage to her mentor, Sarah Orne Jewett, as Rachel is a modern incarnation of Mrs. Todd in *The Country of the Pointed Firs*.

45. For Cather's early habit of "employing the transforming power of dress and disguise" by cross-dressing for several years, see Sharon O'Brien's biography, especially chapter 5, "Enter William Cather" (*Willa Cather: The Emerging Voice* 96).

46. For further analysis of marronage activity during Jacobs's lifetime, see Marcus Nevius, *City of Refuge: Slavery and Petit Marronage in the Great Dismal Swamp, 1763–1856*.

47. For a close analysis of Jacobs's indictment of the Fugitive Slave Act and her profound understanding of the laws of slavery, see Christina Accomando's "*The Regulations of Robbers*": *Legal Fictions of Slavery and Resistance*.

48. "This transaction, effected with the aid of Rev. John B. Pinney of the New York Colonization Society, is explained in a letter from Cornelia Grinnell Willis to Elizabeth Davis Bliss Bancroft [May 3, 1852] in the Bancroft-Bliss Family Papers, Library of Congress" (*Incidents* 291n12). For Jacobs's disheartened and

bitter response in being forced to escape once again from the Norcom family's pursuit of her in New York, see Yellin, *Harriet Jacobs* 114–16.

49. Jacobs never shapes her autobiographical narrative as though she were writing through the voice of an exceptional personage, unlike other well-known enslaved narrators such as Frederick Douglass's 1845 *Narrative of the Life of a Frederick Douglass, An American Slave*.

50. In "Political Science and His'try in *Sapphira and the Slave Girl*," Tomas Pollard writes, "*Sapphira* is the only frame narrative I know of that announces its last framework after 'The End' of the text instead of the beginning, as *My Antonia, Gulliver's Travels, Lalla Rookh, The Scarlet Letter*, and many others do" (47).

51. Marilyn Mobley McKenzie offers a slightly different reading of the mother-daughter reunion beyond white appropriation of Black stories by interrogating more closely Nancy's mother, Till, whose words end the novel: "Till, in other words, gets the last word. . . . Till is represented at the end of the novel as the keeper of the community history, as the storyteller who passed down this troubled but generally happy tale of slavery that the author both owns and disowns. . . . What Till's words represent is the racialized Africanist presence being used to reify the myth of domestic tranquility of the southern past" (87).

52. Citing Joan L. Severa's *Dressed for the Photographer: Ordinary Americans and Fashion, 1840–1900*, Romines explains that "long, narrow coats were fashionable for women in the early 1880s, as was fur trim. Nancy's black silk dress is the classic choice of 'best' dress for a woman of mature years. Felt turbans were mentioned among the fashionable hat styles of the season in a November 1880 fashion magazine. . . . Gold watches had been displayed in photographs of fashionable women since the 1840s; they were still in fashion in the 1880s" ("Explanatory Notes" 521).

Chapter 2

1. I am taking the term *polyphonic* from Mikhail Bakhtin's analysis of Fyodor Dostoevsky's novels in *Problems of Dostoevsky's Poetics*, especially as the term emerges from the field of music to which both Morrison and García are invested. On Morrison's use of polyphony in her novels, see Barbara Hill Rigney's *The Voices of Toni Morrison*, especially chapter 1, "Breaking the Back of Words: Language and Signification," for an excellent overview of how Morrison's works reconstruct ideas about artistic and political revolution in language. See also Nellie McKay's interview with Morrison, who explains that she wishes to accomplish "something that has probably only been fully expressed in music" in "An Interview with Toni Morrison" (426). Taking the biographical story of Margaret Garner as her entrée into writing *Beloved*, Morrison later wrote the English-language libretto for the opera of the same name. (I had the pleasure of attending the

New York City Opera on September 16, 2007, for a performance followed by a Q/A with Morrison.) See La Vinia Delois Jennings's *Margaret Garner: The Premier Performances of Toni Morrison's Libretto*. On Garner's story, see also Reyes, Weisenburger, and Reinhardt.

2. On García's polyphony, see Laura Halperin's "Still Hands: Celia's Transgression in Cristina García's *Dreaming in Cuban*" for an analysis of the influence of French composer Claude Debussy, on Celia's rebellion. In an interview with Iraida H. López, García admits that she only came to Cuban music in adulthood, learning how to dance the salsa from her Puerto Rican boyfriend, who introduced her to Beny Moré and Celia Cruz, both of whom are featured in *Dreaming* ("And There Is Only" 610).

3. In "Changing the Letter: The Yokes, the Jokes of Discourse, or, Mrs. Stowe, Mr. Reed," Hortense J. Spillers explains that the nineteenth-century phrase *peculiar institution* is suggestive in more than one way: "If we think of 'institution' as a specific sum of practices that so configure our sense of 'public' and 'private' that the rift between them is not as substantial as we might flatter ourselves to think, then antebellum slavery in the United States offers a preeminent paradigm of conflicted motives" (25, 28). Echoing Spillers, Gillian Brown offers a corrective to the false notion that slavery undermines women's domestic work by bringing confusion into the marketplace, explaining, "Slavery disregards this opposition between the family at home and the exterior workplace. The distinction between work and family is eradicated in the slave, for whom there is no separation between economic and private status" (505). See chapter 1 on Jacobs and Cather for portrayals of the peculiar institution's disregard for the family at home and the exterior workplace, forcing women to seek drastic measures to separate themselves from the assaultive practices of enslavers on plantation space.

4. As a result of the publication of Toni Morrison's *Beloved*, we have seen a resurgence of interest in the antebellum enslaved woman Margaret Garner and her infanticide, which in 1856 spurred a plethora of newspaper accounts, abolitionist activity, and a fugitive-slave trial. For background on Margaret Garner as an archival source text for Morrison, see Gloria Naylor's "A Conversation: Gloria Naylor and Toni Morrison" (this interview was conducted when Morrison was still working on *Beloved*) and Bill Moyers, "A Conversation with Toni Morrison," in *Conversations with Toni Morrison*. See also the following: Gerda Lerner, ed., *Black Women in White America: A Documentary History*; Cynthia Griffin Wolff, "'Margaret Garner': A Cincinnati Story" in the *Massachusetts Review*; Avery Gordon, *Ghostly Matters: Haunting and the Sociological Imagination*; and J. Brooks Bouson, *Quiet as Its Kept: Shame, Trauma, and Race in the Novels of Toni Morrison*. Inspired by reading Morrison's novel, Steven Weisenburger spent ten years writing the biography of Margaret Garner. See his "My Journey from 'Beloved,'" in *New York City Opera: Playbill* (September 2007): 10–12, 14, 40, and *Modern Medea: A Family Story of Slavery and Child-Murder*. See also Mark Reinhardt's

documentary history, *Who Speaks for Margaret Garner: The True Story That Inspired Toni Morrison's Beloved*.

5. For a fulsome overview of how Morrison adopts a maternal standpoint that is politically motivated, see Andrea O'Reilly's *Toni Morrison and Motherhood: A Politics of the Heart*. O'Reilly examines how Morrison defines motherhood and maternality as emerging from a specific standpoint of Black maternal practice and thought.

6. Homi Bhabha explains that Morrison "insists on the harrowing ethical repositioning of the slave mother" before an analysis of "an emancipation from the ideologies of the slave master" (16). This then, according to Bhabha, accounts for her signifying on historical dates of racial violence but rushing past "the events 'in-themselves'" (16). Avery F. Gordon extends this analysis, explaining that Morrison's oblique focus on "the period in American history we call Reconstruction is instructive here. . . . Twenty years after the Emancipation Proclamation, the characters in *Beloved* are struggling with the knowledge that [quoting from *Beloved*] 'freeing yourself was one thing; claiming ownership of that freed self was another'" (172). See also W. E. B. DuBois, *Black Reconstruction in America* and Eric Foner, *Reconstruction: America's Unfinished Revolution: 1863–1877*.

7. For historical background on fictional responses to the Cuban Revolution, see Isabel Alvarez-Borland's "Displacements and Autobiography in Cuban-American Fiction" and her *Cuban American Literature of Exile: From Person to Persona*; Andrea O'Reilly Herrara's "Women and the Revolution in Cristina García's *Dreaming in Cuban*; and Jorge Duany's "Neither Golden Exile nor Dirty Worm: Ethnic Identity in Recent Cuban-American Novels." See also Ruth Behar's edition, *Bridges to Cuba: Puentes a Cuba*. For histories of Cuba, see Luis A. Perez's *The Structure of Cuban History: Meanings and Purpose of the Past* and *Cuba: Between Reform and Revolution*; and Ada Ferrer's *Freedom's Mirror: Cuba and Haiti in the Age of Revolution*.

8. I take this subheading from Paula Giddings's essential history, "history at its best," as Morrison's front-cover blurb attests of *Where and When I Enter: The Impact of Black Women on Race and Sex in America*. Giddings takes her title from feminist educator Anna Julia Cooper, whose epigraph fronts the book: "Only the BLACK WOMAN can say 'where and when I enter, in the quiet, undisputed dignity of my womanhood, without violence and without suing or special patronage, then and there the whole . . . race enters with me'" (82).

9. See Jean Fagan Yellin's biography for detailed background on Harriet and Louisa Jacobs's post–Civil War contribution to the establishment of free schools under Black leadership in the South. With the establishment in 1865 of the Freedmen's Bureau, Harriet's daughter, Louisa, established Lincoln School in Savannah, Georgia, administered by Black leadership and teachers (*Harriet Jacobs* 199).

10. For a superb analysis of Morrison's use of the rhetoric of trees in *Beloved*, see chapter 8 "'To Get to a Place': Intercorporality in *Beloved*" of Laura

A. Doyle's *Bordering the Body: The Racial Matrix of Modern Fiction and Culture*.

11. Lorraine Liscio reminds us that the name *Sweet Home* is a signification upon and childlike disruption of the euphemism *Home Sweet Home* (38). Avery Gordon calls Sweet Home a cruel caricature, capturing well, quoting Spillers, the "'conflated motives' that is 'antebellum slavery in the United States.' Sweet Home is slavery at home" (167). In the next section of this chapter, I will read the threnody section of part 2 of *Beloved* as Morrison's disruption of that nomenclature through the mother-daughter plot as Sethe's actions prevent her daughter from returning to an underworld eternally imposed by slavocracy.

12. Jean Wyatt explains: "Spatial images that usually function as figures of speech take shape as actions. For example, when Paul D, a formerly enslaved man from the same plantation as Sethe, finds her again after an absence of eighteen years [he asks] 'if there was some space' for him. While his expression seems natural in the circumstances, the situation in the house causes Paul D to make a space for himself more literally than any suitor in literature. . . . Evidently Morrison wants the opening statement of the novel—that '124 was spiteful. Full of baby's venom'—to be taken quite literally . . . [Beloved's] amorphous spirit haunts the house, filling it so completely with her spite that '[t]here was no room for any other thing or body until Paul D . . . broke up the place, making room, . . . then standing in the place he had made'" (477–78).

13. Many scholars on Morrison have offered useful overviews of the concept of rememory, two of which I offer here as they underscore the transhistorical and transgenerational effects of memory. From Avery Gordon: "For Morrison's social memory is not just history, but haunting; not just context, but animated worldliness; not just the hard ground of infrastructural matters, but the shadowy grip of ghostly matters. . . . The picture of the place is not personal memory as we conventionally understand it, private, interior, mine to hoard or share, remember or forget. The picture of the place *is* its very sociality. . . . It is *still out there* because social relations as such are not ours for the owning" (*Ghostly Matters* 165–66). Marianne Hirsch sees a range between what Morrison has called rememory and what Hirsch is defining as postmemory, between on the one hand, a memory that, "communicated through bodily symptoms, becomes a form of repetition and reenactment, and, on the other hand, one that works through indirection and multiple mediation. . . . Morrison's rememory is such a form of 'transposition,' a descent through what Kestenberg calls a 'time tunnel of history' into the world of the dead. Rememory is a noun and a verb, a thing and an action. Communicable, shared, and permanent, because it is spatial and material, tactile, it underscores the deadly dangers of intergenerational transmission" (*The Generation of Postmemory: Writing and Visual Culture after the Holocaust* 82–83).

14. Borrowing from Margaret Homan's notion of literalization characteristic of nineteenth-century Anglo women's writing, Wyatt argues that *Beloved*'s discourse "also tends to resist substitution . . . [W]hen the narrative focuses on

the maternal body or the haunted house, metaphors abandon their symbolic dimension to adhere to a baseline of literal meaning. . . . A similar literalization of spatial metaphors mimics the materializations in the haunted house: the phrase 'she moved him' indicates not that Beloved stirred Paul D's emotions but that she physically moved him, from one location to another" (475).

15. Morrison contributed to *The Black Book*, which includes an oft reproduced photo of the back of an enslaved male, whose healed back lacerations beggar description and serve as a parallel to Sethe's wounding (M. Harris 9). Morrison discussed her editorial involvement on *The Black Book* in "It's Like Growing Up Black One More Time" (*New York Times*, August 11, 1974, 14–24).

16. This diaspora between the years 1959 and 1962 came to be dubbed the "Golden Exile" because most of the refugees came from upper and middle strata of Cuban society. The majority were urban, middle-aged, light-skinned, and white-collar workers (https://journals.openedition.org/pic/464?lang=en).

17. Celia's three children all experience specific kinds of exile: her firstborn, Lourdes, flees Cuba for America with her husband and toddler, Pilar; born second, Felicia remains in Cuba, a mother of three children, twins Luz and Milagro and her son, Ivanito. Felicia becomes infected with syphilis and dies shortly after, despite her long-time friendship with Herminia Delgado who offers Felicia the spiritual ministrations of Santería. Javier, born third, also leaves Cuba for Czechoslovakia, where he works as a biochemistry professor, marries a Czech woman, and has one daughter, Irinita, who remains with her mother after their divorce. Javier returns to the island and dies from alcoholism. All three children are affected by the complex intersection between maternal abandonment and the national division occurring as a result of the Cuban regime. For an examination of the ideological conflicts born of the revolution, see Julee Tate's "Matrilineal and Political Divisions in Cristina García's *Dreaming in Cuban* and *The Agüero Sisters*."

18. For persuasive interpretations of Gustavo as both a lover and a colonizer, see Mary S. Vásquez, who argues that "Since 1959, El Líder has partially taken Gustavo's place" in Celia's life: "All of us who hover around the mid-century of life recall the rumors of multiple seductions by the dictator at the presidential palace. For Celia, these rumors become present reality, with Celia as one of the seduced. He does not age, nor does she" (25).

María DeGuzmán explains that references to the terms *Spain* and *Spaniard* in colonized countries falsely reinforce the idea of "a unified and coherent imperial identity," an illusion that haunts Jorge's life in Cuba (*Spain's Long Shadow: The Black Legend, Off-Whiteness, and Anglo-American Empire* xvii).

19. Laura Halperin explains, "Hands that once played the piano and wrote secret love letters remain still in the mental hospital where Celia—the matriarch . . .—is temporarily confined. Marking a shift from a Celia distinguished by passion to a Celia stripped thereof, the still hands reveal how harmful institutionalization can be. . . . Celia's internment in a mental ward portrays a

troubling alliance among patriarchy, mental health care, and ethno-racial biases that pathologizes and represses *cubana* artistic expression" ("Still Hands" 418–19).

20. McKemmish explains, the archive can move "beyond the boundaries of an individual life and into the collective," thus reinforcing "how evidence of me becomes evidence of us" (175).

21. Laura Halperin is right to conclude that mother and daughter "try to strip Celia of her sanity" ("Still Hands" 421). Andrea O'Reilly Herrara persuasively examines how Celia is abandoned from childhood on, leading to an abusive domestic situation:

> Jorge too "abandons" Celia to his mother and his sister, while he is away on extended business trips. Berta Arango del Pino, who is depicted as a kind of wicked step-mother, and her spinster daughter, Ofelia (whose mad Shakespearean namesake took her own life because of disappointed love) scorn and abuse Celia while Jorge is away, treating her no better than one of their servants. . . . In her depiction of Celia's unhappy marriage and her confinement first in her mother-in-law's house and then in the asylum, García not only portrays women's position before the Revolution, but through the characters of Berta and Ofelia she suggests their complicity in perpetuating the very systems that oppress them. (76)

For an iteration of the Cinderella motif and an intertextual gesture of connection with García, see Sandra Cisneros's *Caramelo* and Bona's "The Portable *Rebozo*: Cisneros's *Caramelo* and Metafictional Histories," in *Women Writing Cloth: Migratory Fictions in the American Imaginary*.

22. Vásquez asserts, "Celia is a failed and even lethal mother. . . . Yet there is another Celia. . . . A fervent critic of earlier Cuban regimes and keenly aware of social injustice, Celia has stopped national time at the moment of this regime's triumph, a device that obviates the need to record, assess, and finally judge its history" (25).

23. See D. W. Winnicott, *On the Child*. I am grateful to Maggie Nelson's work, *The Argonauts*, for her reference to this passage.

24. I borrow this term, *mis-love*, from Zora Neale Hurston's *Their Eyes Were Watching God*.

25. Gordon explains, "Sethe runs not when she learns to read and write, but when she learns how she will be read and written. . . . Morrison rejects literacy as the supreme measure of humanity, but more significantly, she refuses the task of having to prove the slave's (and by implication her descendants') humanity" (147).

26. Boelhower quotes from Morrison's *Song of Solomon*, in which the protagonist thinks, "For a long time now he knew that anything could appear to be something else and probably was" to explain that Guitar eventually learns

that "one's interpretive gaze is only as long as one's ethnic memory" (*Through a Glass Darkly* 88).

27. Morrison inserts only one section in *Beloved* (toward the end of part 1, 148–53) in which the point of view is told solely from the enslavers and is underwritten by the Fugitive Slave Law. However, Morrison's conclusion to that section takes an absurdist turn, riffing on Stephen Crane's critique of war in *The Red Badge of Courage* by juxtaposing the horrific event that just occurred (Sethe's attempt to kill all her children when she sees schoolteacher enter her yard) against a white boy child's request to Baby Suggs to meet a sharp deadline on the high-topped shoes he puts in her cobbler's hands (153).

28. I take this terminology from Gilles Deleuze and Félix Guattari to suggest a less hierarchical understanding of family histories, insisting on a multiplicity that resists structures of domination. The concept of a rhizome therefore can be a more expansive metaphor in that "the rhizome is an antigenealogy," and trees are genealogical (21). Unlike Deleuze, I will not stop believing in trees as Morrison shows in *Beloved* that their function transcends binary thinking.

29. I am guided here by Marianne Hirsch's reference to Gayatri C. Spivak's reading of Ma'am's slap:

> "Even between mother and daughter, a certain historical withholding intervenes." And yet . . . "it *is* passed on with the mark of untranslatability on it, in the bound book of *Beloved* that we hold in our hands." The implication, on the one hand, that interest and empathy are heightened within the matrilineal family in particular, and the articulation, on the other, of the "historical withholding" *even* between mothers and daughters, make of Morrison's novel a theoretical text for the contradictions that define the intergenerational legacy of trauma and familial postmemory in particular. (*The Generation* 81)

30. Gordon writes, "Denver is named after the white girl who delivered her; Sethe is named after the only man her mother 'put her arms around'; Baby Suggs names herself after her husband; Stamp Paid signs himself all accounts paid; . . . each name also offers a story of why the people who hold those names are anonymous, why they have not counted" (188–89).

31. Deborah Horvitz examines the multiple meanings of Morrison's term, *disremembered*:

> The American and African Beloveds join forever in the last two pages of the novel as symbols of the past—exploding, swallowing, and chewing—body exploding, dissolving, or being chewed up and spit out links each enslaved Beloved with her sister in captivity. . . .The imagery emphasizes, too, those African women who did not survive

the Middle Passage—those who were chewed up, spit out, and swallowed by the sea—those whose bodies and stories were never recovered. Morrison, speaking of the women whose stories are lost, says they are 'disremembered' . . . meaning not only that they are forgotten, but also that they are dismembered, cut up and off, and not re-membered. (164–65)

32. For an excellent analysis of the dynamics of shame and pride in the "master-slave" relationship and its import in Morrison's *Beloved*, especially regarding Sethe's central shame event, the assault in the barn by schoolteacher's nephews, see J. Brooks Bouson's *Quiet as It's Kept: Shame, Trauma and Race in the Novels of Toni Morrison*.

33. In her reading of Penelope, for example, Cavarero argues that through "dilated time, . . . endless, cadenced sameness," Penelope weaves impenetrable time in the weaving room with her complicitous handmaids (14). In her reading of Demeter, Cavarero references Luce Irigaray, writing, "The myth of Demeter speaks precisely of an interruption in a feminine genealogy, violently overpowered by the patriarchal order. This order is oblivious to birth and emphasizes death" (59). Morrison implicitly utilizes both mythological figures, Penelope and Demeter, in the threnody section of *Beloved*.

34. In Hawthorne's *The Scarlet Letter*, Hester Prynne is forced by the Puritan patriarchs to stand before the condemning crowd after she steps from the threshold of the prison with an illegitimate baby in her arms, refusing to reveal the child's paternity. Morrison's intertextual nods are generous here with regard to Hester's infanticidal impulses, her community banishment; and her subversion of the Puritan community's representational codes.

35. In more than one interview, Morrison was asked to judge Sethe's actions, to which she has replied, "For me it was an impossible decision. Someone gave me the line for it at one time and I found it useful. 'It was the right thing to do, but she had no right to do it'" (Moyers 272).

36. Morrison describes this section to Martha Darling as "a kind of threnody," in which they "exchange thoughts like a dialogue, or a three-way conversation, but unspoken—I mean unuttered" (5).

37. Like Morrison, García's intertextual references are vast, inclusive of other Latina writers, particularly Sandra Cisneros, whose *House on Mango Street* was a formidable influence on *Dreaming in Cuban*. See Rafael Dalleo's keen analysis of the intertextual relationship between García's *Dreaming in Cuban* and Cisneros's *House on Mango Street* in "How Cristina Garcia Lost Her Accent, and Other Latina Conversations," for his discussion of how García translates Cisneros geographically in her novel.

38. For a brief list of writers who insert family trees in their novels for historical, metafictional, and geographical purposes, see Louise Erdrich's *Love Medicine*, Gloria Naylor's *Mama Day*, Julia Alvarez's *In the Name of Salomé*, Juliet

Grames's *The Seven or Eight Deaths of Stella Fortuna*, and Ung Loung's *First They Killed My Father*. See also Shirlee Taylor Haizlip's *The Sweeter the Juice: A Family Memoir in Black and White*, an extended family tree culled from multiple archives, unearthing six generations of maternal lineage.

39. As Andrea O'Reilly Herrera explains, "Lourdes miscarries a son shortly after she is raped at knife-point by a revolutionary soldier. Because rape is yet another form of loss, and the knife the soldier uses to carve the inexplicable message in Lourdes's belly is an obvious symbol of male power, this scene implies that the victimization of the female is tantamount to the abuse which continues to characterize Castro's authoritarian, paternalistic government" (73).

40. In "Matrilineal and Political Divisions in Cristina García's *Dreaming in Cuban* and *The Agüero Sisters*," Julee Tate explains, "Thus Lourdes's relationship with Celia is emblematic of her relationship with Cuba: she is estranged from both" (153).

41. McCracken explains, "The public admission of this complicity with violent patriarchy, both to his daughter on the diegetic level and to readers on the pages of the novel, constitutes a ruptural feminism that overcodes the magical elements of the novel and thereby resists their containment as the exotic" (26). See also Inger Pettersson's use of Roman de la Campo's term *cross-over aesthetics* to describe García's "acts of cultural translation . . . [that] resemble magical realism, but this approach destablises the typical irrationality of magical realist occurrences, lending them instead an unexpected rationality" (52).

42. Pettersson uses trauma theory to examine Lourdes, arguing that her exile and exodus from Cuba are signified by the scar on her stomach, "the visible representation of her trauma," and García's "traumatically marked literary language used to depict Lourdes's experiential world" (44). Pettersson also argues that Lourdes is in safe space when in Jorge's company, which is arguable since her father's withholding stalls her healing process to begin with.

43. I rephrase the term *hyperassimilation* to echo Ellen McCracken's description of Lourdes's "hyper-Americanism." As McCracken explains, "García critiques the excessive appropriation of U.S. economic and cultural models by the fanatical Cuban exiles in a series of parodical images that foreground the gender issue of the eating disorder" (25).

44. References to milk abound in *Dreaming in Cuban*. Andrea O'Reilly Herrera's description suffices: "Rufino is in Havana ordering a cow-milking machine for the Puentes' *dairy* farm (my stress), which is confiscated (lost) in accordance with the Agrarian Reform Bill (1959); and in a parallel scene, the muggers in Morningside Park, who hold Pilar at knife-point, abuse the latter by fondling and suckling her breasts. In the same vein, Jorge is hit by a *milk* truck on his work route as he peddles American goods" (87).

45. The meanings of Beloved as a character and a phenomenon accumulate throughout the narrative. J. Brooks Bouson relates, "Her unsated hunger helps Sethe recall and talk about her painful past; it also brings with it the recovery of

unspeakable secrets [and] *[l]eads to regressive disorganization*. . . . Beloved is also more than the murdered and resurrected daughter of Sethe; she is an excessive character that mobilizes and accumulates meaning after meaning as the narrative unfolds: she embodies the sexual shame of the slave woman, . . . a kind of literary container for the shaming stereotypes used by hegemonic culture to define the racial and sexual Otherness of black female identity" (151–52).

46. As Jorge Duany explains in "Cuban Communities,"

> The mass migrations of Cubans from Mariel harbor to Key West, Florida, took place between April and September of 1980. The sudden and dramatic outflow partly resulted from the visits of more than 100,000 exiles to Cuba in 1989, which familiarized their relatives with economic opportunities in the United States. The immediate cause of the boat lift was the take-over of the Peruvian embassy in Havana by more than 10,000 Cubans. Fidel Castro resented that the Peruvian government failed to return some Cubans who had invaded the embassy requesting political asylum. So he removed its police custody and exhorted all those wishing to leave the country to go to the embassy. (4)

García's final section of *Dreaming*, "The Languages Lost (1980)," includes the section "Six Days in April," which scrupulously sticks to the facts of this event, showcasing her journalist's skills.

47. García's follow-up novel to *Dreaming in Cuban*, *Vanishing Maps* (2023), reprises the Del Pino family twenty years later with a very much living Celia Del Pino traveling to Spain for what unsurprisingly turns out to be a disappointing reunion with her former Spanish lover.

48. Arguing that García draws on dominant ideologies "that frame creativity and madness together" (418), Halperin underscores how Celia is mistreated: "García broadens and even challenges the portrait of the archetypal literary madwoman by forcing readers to confront her racialization, allying Celia with a certain Afro-*cubinidad*—reflected in her name, the blackness of her passion, her fascination with the Moorish city of Granada, [and] the *duende's* black sounds" ("Still Hands" 430). For the influences of figures of Spain and Spaniards on American literature more largely, see María DeGuzmán's *Spain's Long Shadow*. For a foundational essay on the concept of *cubanidad* given as a lecture to students in 1939 at the University of Havana (and published in 1940), see Fernando Ortiz, "The Human Factors of Cubanidad."

49. María DeGuzmán's definition of *duende* is pertinent here, especially as it relates to Celia's artistry and her death: "a mysterious or compelling spirit or force of enhancement and engagement" (326n13).

50. García Lorca published many volumes of poetry during his lifetime and incorporated "elements of Spanish folklore, Andalusian flamenco and Gypsy

culture, and *cante jondes*, or deep songs, while exploring themes of romantic love and tragedy" (https://www.poetryfoundation.org/poets/federico-garcia-lorca). He was arrested in 1936 at the onset of the Spanish Civil War and executed by a firing squad that same year. DeGuzmán suggests that the identification with realness might have been what prompted Andalusian poet from Granada, Federico García Lorca to associate the blues and African American rituals with *duende* (326n13).

51. In an interview with Toni Morrison, Bill Moyers admits to finding incredible Sethe's willingness to kill her daughter, Beloved, to prevent schoolteacher from kidnapping her, to which Morrison replies: "That was Margaret Garner's story. She was a slave woman who escaped from Kentucky and arrived in Cincinnati to live with her mother-in-law. . . . She became a *cause-célebrè* for the abolitionists because they were attempting to get her tried for murder. That would have been a bit of a coup because it would have assumed she had some responsibility over those children. But the abolitionists were unsuccessful. She was tried for the "real" crime, which was stolen property, and convicted and returned to the same man" (Taylor-Guthrie 271–72).

52. I am grateful to Samantha L. McAuliffe, who postulates that García's novel might be persuasively read through Mary Louise Pratt's idea of contact zones, permitting an "insider view of what being Cuban American really means" (1–2).

Chapter 3

1. I am guided in my use of the term *life writing* by Sidonie Smith and Julia Watson, who argue that the terms *life writing* and *life narrative* "are more inclusive of the heterogeneity of self-referential practices" as such work includes writing that "occurs within a dialogic exchange between writer and reader/viewer rather than as a story to be proved or falsified" (4). Monica B. Pearl explains that Lorde's *Zami* is a narrative "seeking a home—a generic home; it is a text looking for language and looking for a way of saying something that has not been said before" (311).

2. "The Uses of the Erotic: The Erotic as Power" was originally delivered as a lecture in 1978 at the Fourth Berkshire Conference on the History of Women at Mount Holyoke College. Published thereafter as a pamphlet at small presses, the essay is collected in Lorde's *Sister Outsider: Essays and Speeches*.

3. When referencing their constructed personae within their works, I refer to the authors' first names; when referencing the authors' mediated responses to their stories, I use the authors' surnames.

4. I am grateful to Smith and Watson for their referencing "memory theaters" in *Reading Autobiography*, to describe an intersection of pertinence to this chapter: memory and space.

5. In her analysis of the intersections between life writing and theory, Susan Driver counterpoises the works of Luce Irigaray, Trinh Ti Minh-ha, and

Audre Lorde to illustrate how these writers "mobilize mother daughter desires as a personally and politically engaging process of representation" to interrupt "the symbolic grip of monological maternal ideologies . . . [and to recover] those dimensions of desiring maternal selves left out of official discourses. Mothers are explored . . . as cultural signs, psychic figures, and embodied selves" ("Between Theories" 348).

6. Kaplan applies Derrida's version of genre production to deconstruct rules undergirding the canonized Western literary genre of autobiography, a genre that maintains its hegemony as the provenance of white masculine convention and entrenched ideas about the canon. Referencing Derrida's "The Law of Genre," Kaplan explains that such a law, with its limits and exclusions, is simultaneously based on a "counterlaw," undermining "the impossibility of maintaining those limits" (116–17). Thus, within the proscription "genres are not to be mixed," outlaw productions will emerge and "break obvious rules of genre. . . . These emerging outlaw genres require more collaborative procedures that are more closely attuned to the power differences among participants in the process of producing the text. Thus, instead of a discourse of individual authorship, we find a discourse of situation; a 'politics of location' " (Kaplan 119).

7. Several scholars have examined Lorde's plurality of voices in *Zami*. As Charlene Ball explains, "the plural voice is the communal voice of all the acknowledged selves. This voice moves in the narrative among memory, fantasy-dream, collective myth, and personal myth to create a community of voices" (67).

8. The edition I am using of *Zami: A New Spelling of My Name* was first published by the Crossing Press under its feminist series imprimatur. Like many of her feminist sisters writing in the 1980s (e.g., Gloria Anzaldúa, Cherríe Moraga, and Leslie Marmon Silko), Lorde supported the activist efforts of small-press publishing. As Barbara Smith explains, all of Lorde's "works of prose have been published by independent women's presses" (244n3), though in conversation with Lorde, Smith also learned that "*Zami: A New Spelling of My Name* was rejected by at least a dozen commercial presses" (244n3). See Smith's "The Truth That Never Hurts: Black Lesbians in Fiction in the 1980s."

9. I am indebted to Claudia Tate's reading of the self-parodic use of the traditional signatory in Harriet E. Wilson's 1859 novel, *Our Nig*, in which "The lexical identity established between the novel's principal title—*Our Nig*—and its pseudonymous authorial signatory—"Our Nig"—inscribes a sophisticated mode of self-reflexive irony that extenuates direct public censure" (*Domestic Allegories* 40).

10. Lorde described herself as "legally blind" without corrective lenses, and she did not begin wearing glasses until she was four years old. "Despite my nearsightedness, or maybe because of it, I learned to read at the same time I learned to talk, which was only a year or so before I started school" (*Zami* 21). In an interview with Adrienne Rich, Lorde said, "Until I got spectacles, when I was four, I thought trees were green clouds" ("An Interview" 85).

11. Pearl persuasively argues that Lorde's biomythography "actually derives from two extant American literary traditions—the African American narrative of enslavement and the lesbian coming out story—rendering it, after all, not a marginal text, but rather a text that falls obviously and firmly in the tradition of American literature" (297).

12. Lorde's biographer, Alexis De Veaux, explains: "She'd call herself 'black, feminist, lesbian, mother, poet warrior.' Over the course of her life, Lorde used these multiple identities as passports between an array of sisterhoods, declaring within each of them, 'I am your sister'" (367). My manuscript went into production before the publication of Alexis Pauline Gumbs's recent biography of Audre Lorde, *Survival Is a Promise: The Eternal Life of Audre Lorde*.

13. On Lorde's immigrant parents and Audre Lorde's first decades, see DeVeaux.

14. As Stephanie Li explains, subject positions derived from family are fluid "such that Lorde may understand herself as both mother to her mother and mother to herself" ("Becoming her Mother's Mother" 142).

15. Also known as the regal moth or royal walnut moth the *Citheronia regalis* is a North American moth, whose caterpillars are known as hickory-horned devils, "their frightening appearance is purely a ruse; the spines, though prickly, do not sting" ("Citheronia regalis").

16. The black/white cover imagery also might signify Lorde's overexposure when she works as an assembly-line worker in a Connecticut factory which exposed her to harmful X-ray machines:

> Audre was constantly exposed to carbon tetrachloride—overexposure can destroy the liver and cause cancer of the kidneys. She was also exposed to X-ray machines . . . as one of the coveted jobs in the 'Reading Room' and logged in a certain amount of crystals above the expected base count [and was thus "rewarded" with a bonus]. It was low-wage work, a health risk which many of the workers, poor women without other options, succumbed to as they rationalized about the seconds they saved by not pulling down the shields over the X-ray machines. (DeVeaux 40)

17. The mortar-and-pestle passage is one of the most analyzed scenes in *Zami*. Claudine Raynaud discusses the connection between the ritual of hair combing and the pounding of spices with a pestle to prepare a Caribbean dish: "Lorde is holding her mother's mortar against her, '*Thud push rub rotate up.*' . . . Making *souse* is a means for Lorde of recovering a world of scent, sensation, rhythm, and sound. The grinding of the spices on the day when she first menstruates becomes a ritual 'a piece of old and elaborate dance between [her] mother and [herself]'" (229). For other excellent readings, see Chinosole, Li, Holland, and Musser, who

analyzes the phrase "like a nutmeg nestled inside its covering of mace" in the context of where it occurs in *Zami*, the hair-combing scene between mother and daughter (177).

18. In the next chapter, I shall implicitly reprise an analysis of the "closet of white decadence" but with a focus on gay male suffering during the AIDS crisis (Chinosole 386).

19. In "Coming Home," Anne-Marie Fortier builds on Avtar Brah's concept of homing desire to advance her argument through an analysis of Italian American queer narratives.

20. Taking her cue from Fortier, Stella Bolaki argues that the home can be

"intensely queer, and queer, utterly familiar," and this becomes obvious when we consider ethnic-diasporic formations across multiple axes of difference. . . . [The] frustrating and guilt-ridden process of "unlearning" that accompanies moving out, is not given any space in *Zami*. Becoming queer for Lorde is not necessarily engendered in the movement away from home or through 'unlearning.' It emerges, rather, from the very fabric of queer (in the broader sense) family home and through a process that resembles translation. The familial home, situated in a liminal space of in-betweenness given its diasporic status within white mainstream America, becomes a useful tool in fashioning a queer identity. (779)

21. I take the metaphor of *centrifugal reading* from Robert Scholes, who states, "Centripetal reading conceives of a text in terms of an original intention located at the center of that text. . . . Centrifugal reading, on the other hand, sees the life of the text as occurring along its circumference, which is constantly expanding, encompassing new possibilities of meaning. The paired notions of centrifugality and centripetality constitute a 'better metaphor' of reading than backward-and forward-looking" (*Protocols of Reading* 8).

22. The Johnson-Reed Act, also known as the Immigration Restriction Act of 1924, halted migrations from eastern and southern Europe, and the federal act also included the Chinese Exclusion Act and the National Origins Act, preventing immigration from Asia. This legislation was described in a 1924 *Los Angeles Times* headline as a "Nordic Victory" (Higham 300). Such restrictions occurred simultaneously alongside the Jim Crow era of enforced racial segregation, which both Lorde and Ragusa represent in their narratives.

23. Wong takes William Boelhower to task in his *Immigrant Autobiography in the United States: Four Versions of the Italian American Self* for modeling his analysis of immigrant autobiography on "nothing more than a genotype of American autobiography," for example, portraying a protagonist's Americanization and "telescoping . . . first and second generations into a 'single immigrant experience'" (299, 301). In her examination of Chinese immigrant autobiographies, by contrast,

Wong observes a devotion to "preimmigration life in China," and the mediated status of American-born children, whose "understanding of Old World culture" is influenced by the often besieged memories of their parents. Wong's observation also extends to many fictional and autobiographical narratives, including *Zami* and *The Skin Between Us* (299, 301).

24. As Tony Murray explains, since a "sense of loss [is] often engendered by migration," emigrants often experience separations sometimes "twice over," as in the case of migrating young adults, who lose twice as children and then as parents (88). See Mari Tomasi's *Like Lesser Gods*, Maxine Hong Kingston's *The Woman Warrior*, and Tina De Rosa's *Paper Fish* for European- and Asian-descended novels at odds with the logic of Eurocentric thinking, responding antithetically to Western constructions of culture.

25. I take this phrase from the immigrant mother in Paule Marshall's 1959 novel, *Brown Girl, Brownstones*, a young mother whose migratory experiences parallel Lorde's mother in *Zami*. *Brown Girl* portrays first-generation Barbadian immigrants living in a Brooklyn neighborhood during the 1940s. Irma Watkins-Owens also references Marshall's novel to highlight the fact that "many immigrants could be detached from and defiant about America—viewing it as someone else's country—while at the same time recognizing it as a place that offered a chance to overcome the severe economic constraints at home" ("Early Twentieth-Century-Caribbean Women" 27). See also Watkins-Owens's full-length study, *Blood Relations: Caribbean Immigrants and the Harlem Community: 1900–1930*.

26. Felski explains, "The longing for intimacy emerges as a defining feature of the feminist confession at two interconnected levels: in the actual representation of the author's own personal relationships and in the relationship between author and reader established by the text . . . In one sense . . . the feminist confession documents the failure of intimacy. Yet clearly the production of the text itself functions as an attempted compensation for this failure, generating in the relationship between reader and author the erotic mutuality which cannot otherwise be realized" (89).

27. I contacted the author to seek permission to include this photograph of Kym with her grandmothers in this chapter since the Norton print staff could not locate it. Ragusa replied to say she no longer has the photo: "It's been many years, many moves, and last year a flood that destroyed boxes of my photos and other archives. I hope it's still floating around somewhere, but for now, the image in the book is all we have." E-mail to the author, January 5, 2023.

28. In "Southern Encounters in the City: Reconfiguring the South From the Liminal Space," Evelyn Ferraro extends sociologist Franco Cassano's spatial rethinking of Southern Italy to examine "other historically displaced and imagined Souths," connecting the Mediterranean to a reading of Ragusa's memoir (219).

29. I am quoting from the title of Pasquale Verdicchio's book, *Bound by Distance: Rethinking Nationalism through the Italian Diaspora*. I discussed this metaphor with the author whose explanation encapsulates both Lorde's and

Ragusa's struggles to belong to certain communities (including their families of origin) as they are coming of age:

> In the end, that is probably the only way that we can define ourselves, through our communities and the traits and practices that we find comfortable, comforting, welcoming. . . . It's the conundrum of identity, I guess, amplified by the fact that most of the time we are more likely to be defined from outside, by others' perception of who we might be. I knew that I wanted to approximate that notion of the impossibility of belonging to a construct that denied one's belonging and being within it . . . and the struggles involved in that attempt. (E-mail to the author, July 18, 2020)

30. Ragusa includes the full spelling of the negative epithet used against African Americans in the United States on her list, but I cannot do so as my location as a white, Sicilian/Abruzzian Italian American does not permit this. I do include the racialized slur *Guinea* as it was also used against Italian immigrants in America. The word *Guinea* is a reference to a region on the west coast of Africa and came to be used as a derogatory term toward Italians in America; likewise, the slur *Dago*, also an offensive epithet, was used regularly against Italians in the nineteenth and twentieth centuries. See David Roediger's "Guineas, Wiggers, and the Dramas of Racialized Culture."

31. Tenzer summarizes key features of *Passing*, Ragusa's documentary on her maternal grandmother, which focuses on the story Miriam told Kym about a trip she took from New York City to Florida in 1959: "Traveling with an African American male friend (her then lover), her grandmother encounters the segregated and racially hostile South for the first time when her companion sends her into a diner in North Carolina to purchase food for a picnic. Inside, two white male customers repeatedly confront her with the question 'What side of the tracks are you from?'" (213).

32. Baldo makes a persuasive connection between Kym Ragusa's trip to Sicily and the translation of *The Skin Between Us* into Italian, both examples of a return home, and, quoting translator, Caterina Romeo, "a way of migrating again backwards" (9).

33. Examining the degree and nature of the of opposition that may have existed between early first-generation African Caribbean immigrants and members of the proximal host society, African Americans, Oswald Warner shows how in such a context "these Afro-Caribbeans invoked certain ethnic markers in order to racialize their ethnicity so as to separate themselves, that is, to make racial space, by constructing ethnic boundaries, from the more racially encompassing black American racial identity" (78–79). As Warner explains, first-generation Afro-Caribbean immigrants comprised "the overall majority of the 143,797 black

immigrants who entered the US between 1899 and 1937" (71). As census data show "by 1930, 57% of all Caribbean immigrants lived in New York City, especially in Harlem, the home of 47,000"; the first wave of Caribbean immigrants coincided with the " 'Great Migration' of African Americans from southern states to northern US cities" (72).

34. Kim D. Butler, from whom I take *diasporan consciousness*, explains that this phrase "implies recognition of the historical and cultural connection to the homeland[;] it necessarily includes a simultaneous recognition of the unique community existing between members of the diasporan group" (208).

35. Jennifer Guglielmo explains, "Historian David Roediger notes that Baldwin was one of many African American writers who expertly critiqued how participants in the life of white supremacy 'helped to steal the vitality from immigrant communities of the Irish, Italians, Jews, Poles, and others', since it required the desperate hope that all the fear, exclusion, hatred, violence, and terror upon which whiteness is consolidated would be worth it" (3). Fred Gardaphé asserts that Italian Americans are an invisible people because "they refuse to be seen. Italian Americans became invisible the moment they could pass themselves off for being white" (1). For studies on race as it relates to Italian immigrants in America, see also Jacobson, Gabaccia, T. Guglielmo, Orsi, Luconi, and Richards.

36. For a good overview of the two streams of Italian positivism that emerged during the Risorgimento when Italy became a nation-state in 1861, see Donna Gabaccia, "Race, Nation, Hyphen: Italian Americans and American Multiculturalism in a Comparative Perspective." As Gabaccia explains, "Just as Italy became a nation-state and Argentina and the United States ended their civil wars, the 1859 publication of Charles Darwin's *Origins of Species* sparked international debates among the scientific racists we now usually call social Darwinists in the English-speaking world and positivists elsewhere" (51).

37. See writers Louise DeSalvo and Diane di Prima, who illuminate the racialized landscape of the Italian American imaginary. DeSalvo explicates the racialization of Italians in governmental documents such as DeSalvo's grandmother's naturalization papers in "Color: White/Complexion: Dark," and more fully her parents' ethnic shame in her memoir, *Crazy in the Kitchen: Food, Feuds, and Forgiveness in an Italian American Family*. For the "pseudo 'white' identity" of Di Prima's Italian American parents, see *Recollections of My Life as a Woman: The New York Years*. It is more than a bit fortuitous that DeSalvo and di Prima had important and life-sustaining relationships with the authors I discuss in this chapter. See Kym Ragusa's "On Vulnerability and Risk: Learning to Write and Teach Memoir as a Student of Louise DeSalvo," in *Personal Effects*. For further details about the relationship between poets Di Prima and Lorde and the life-changing phone call that Diane made to Audre in the early years, see De Veaux's *Warrior Poet* (93–94, 157–58).

38. In *Preoccupied Spaces: Remapping Italy's Transnational Migrations and Colonial Legacies*, Fiore explains, "Conceivable as foundational movements for

the two nations of Italy and the United States, emigration and slavery are thus presented as histories that can foster a more profound awareness of the present, including the racial conflicts characterizing the multiracial society like the United States or prompted by recent migration as in the case of Italy" (58).

39. For historical background on the 1950s lesbian bar scene in New York City and, more largely, histories of LGBTQ* lives, see Martin Duberman's *Stonewall: The Definitive Story of the LGBTQ Rights Uprising That Changed America* and Lillian Faderman's *Odd Girls and Twilight Lovers: A History of Lesbian Life in Twentieth-Century America*, especially chapter 7, "Butches, Femmes, and Kikis: Creating Lesbian Subcultures in the 1950s and '60s." See also *The Encyclopedia of New York City* (733–34), which includes references to the lesbian bars Lorde visited in the 1950s: the Bagatelle, Three Page, Pony Stable, and Swing Rendezvous. For a recent urban-studies perspective, see Zoe Wennerholm's "'It's Your Future, Don't Miss It': Nostalgia, Utopia and Desire in the New York Lesbian Bar." For a historical geography of lesbian and queer spaces in New York and an accounting of their disappearance through rapid gentrification, see Jen Jack Gieseking's *A Queer New York: Geographies of Lesbians, Dykes, and Queers*. For analysis on Lorde's portrayal of the Black lesbian bar scene, see also Barbara Smith, "The Truth that Never Hurts: Black Lesbians in Fiction in the 1980s," and Katie King, "Audre Lorde's Lacquered Layerings: The Lesbian Bar as a Site of Literary Production."

40. As Charlene Ball explains, "The crossroads is where Esu/Elegbara stands, god of travelers and strangers. . . . Like the avatar of Esu/Elegbara that she is, Afrekete/Kitty embodies chance and uncertainty. Her appearance in Audre's life is unplanned and unexpected, and so is her disappearance. . . . Audre has learned how to give up persons in real time but to keep them forever in mythic time" (73–74).

41. Lorde eroticizes food throughout *Zami*, so we should not be surprised to read Audre's description of the sensual arrangement and erotically sculptured selections of food at the private home party. In its vulvar evocation, Lorde's description echoes Judy Chicago's *Dinner Party* in acknowledgment of women's genitalia. Though no overt allusion is made to the mortar-and-pestle scene, Lorde has succeeded in establishing a close relationship between the material culture of her mother and the Black lesbian erotic, often revolving around food.

42. According to Kara Provost, Lorde borrows selectively from the Mawulisa pantheon of African gods, choosing to identify with a lesser-known, overtly female manifestation of the goddess Afrekete as a supplement to the phallic Eshu, focusing specifically on "the trickster's multivocality and ability to act as translator. . . . Afrekete [is] the youngest *daughter*, a figure Lorde associates with linguistic skill and black female strength, intelligence, and sexuality" (46). On Lorde's discussing her shift from Eshu (utilized in her first book of poetry, *The Black Unicorn*) to Afrekete in *Zami*, see Judy Grahn, *Another Mother Tongue: Gay Words, Gay Worlds*. See also Ball's additional commentary on the archetypal qualities

characteristic of Afrekete's multidimensionality: "Afrekete combines aspects of the Maiden and the Mother, . . . the Green-World Lover . . . as well as the Queen of the World. She is a daughter, a young girl like Persephone, . . . Like Demeter, she is a mother, and a maternal aspect of the triple Goddess, associated with fruits and the earth. She brings Audre nurturance, fruits, and vegetables from 'under the bridge,' as Audre's own mother did" (75). While my list is not exhaustive, see the following scholars on African mythological gods as tricksters and linguistic magicians: Gates, Keating, Provost, Ball, Chinosole, and Russell.

43. For a religious and community history of Italian Harlem, see Robert Orsi's *The Madonna of 115th Street: Faith and Community in Italian Harlem, 1880–1950*. On Italian immigrants' anticlericalism, see Mary Elizabeth Brown's "Religion." On Italian feste, leading to its culmination in the procession, see Kay Turner's "The Virgin of the Sorrows Procession: A Brooklyn Inversion" and Joseph Sciorra's "'We Go Where the Italians Live': Religious Processions and Ethnic and Territorial Markers in a Multi-Ethnic Brooklyn Neighborhood."

44. On the relationship between text and textile, see Edvige Guinta and Joseph Sciorra, eds., *Embroidered Stories: Interpreting Women's Domestic Needlework from the Italian Diaspora*.

45. Imagining Gilda arranged in marriage, Ragusa writes, "She's put out her best *biancheria*, the embroidered white linens that had been part of her dowry as a young bride, handmade by her own mother: lacy antimacassars for the couch and chairs, crisp, perfectly folded napkins, and a long tablecloth appliquéd with hearts and lovebirds that she saved just for this moment. This is a seduction of the highest order, a mother's seduction" (*Skin* 126). Simone de Beauvoir early noted, "For the woman[,] her complicity is invited"; from a young age, a girl is offered inducements to be complicit in her destiny, "imposed on her from the exterior" (312).

46. Robert Orsi explains that Italians secured through their enactment of festivals and outdoor processions boundaries *against* darker-skinned newcomers like Puerto Ricans, "who were too much like them for comfort [incorporating them] into an overarching narrative that held them responsible for the demise of the community. . . . [T]he narrative was a theodicy, a story that endeavored to make sense of the great chance, to account for the decisions to leave, respond to the genuine sorrow people felt at the passing of a once thriving Italian world, and repair the fragmenting moral order" ("The Religious Boundaries" 337).

47. Reclaiming the maternal through women's participation in ritualized performances such as religious processions, see Susan Caperna Lloyd's memoir, *No Pictures in My Grave: A Spiritual Journey in Sicily*, and Alison D. Goeller's essay "Persephone Goes Home: Italian American Women in Italy."

48. As Ball explains, "Aphrodite, Oya, and Aflakete are all related to the ocean. Linda, Audre's mother, also comes from an island and is connected to the ocean. And Kitty's apartment invokes the movement and mystery of ocean" (69).

49. For an analysis of the shoreline as a site of "transoceanic becoming . . . as an African diaspora being," see Ashley Taylor Coleman's "Religio-erotic Experience and Transoceanic Becoming at the Shoreline in Audre Lorde's *Zami*."

Chapter 4

1. I employ Elizabeth Freeman's description of "queer kinship" to enlarge understandings of the LBGTQ* community. Freeman offers a different sense of "what kinship might be," as in "practical strategies for accommodating all the possible ways one human being's body can be vulnerable and hence upon that of another, and for mobilizing all the possible resources one body has for taking care of another" ("Queer Belongings" 297, 298). For a recent collection on queer kinship that uses queer and trans theory to examine how dominant theories of kinship ignored the harmful effects of chattel slavery, settler colonialism, and white supremacy, see *Queer Kinship: Race, Sex, Belonging, Form*, edited by Tyler Bradway and Elizabeth Freeman. For a sociocultural essay in this collection on trans history from the stories of maternal women with trans experience, see Dilara Çalişkan's "World Making: Family, Time, and Memory among Trans Mothers and Daughters in Istanbul."

2. Both authors pay homage to specific ethnic identities. Maso mirrors codes of ethnic identity to advance a queer aesthetic she has developed over the course of four decades of writing. Maso highlights her investment in representing ethnic groups migrating from Europe to America, including Italian, Irish, German, Armenian, and Jews, for example. Maso's approach to mirroring ethnic codes illuminates her complex portrayals of queer desire, especially in the "Last Supper" scene between her protagonist Caroline and Stephen. Makkai explores the brief marriage of her Hungarian grandparents in her essay "Other Types of Poison," which is fictionalized in her short-story collection, *Music for Wartime*, several stories of which are about Jewish refugees. Makkai later discovered that her grandfather was principal author and proponent of Hungary's Second Jewish Law of 1939, a major piece of antisemitic legislation that restricted Jews from economic and public participation in pre-Nazi Hungary. Makkai's portrayal of Yale Tishman and Fiona's Great-Aunt Nora are creative composites of Makkai's interest in the Lost Generation after the first world war (including lost artistic voices) and the AIDS era, which metonymically recalls the Holocaust of World War II.

3. See Eve Sedgwick's "Paranoid Reading, Reparative Reading: or, You're So Paranoid You Probably Think This Introduction Is about You" in *Novel Gazing: Queer Readings in Fiction*. Sedgwick locates the AIDS crisis as a central locus for her thoughts on interpreting queer texts through the lens of paranoia (which became a privileged site of antihomophobic readings by the mid-1980s), examining paranoid and reparative positions as critical practices that are "changing

and heterogenous" (6, 8). Maso and Makkai offer complex versions of reparative stances in their novels fully aware of the privileged site of paranoia to expose the mechanisms "of homophobic and heterosexist enforcement against" homosexuality (Sedgwick 5).

4. While there is a semantic difference between the terms *epidemic* and *pandemic* (*epidemic* typically refers to an outbreak, and *pandemic*, to a spread across several countries), epidemiologists have used both terms to describe the effects of AIDS globally. In this chapter, I use both terms to express both the global range of the disease and its ongoing effects today. Early in its history, HIV infection was referred to as the gay plague, and, once named as AIDS, was understood in a premodern way; as Susan Sontag has explained, as "a disease incurred by people both as individuals and as members of a 'risk' group—that neutral-sounding, bureaucratic category which also revives the archaic idea of a tainted community that illness has judged" (*AIDS and Its Metaphors* 46). I use the term *plague* only in relation to how this illness was named in the early years of its existence.

5. Overwhelmed by her childhood friend's diagnosis, Maso stopped writing *The Art Lover* for a year, explaining in the autobiographical section of the novel: "My chest began to hurt. I imagined the lining of my heart to be inflamed" (200). From the French *couver*, "to brood, hatch," couvade syndrome is informally referred to as sympathetic pregnancy whereby men experience symptoms of pregnancy at the time their partner is pregnant. It was coined by anthropologist E. B. Taylor in 1865 to refer to certain rituals fathers adopt during pregnancy. For a historical overview of shifting interpretations of couvade, see Elizabeth Prine Pauls, "Couvade."

6. I deliberately echo here the lexicon surrounding nineteenth-century motherhood and play on the "cult-of-true-womanhood" ideology that pervaded the discourse and that Harriet Jacobs brilliantly deploys through Linda Brent in *Incidents in the Life of a Slave Girl* as referenced in chapter 1.

7. See also Michael Butter's "Historiographic Metafiction" in *The Encyclopedia of Twentieth-Century Fiction*, edited by Patrick O'Donnell, David W. Madden, and Justus Nieland. Also, see Brian McHale's *Postmodernist Fiction*, Barry Pomeroy's *Historiographic Metafiction or Lying with the Truth*, and Patricia Waugh's *Metafiction: The Theory and Practice of Self-Conscious Fiction*.

8. As Linda Hutcheon explains, "we cannot know the past except through its texts: its documents" (*Poetics* 16).

9. From Terry Pitts's blog, *Vertigo*, "where literature and art intersect, with an emphasis on W. G. Sebald and literature with embedded photographs." See especially, "'There Is So Much Pain in the World': Carole Maso's 'The Art Lover,'" posted on March 22, 2016.

10. Gary Falk (1954–1986) was a painter and assemblage artist in New York. According to the biographical note in his archive, "Falk developed a personal sign system in his works of art, and often worked in enamel and acrylic on Plexiglass

and aluminum" ("Gary Falk papers"). Falk exhibited his art at several New York galleries and at the New Museum. For more information about his oeuvre, see the Falk entry in the American Smithsonian Archives of American Art.

11. In "A Conversation with Rebecca Makkai," she writes, "[M]y main character, Yale Tishman, is someone I keep thinking of like a friend I lost. When I get good news about the novel, I wish I could tell him about it. That might make me sound unbalanced, but it was important to my process that I get to the point of thinking of him as a real person" (*Great Believers* 5).

12. According to David Artavia and Diane Anderson-Minshall,

> The disease that later became known as AIDS was first identified in medical journals in 1981 (President Ronald Reagan's first year in office). As AIDS became a national health crisis, Reagan's administration remained silent. Despite more than 16,000 Americans dying from complications of AIDS between 1981–1986, Reagan did not use the term "AIDS" in public until nearly five years into his administration.... In the background, religious leaders like Rev. Jerry Falwell told followers 'AIDS is the wrath of God upon homosexuals,'... and Reagan's own communications director, Pat Buchanan, argued that AIDS was nature's revenge on gay men. By the time Reagan addressed the issue of AIDS at the Third International Conference on AIDS in Washington, D.C., ... nearly 21,000 had died from the disease and it had already spread to 113 countries with over 50,000 cases worldwide. Reagan's acknowledgment of the disease proved to be too late to stop the epidemic, and his response was almost entirely ineffective. ("Queer Life in the '70s and '80s: Art, Activism, & AIDS")

13. As I wrote in the introduction, I take the term *reparenting* from Rachel Blau Du Plessis's *Writing beyond the Ending: Narrative Strategies of Twentieth-Century Women Writers*, but I diverge from Du Plessis's focus on the Oedipal crisis within a heterosexual paradigm; nonetheless, the narrative strategy remains the same as it aims to "forge an alternative fictional resolution [to end] sexual polarization ... to construct from available male and female roles, sibling and parent-child ties, some set of relationships that would be less emotionally damaging" (83).

14. Arthur Kleinman, MD, makes useful distinctions between the terms *illness*, *disease*, and *sickness*: "*Illness* refers to how the sick person and the members of the family or wider social network perceive, live with, and respond to symptoms and disability.... [D]*isease* is reconfigured *only* as an alternative in biological structure or functioning.... [S]*ickness* [is] the understanding of a disorder in its generic sense across a population in relation to macrosocial (economic, political, institutional) forces" (Frank 3–6).

15. See Ahmed, "Feminist Futures" 238, 239. In his review of *The Great Believers*, Brian Bromberger quotes from Fiona's ninety-year-old Great-Aunt Nora, an artist herself during World War I, who donates a treasure trove of paintings to Northwestern University, the gallery where Yale works as the development director. Nora insists on including artwork of her former lover, who committed suicide after the war, explaining, "When someone's gone and you're the primary keeper of his memory, letting go would be a kind of murder" (Bromberger).

16. One unabashedly humorous comment made by Caroline occurs when she addresses her father, who has benefitted from his status as a white, heterosexual man from an era that gifted him with economic and educational uplift: "Max, last night I dreamt that a B movie actor decided as a joke to run for president and got elected and then started a zany military program called Star Wars, like the movie, while everyone on earth was dying or starving to death. A big dome in the sky that would keep out all the bad guys" (183). As Lillian Faderman explains,

> Reagan himself would not utter the word AIDS until his good friend from Hollywood days, Rock Hudson, died of it in 1985. The year before, however, when three hundred thousand of Americans had already been diagnosed with the disease and Ronald Reagan was running for reelection, he told a group that kept tally of a 'presidential Biblical scoreboard' that his administration would continue to resist all attempts to 'obtain any government endorsement of homosexuality.' That seemed to include any effort to help save homosexual lives. (*The Gay Revolution* 418)

17. And brutal they are: at an ACT UP protest four years after testing positive for HIV, Yale suffers a broken rib after being pinioned to the ground, knelt on, cuffed, and put in the paddy wagon by Chicago police, sending him to the hospital.

18. St. Vincent's opened in 1984, a year after San Francisco's General Hospital opened the first AIDS ward in the United States. See Michael J. O'Loughlin's retrospective, "The Catholic Hospital That Pioneered AIDS Care," in *America: The Jesuit Review*. "It was through this commitment [to ensure that AIDS patients from the neighborhood could be served with dignity and respect] that a Catholic institution became perhaps the most iconic hospital in the history of H.I.V. and AIDS care in the United States" (O'Loughlin). See also Andrew Boynton's comments: "St. Vincent's soon became the ground zero in the city's AIDS crisis," in "Remembering St. Vincent's."

19. This chapter was primarily written during another pandemic (COVID-19), so I want to recognize the work of caretakers, especially nurses in the early days, who functioned in multiple ways during patients' final stages of illness. The

parallels between the AIDS epidemic and COVID-19 across macrosocial lines is especially relevant as the sick in both eras often died with only a gloved and masked nurse by their side.

20. In this chapter, I use the terms *caretaker* and *caregiver* interchangeably, though I am aware of their nuanced differences; according to the *OED*, *caretaker* has been used in the English language since the early 1800s; *caregiver*, by contrast, entered the lexicon of American English much later, in the 1960s, and can connote a more transactional form of tending to another as in a person hired to look after elderly or people with disabilities who need help. I am using these terms to suggest both meanings as I believe that Maso and Makkai characterize their protagonists engaging in nurturing activities traditionally aligned with motherhood and extending that meaning to include nonaffiliated maternal figures whose nurturing compels a reconsideration of the meanings of love and fidelity beyond natality.

21. While not strictly aligning their narratives with apocalyptic witnessing, Maso and Makkai focus rather on the act of sitting vigil at the bedside of the dying, enabling both authors to represent death in a premodern way. About the existence (or not) of an afterlife, Sandra Gilbert distinguishes between two ways of "*telling* death": "expiration," which harbors spiritual overtones, and "termination," which lacks transcendence. The antipodal words loosely characterize premodern and modern perceptions of death and ultimately represent two ways of "thinking about death" (106). While engaging in but not strictly submitting to the meanings of either word, Maso and Makkai focus rather on the act of maternal witnessing by women who are overwhelmed, as Shoshana Felman and Dori Laub explain, "by occurrences that have not settled into understanding or remembrance" (as qtd. in Gilbert 98).

22. In *The Wounded Storyteller*, Arthur Frank generates a typology of four ideal body types to examine illness narratives: the disciplined body, the mirroring body, the dominating body, and the communicative body. He further explains, "Actual body selves represent distinctive mixtures of ideal types" (29). In their maternal roles, Caroline and Fiona mirror and communicate illness narratives with their loved ones.

23. To reiterate Marianne Hirsch's explanation: "Postmemory's connection to the past is thus actually mediated not by recall but by imaginative investment, projection, and creation. . . . These events happened in the past, but their effects continue into the present. This is, I believe, the structure of postmemory and the process of its generation" (*The Generation of Postmemory* 5).

24. Hirsch sees a range between what Toni Morrison has called "rememory," which I discussed in chapter 2, and what she defines as " 'postmemory'—between, on the one hand, a memory that, communicated through bodily symptoms, becomes a form of repetition and reenactment, and, on the other hand, one that works

through indirection and multiple mediation. Within the intimate familial space of mother/daughter transmission, however, postmemory always risks sliding into rememory, traumatic reenactment, and repetition" (*The Generation of Postmemory* 82–83). In Makkai's *The Great Believers*, Fiona's daughter, Claire, suffers from this slippage, reenacting her mother's trauma through imaginative projection. See also Robin Silbergleid's article on Carole Maso's novel *AVA*, which was published after *The Art Lover* and more overtly functions as a post-Holocaust narrative that uses postmemory as a major device to represent Ava's interior thoughts: "'Treblinka: A Rather Musical Word': Carole Maso's Post Holocaust Narrative."

25. Unlike Caroline of *The Art Lover*, whose mourning enables her movement toward healing (and the possibility of representing it), Fiona's melancholia in *The Great Believers* prevents her from moving into the twenty-first century as she continues to fantasize about the days before AIDS. In this way, Fiona's struggle bears comparison with Maso's fourth novel, *The American Woman in the Chinese Hat*, in which Catherine destroys her manuscript and ends romantic relationships after learning that her brother has the deadly AIDS virus. For an analysis on the relationship between metafictional technique and grief work that applies the Freudian paradigm of mourning and melancholy to Maso's *The Art Lover*, see Grant Stirling's "Mourning and Metafiction: Carole Maso's '*The Art Lover.*'" Stirling ascribes to Caroline an unprocessed mourning that becomes a form of melancholic stasis, though Caroline refuses to use art as an aesthetic retreat to preserve the lost object. I do not read Caroline's mourning as anything other than an active process and argue instead that Maso represents her protagonist's mourning as a form of lamentation that actively seeks closure. In this viewpoint, I am more aligned with that of Robin Silbergleid, who interprets melancholy in *Narratives of Loss* not as an aesthetic retreat but as a "retreat from the aesthetic" (99). Like Silbergleid, I interpret Maso's lavish use of graphics and deliberate shift from fictional to autobiographical narrative as the author's attempt to represent "'the thing itself' as suggested in the narrative's last moment, an image of Carole and Gary, the 'truest' representation" (*Narratives of Loss* 99).

26. On the most basic level, the term *antinarrative* describes a refusal to adhere to typical conventions of narrative. Maso and Makkai represent loss of faith in fictional narrative in different ways, but both deploy antinarrative techniques in response to the extremity of the AIDS crisis.

27. Roof examines the reciprocal relation between narrative and sexuality, demonstrating how such a marriage produces sexual categories "whose existence and constitution depend upon a specific reproductive narrative heteroideology which depends on literary configurations of the heteronarrative" (xxvii).

28. Alongside Hirsch's *The Generation of Postmemory*, other works useful to my analysis are James Young's "The Holocaust as Vicarious Past: Restoring the Voices of Memory to History" in *Judaism*; Ellen S. Fine's "Transmission of

Memory: The Post-Holocaust Generation in the Diaspora," in *Breaking Crystal*; and Gabriele Schwab's *Haunting Legacies Violent Histories and Transgenerational Traumas*.

29. For an excellent article on Maso's critique of modernism, especially her critique of art historians' devotion to modernist interpretations, see Charles B. Harris, "The Dead Fathers: The Rejection of Modernist Distance in *The Art Lover*." Harris analyzes Maso's use of four details of Giotto's fresco *Noli Me Tangere* ("Don't Touch Me") and an inserted page from art historian James H. Stubblebine. Harris interprets Maso's position this way: "This modernist view of art with its false assurances of orderliness and transcendence, must be forsaken, the novel's final two sections make clear, before these lovers can get on with their lives" (159).

30. One of many contemporary US writers to pay homage to Virginia Woolf, Maso establishes a genealogy with Woolf through the maternal, recalling Woolf's famous line in *A Room of One's Own*: "A woman writing thinks back through her mothers" (96).

31. In *By the Breath of Their Mouths: Narratives of Resistance in Italian America*, I place *The Art Lover* in conversation Dorothy Calvetti Bryant's *A Day in San Francisco* to examine how these authors portray the AIDS crisis contemporaneously, documenting illness through the lens of wounded storytellers who hold diametrically different responses to their dying.

32. On the relations between lesbians and gay men in ACT UP, see Ann Cvetkovich's *An Archive of Feelings: Trauma, Sexuality, and Lesbian Public Cultures*, especially "AIDS Activism and Public Feelings: Documenting ACT UP's Lesbians."

33. Maso attributes her refusal to succumb to fear to Gary's supportive friendship, even while he lay dying. She writes of her conviction "to living, working—loving with a new recklessness, abandon, urgent, urgent. Gary who taught me to do everything, to be everything, to want, to have, to try everything—to not be afraid anymore" (*Break Every Rule* 9–10).

34. In "Testimony," Timothy F. Murphy maintains that writing about those who have died of AIDS need not only advance a political or medical reform; this, in contrast to Douglas Crimp who then wrote, "*Anything said or done about AIDS that does not give precedence to the knowledge, the needs, and the demands of people living with AIDS must be condemned*" (Murphy 307).

35. As I commented in chapter 3, I apply the idea of "diasporan consciousness" to the movements of Lorde and Ragusa. Likewise, for members of the queer community whose movements have often required migration if not repatriation to another country, Kim D. Butler explains that, while the phrase "implies recognition of the historical and cultural connection to the homeland, it necessarily includes a simultaneous recognition of the unique community existing between members of the diasporan group" (208).

36. In her interview with Rich Fahle at the 2019 AWP Book Fair, Makkai said that she read every issue of *Windy City Times* from 1985 through 1992, housed in the Harold Washington Library archives.

37. Elizabeth Freeman connects the idea of resisting narrative progress with the notion of "temporary drag," which parallels Makkai's recursive practices in *The Great Believers*: Makkai pulls generations backward to challenge ideas about generational succession/success (*Time Binds* 65). I am grateful to Matt Franks for applying Freeman's notion to how Virginia Woolf enacts queer temporality in *To the Lighthouse* in relation to the Mrs. Ramsay–Lily Briscoe bond by using techniques of delay and synchronicity rather than through generational succession and progress (Franks 15–17).

38. In one of the epigraphs to the novel, Makkai quotes from F. Scott Fitzgerald's "My Generation": "We were the great believers. I have never cared for any men as much as for these who felt the first springs when I did, and saw death ahead, and were reprieved—and who now walk the long stormy summer."

39. As Albert Williams says, 1985 was "a turning point in the AIDS crisis" and Makkai was seven years old at the time. In reply, Makkai says, "The timing thing is really interesting to me. I think you're the first person to ask me about the timing. Nineteen eighty-five, as you know, is a pivotal year—. . . As much as I know, I can never perfectly capture this world, I would love people who lived through this to feel some recognition, to feel some catharsis" (Williams).

40. See MK Czerwiec's graphic memoir, *Taking Turns: Stories from HIV/AIDS Care Unit, 371*, where she served for seven years as a nurse at the HIV/AIDS care unit at Illinois Masonic Hospital, the first dedicated AIDS unit in Chicago (and the Midwest). This is the very setting for Makkai's AIDS victims in *The Great Believers*.

41. Alongside reading all the issues between 1985 and 1992 of the *Windy City Times* housed at the Harold Washington Library archives, Makkai also researched early AIDS medical history at the Gerber/Hart Library and Archives lesbian and gay resource center in Rogers Park in Chicago (Eakin).

42. Bouson is quoting from several theorists on trauma, two of which I reference from her book: Bessel van der Kolk's and Onno van der Hart's "Intrusive Past: The Flexibility of Memory and the Engraving of Trauma"; and Dori Laub's "Bearing Witness, or the Vicissitudes of Listening."

43. During her interview with Rich Fahle in 2019, Makkai shared that she continues to display a black-and-white photograph on her laptop screensaver of four men at a candlelight vigil, a constant reminder that this disease not only stole a generation of men, but continues to take the lives of many people globally. Makkai discussed the global dimensions of AIDS, addressing the racism inherent in the continued silence in response to this disease in the twenty-first century; according to Makkai, 35 million people suffer from HIV globally (1.1 million in the United States), and 45 million have died ("Makkai on 'The Great Believers'").

44. Freeman explains:

The flip side of an understanding of kinship in terms of dependency is what I will call the technique of renewal: as a practice, kinship can also be viewed as the process by which bodies and the potential for physical and emotional attachment are created, transformed, and sustained over time. . . . Longing to belong, . . . encompass[es] not only the desire to impossibly extend our individual existence or to preserve relationships that will invariably end, but also to have something queer exceed its own time, even to imagine that excess *as* queer in ways that getting married or having children might not be. ("Queer Belongings" 298, 299)

45. José Esteban Muñoz said, "Queerness is utopian and there is something queer about the utopian" (457).

46. See Susan Sontag's *On Photography*.

Bibliography

Abbott, Traci B. "'A Good Girl Like Nancy': Willa Cather's *Sapphira and the Slave Girl.*" *Southern Quarterly*, vol. 46, no. 1, Fall 2008, pp. 26–45.

Accomando, Christina. *"The Regulations of Robbers": Legal Fictions of Slavery and Resistance*. Ohio State University Press, 2001.

"Adrienne Rich's Later Work." Edited by Cynthia R. Wallace, *Arizona Quarterly: A Journal of American Literature, Culture, & Theory*, vol. 78, no. 2, Summer 2002.

Ahmed, Sara. "Feminist Futures." *Feminist Futures: A Concise Companion to Feminist Theory*, edited by Mary Eagleton, Blackwell, 2003, pp. 236–54.

Ahmed, Sara. "Orientations: Toward a Queer Phenomenology." *GLQ: A Journal of Lesbian and Gay Studies*, vol. 12, no. 4, 2006, pp. 543–74.

Alvarez, Julia. *In the Name of Salomé*. Plume, 2001.

Alvarez-Borland, Isabel. *Cuban American Literature of Exile: From Person to Persona*. University Press of Virginia, 1998.

Alvarez-Borland, Isabel. "Displacements and Autobiography in Cuban-American Fiction." *World Literature Today*, vol. 68, no. 1, Winter 1994, pp. 43–48.

Ammons, Elizabeth. *Conflicting Stories: American Women Writers at the Turn into the Twentieth Century*. Oxford University Press, 1992.

Andrews, William L. *To Tell a Free Story: The First Century of Afro-American Autobiography, 1760–1865*. University of Illinois Press, 1986.

Anzaldúa, Gloria. *Borderlands/La Frontera: The New Mestiza*. 2nd edition, Aunt Lute, 1987.

Anzaldúa, Gloria. *The Gloria Anzaldúa Reader*. Edited by AnaLouise Keating, Duke University Press, 2009.

Arnold, Marilyn. "'Of Human Bondage': Cather's Subnarrative in *Sapphira and the Slave Girl.*" *Mississippi Quarterly*, vol. 40, no. 3, Summer 1987, pp. 323–38.

Artavia, David and Diane Anderson-Minshall. "Queer Life in the '70s and '80s: Art, Activism, & AIDS." *The Advocate*, 4 May 2017, https://advocate.com/advocate50/2017/5/04/queer-life-70s-and-90sart-activism-aids.

Auden, W. H. "In Memory of W. B. Yeats." *W. H. Auden: Collected Poems*. Edited by Edward Mendelson, revised edition, Modern Library, 2007, p. 245.

Auden, W. H. "Their Lonely Betters." *W. H. Auden: Collected Poems*. Edited by Edward Mendelson, revised edition, Modern Library, 2007, p. 580.

Audre Lorde: The Berlin Years, 1984-1992. Directed by Dagmar Schultz, 2012.

Bakhtin, Mikhail. *The Dialogic Imagination: Four Essays*. University of Texas Press, 1981.

Bakhtin, Mikhail. *Problems of Dostoevsky's Poetics*. Edited and translated by Caryl Emerson, University of Minnesota Press, 1984.

Baldo, Michela. "Painful Italianness: Translating the (Post)migrant Female Body." Institute of Modern Languages Research, 18 June 2014, University of London.

Baldwin, James. "On Being 'White' . . . and Other Lies." *Black on White: Black Writers on What It Means to Be White*, edited with an introduction by David R. Roediger, Schocken Books, 1998, pp. 177-80.

Ball, Charlene M. "Old Magic and New Fury: The Theaphony of Afrekete in Audre Lorde's 'Tar Beach.'" *NWSA Journal*, vol. 13, no. 1, Spring 2001, pp. 61-85.

Barker, Wesley N. "Is Mother Other? Desire and the Ethics of Maternality." *Theology and Sexuality*, vol. 19, no. 3, 2013, pp. 203-26.

Basile, Giambattista. *Il Pentamerone: or, The Tale of Tales*. 1893. Translated by Richard F. Burton, H Liveright, 1927.

Baym, Nina. *Women's Fiction: A Guide to Novels by and about Women in America: 1820-1870*. Cornell University Press, 1978.

Behar, Ruth. *Bridges to Cuba: Puentes a Cuba*. University of Michigan Press, 1995.

Bhabha, Homi. *The Location of Culture*. Routledge, 1994.

Bhattacharjee, Tuhin. "Antigone/Mother's Second Death and the Maternal in Lacan and Cavarero." *philoSOPHIA*, vol. 10, no. 2, 2021, pp. 190-206, Project MUSEdoi:10.1353/phi.2021.0003.

Birnbaum, Lucia. *Black Madonnas: Feminism, Religion, & Politics in Italy*. Northeastern University Press, 1993.

Boelhower, William. "The Ethnic Trilogy: A Poetics of Cultural Passage." *MELUS*, vol. 12, no. 4, Dec. 1985, pp. 7-23.

Boelhower, William. *Immigrant Autobiography in the United States: Five Versions of the Italian American Experience*. 1982. Bordighera, 2021.

Boelhower, William. *Through a Glass Darkly: Ethnic Semiosis in American Literature*. Oxford University Press, 1987.

Bolaki, Stella. "'New Living the Old in a New Way': Home and Queer Migrations in Audre Lorde's *Zami*." *Textual Practice*, vol. 25, no. 4, Aug. 2011, pp. 779-98.

Bona, Mary Jo. *By the Breath of Their Mouths: Narratives of Resistance in Italian America*. State University of New York Press, 2010.

Bona, Mary Jo. "Queer Daughters and Their Mothers: Maso, Cappello and Bechdel Write Their Way Home." *La Mamma: Interrogating a National Stereotype*, edited by Penelope Morris and Perry Willson, Palgrave Macmillan, 2018, pp. 185-214.

Bona, Mary Jo. "Whites Only: Race and Mobility in Kym Ragusa's *The Skin Between Us: A Memoir of Race, Beauty, and Belonging* and Claudia Rankine's *Citizen: An American Lyric*." *Italian American Review*, vol. 13, no. 1, 2023, pp. 31–53.

Bona, Mary Jo. *Women Writing Cloth: Migratory Fictions in the American Imaginary*. Lexington Books, 2016.

Bouson, J. Brooks. *Quiet as Its Kept: Shame, Trauma, and Race in the Novels of Toni Morrison*. State University of New York Press, 2000.

Boynton, Andrew. "Remembering St. Vincent's." *New Yorker*, 16 May 2013, https://www.newyorker.com/culture-desk/remembering-st-vincents.

Bradway, Tyler and Elizabeth Freeman, editors. *Queer Kinship: Race, Sex, Belonging, Form*. Duke University Press, 2022.

Brah, Avtar. *Cartographies of Diaspora: Contesting Identities*. Routledge, 1996.

Braxton, Joanne M. "Ancestral Presence: The Outraged Mother Figure in Contemporary Afra-American Writing." *Wild Women in the Whirlwind: Afra-American Culture and the Contemporary Literary Renaissance*, edited by Joanne M. Braxton and Andrée Nicola McLaughlin, Rutgers University Press, 1990, pp. 299–315.

Bromberger, Brian. "Plague Years." *The Bay Area Reporter: Arts & Culture*, 3 Oct. 2018, https://www.ebar.com/arts&culture/books.

Brown, Gillian. "Getting in the Kitchen with Dinah: Domestic Politics in *Uncle Tom's Cabin*." *American Quarterly*, vol. 36, no. 4, Fall 1984, pp. 503–23.

Brown, Mary Elizabeth. "Religion." *The Italian American Experience: An Encyclopedia*, edited by Salvatore La Gumina, Frank J. Cavaioli, Salvatore Primeggia, and Joseph A. Vafacalli, Garland, 2000, pp. 538–42.

Bryant, Dorothy Calvetti. *A Day in San Francisco*. Ata Books, 1982.

Bryce-Laporte, Roy Simon. "Black Immigrants: The Experience of Invisibility and Inequality." *Journal of Black Studies*, vol. 3, no. 1, 1972, pp. 29–55.

Butler, Judith. "Imitation and Gender Insubordination." *Inside/Out: Lesbian Theories, Gay Theories*, edited by Diana Fuss, Routledge, 1991, pp. 13–31.

Butler, Kim D. "Defining Diaspora, Refining a Discourse." *Diaspora: A Journal of Transnational Studies*, vol. 10, no. 2, Fall 2001, pp. 189–219.

Butter, Michael. "Historiographic Metafiction." *The Encyclopedia of Twentieth-Century Fiction, Volume II American Fiction: A-Z*, edited by Patrick O'Donnell, David W. Madden, and Justus Nieland, Wiley-Blackwell, 2011, pp. 626–30.

Butterfield, Sherri-Ann. P. " 'We're Just Black': The Racial and Ethnic Identities of Second-Generation West Indians in New York." *Becoming New Yorkers: Ethnographies of the New Second Generation*," edited by Philip Kasinitz, John H. Mollenkopf, and Mary C. Waters, Russell Sage, 2004, pp. 288–312.

Byrd, Rudolph P., Johnnetta Betsch Cole, and Beverly Guy-Sheftall, editors. *I am Your Sister: Collected and Unpublished Writings of Audre Lorde*. Oxford University Press, 2009.

Camacho, Roseanne V. "Whites Playing in the Dark: Southern Conversation in Willa Cather's *Sapphira and the Slave Girl*." *Willa Cather's Southern Connections: New Essays on Cather and the South*, edited by Ann Romines, University Press of Virginia, 2000, pp. 65–74.

Carby, Hazel V. *Reconstructing Womanhood: The Emergence of the Afro-American Woman Novelist*. Oxford University Press, 1987.

Caruth, Cathy. "Introduction." *Psychoanalysis, Culture and Trauma, American Imago*, vol. 48, no. 1, Spring 1991, pp. 1–12.

Cather, Willa. *My Antonia*. Vintage, 2018.

Cather, Willa. "The Novel Démeublé." 1922. *Not Under Forty*, University of Nebraska Press, 1968. pp. 43–51.

Cather, Willa. *Sapphira and the Slave Girl*. Historical essay and explanatory notes by Ann Romines, textual essay and editing by Charles W. Mignon, Kari A. Ronning, and Frederick M. Link, University of Nebraska Press, 2009.

Cavarero, Adriana. *In Spite of Plato: A Feminist Rewriting of Ancient Philosophy*. Foreword by Rosi Braidotti, Polity, 1995.

Chicago, Judy. *Dinner Party*. Elizabeth A. Sackler Center for Feminist Art, Brooklyn Museum, 1974–79.

Chinosole. "Audre Lorde and Matrilineal Diaspora: 'Moving History beyond Nightmare into Structures for the Future . . .'" *Wild Women in the Whirlwind: Afra-American Culture and the Contemporary Literary Renaissance*, edited by Joanne M. Braxton and Andrée Nicola McLaughlin, Rutgers University Press, 1990, pp. 379–94.

Chodorow, Nancy. "Family Structure and Feminine Personality." *Woman Culture & Society*, edited by Michelle Zimbalist Rosaldo and Louise Lamphere, Stanford University Press, 1974, pp. 43–66.

Chodorow, Nancy. "Gender, Relation, and Difference in Psychoanalytic Perspective." *Feminist Social Thought: A Reader*, edited by Diana Tietjens Myers, Routledge, 1997, pp. 8–20.

Chodorow, Nancy. "Reflections on *The Reproduction of Mothering*—Twenty Years Later." *Studies in Gender and Sexuality*, vol. 1, no. 4, 2000, pp. 337–48.

Chodorow, Nancy. *The Reproduction of Mothering*. 1978. University of California Press, 1999.

Cisneros, Sandra. *Caramelo*. Knopf, 2002.

Cisneros, Sandra. *House on Mango Street*. McGraw-Hill, 2000.

"Citheronia regalis." Wikipedia. https://en.wikipedia.org/wiki/Citheroniaregalis.

Cixous, Hélène. "The Laugh of the Medusa." *Signs*, vol. 1, no. 4, Summer 1976, pp. 879–93.

Collins, Patricia Hill. *Black Feminist Thought: Knowledge, Consciousness, and the Politics of Empowerment*. 3rd edition, Routledge, 2022.

Collins, Patricia Hill. "The Meaning of Motherhood in Black Culture and Black Mother/Daughter Relationships." *SAGE*, vol. 4, no. 2, Fall 1987, pp. 3–11.

Collins, Patricia Hill. "Shifting the Center: Race, Class and Feminist Theorizing about Motherhood." *Maternal Theory: Essential Readings*, edited by Andrea O'Reilly, Demeter Press, 2007, pp. 45–65.
Conelli, Linnea. *Symbols of English Identity: The Country House and Representations of Maternity in Modern British Fiction*. 2020. State University of New York at Stony Brook, PhD dissertation.
Cooley, Nicole. "Carole Maso: An Interview." *The American Poetry Review*, vol. 24, no. 2, March/April 1995, pp. 32–35.
Crane, Stephen. *The Red Badge of Courage*. Edited by Donald Pizer. 3rd edition, W. W. Norton, 1994.
Cvetkovich, Ann. *An Archive of Feelings: Trauma, Sexuality, and Lesbian Public Cultures*. Duke University Press, 2003.
Czerwiec, MK. *Taking Turns: Stories from HIV/AIDS Care Unit 371*. Pennsylvania State University Press, 2017.
Dalleo, Raphael. "How Cristina Garcia Lost Her Accent, And Other Latina Conversations." *Latino Studies*, vol. 3, no. 1, 2005, pp. 3–18.
Darling, Marsha Jean. "In the Realm of Responsibility: A Conversation with Toni Morrison by Marsha Jean Darling." *Women's Review of Books*, vol. 5, no. 6, Mar. 1988, pp. 246–54.
Davies, Carole Boyce. *Black Women, Writing, and Identity: Migrations of the Subject*. Routledge, 1994.
Davis, Rocio. "Back to the Future: Mothers, Languages and Homes in Cristina García's *Dreaming in Cuban*." *World Literature Today*, vol. 74, no. 1, Winter 2000, pp. 60–68.
de Beauvoir, Simone. *The Second Sex*. 1949. Translated by Constance Borde and Sheila Malovany-Chevallier, Vintage Books, 2010.
DeGuzmán, María. *Spain's Long Shadow: The Black Legend, Off-Whiteness, and Anglo-American Empire*. University of Minnesota Press, 2005.
Deleuze, Gilles and Félix Guattari. *A Thousand Plateaus: Capitalism and Schizophrenia*. Translated by Brian Massumi, University of Minnesota Press, 1987.
De Rosa, Tina. *Paper Fish*. Feminist, 1996.
DeSalvo, Louise. "Color: White/Complexion: Dark." *Are Italians White? How Race Is Made in America*, edited by Jennifer Guglielmo and Salvatore Salerno, Routledge, 2003, pp. 17–28.
DeSalvo, Louise. *Crazy in the Kitchen: Food, Feuds, and Forgiveness in an Italian American Family*. Bloomsbury, 2004.
DeVeaux, Alexis. *Warrior Poet: A Biography of Audre Lorde*. W. W. Norton, 2004.
Di Prima, Diane. *Recollections of My Life as a Woman: The New York Years*. Viking, 2001.
Douglass, Frederick. *Narrative of the Life of Frederick Douglass, An American Slave*. 1845. Edited by William L. Andrews and William S. McFeely, W. W. Norton, 1997.

Doyle, Laura A. *Bordering on the Body: The Racial Matrix of Modern Fiction and Culture*, Oxford University Press, 1994, pp. 206–30.

Doyle, Nora. *Maternal Bodies: Redefining Motherhood in Early America*. University of North Carolina Press, 2018.

Driver, Susan. "Between Theories and Life-Writings: Feminist Daughters Communicating Desires across Generational Differences." *Women's Studies*, vol. 35, no. 4, Aug. 2006, pp. 347–74.

Driver, Susan. "Reading Adrienne Rich's *Of Woman Born* as a Queer Feminist Daughter." *Journal of the Association for Research on Mothering*," vol. 8, no. 1.2, 2006, pp. 109–22.

Duany, Jorge. "Cuban Communities in the United States: Migration Waves, Settlement Patterns and Socioeconomic Diversity." *Pouvoir dans la Caraïbe*, Nov. 1999, pp. 69–103, https://doi.org/10.4000/plc.464.

Duany, Jorge. "Neither Golden Exile nor Dirty Worm: Ethnic Identity in Recent Cuban-American Novels." *Cuban Studies*, vol. 23, 1993, pp. 167–83.

Duberman, Martin. *Stonewall: The Definitive Story of the LGBTQ Rights Uprising That Changed America*. 1993. Revised edition, Plume, 2019.

Du Bois, W. E. B. *Black Reconstruction in America*. 1935. Atheneum, 1992.

DuPlessis, Rachel Blau. *Writing beyond the Ending: Narrative Strategies of Twentieth-Century Women Writers*. Indiana University Press, 1985.

Edelmen, Lee. *No Future: Queer Theory and the Death Drive*. Duke University Press, 2004.

Erdrich, Louise. *Love Medicine*. 1984. New and expanded version. Harper Perennial, 1993.

Erickson, Amy Louise. "Possession—and the other one-tenth of the Law: Assessing Women's Ownership and Economic Roles in Early Modern England." *Women's History Review*, vol. 16, no. 3, July 2007, pp. 369–85.

Evans, Stephanie Y. *Black Women's Yoga History*. State University of New York Press, 2021.

Faderman, Lillian. *The Gay Revolution: The Story of Struggle*. Simon & Schuster, 2015.

Faderman, Lillian. *Odd Girls and Twilight Lovers: A History of Lesbian Life in Twentieth-Century America*. Penguin, 1991.

Farwell, Marilyn. *Heterosexual Plots and Lesbian Narratives*. New York University Press, 1996.

"Federico García Lorca." *Poetry Foundation*, 2022, https://www.poetryfoundation.org/search?query=Federico+Garc%C3%ADa+Lorca.

Felman, Shoshana and Dori Laub, MD. *Testimony: Crises of Witnessing in Literature, Psychoanalysis, and History*. Routledge, 1992.

Felski, Rita. "On Confession." *Women, Autobiography, Theory: A Reader*, edited by Sidonie Smith and Julia Watson, University of Wisconsin Press, 1998, pp. 83–95.

Ferraro, Evelyn. "Southern Encounters in the City: Reconfiguring the South from the Liminal Space." *Small Towns, Big Cities: The Urban Experience of Italian Americans*, edited by Dennis Barone and Stefano Luconi, American Italian Historical Association, 2010, pp. 219–27.

Ferrer, Ada. *Freedom's Mirror: Cuba and Haiti in the Age of Revolution*. University of North Carolina Press, 2014.

Fine, Ellen S. "Transmission of Memory: The Post-Holocaust Generation in the Diaspora." *Breaking Crystal*, edited by Efraim Sicher, University of Illinois Press, 1998, pp. 185–200.

Fiore, Teresa. *Preoccupied Spaces: Remapping Italy's Transnational Migrations and Colonial Legacies*. Fordham University Press, 2017.

Foner, Eric. *Reconstruction: America's Unfinished Revolution: 1863–1877*. Harper & Row, 1988.

Foner, Nancy. "Introduction: New Immigrants in a New New York." *New Immigrants in New York*, edited by Nancy Foner, Columbia University Press, 2001, pp. 1–32.

Foreman, Gabrielle P. *Activist Sentiments: Reading Black Women in the Nineteenth Century*. University of Illinois Press, 2009.

Fortier, Anne-Marie. "'Coming Home': Queer Migrations and Multiple Evocations of Home." *European Journal of Cultural Studies*, vol. 4, no. 4, Nov. 2001, pp. 405–24.

Foster, Frances Smith. *Written by Herself: Literary Production by African American Women, 1746–1892*. Indiana University Press, 1993.

Frank, Arthur W. *The Wounded Storyteller: Body, Illness and Ethics*. 2nd edition, University of Chicago Press, 2013.

Franks, Matt. "Mrs. Ramsay's Queer Generationality." *Virginia Woolf Miscellany*, vol. 82, Fall 2012, pp. 15–17.

Freeman, Elizabeth. "Queer Belongings: Kinship Theory and Queer Theory." *A Companion to Lesbian, Gay, Bisexual, Transgender, and Queer Studies*, edited by George E. Haggerty and Molly McGarry, Blackwell, 2007, pp. 295–314.

Freeman, Elizabeth. *Time Binds: Queer Temporalities, Queer Histories*. Duke University Press, 2010.

Fullerton, Romayne Smith and M. J. Patterson. "Procrustean Motherhood: The Good Mother during Depression (1930s), War (1940s) and Prosperity (1950s)." *The Canadian Journal of Media Studies*, vol. 8, Dec. 2010, pp. 1–30.

Gabaccia, Donna. "Race, Nation, Hyphen: Italian–Americans and American Multiculturalism in a Comparative Perspective." *Are Italians White? How Race Is Made in America*, edited by Jennifer Guglielmo and Salvatore Salerno, Routledge, 2003, pp. 44–59.

Gallop, Jane. *The Daughter's Seduction: Feminism and Psychoanalysis*. Macmillan, 1982.

García, Cristina. *Dreaming in Cuban: A Novel*. Ballantine Books, 1992.

García, Cristina. *Vanishing Maps: A Novel*. Alfred A. Knopf, 2023.
Gardaphé, Fred. "Introduction: Invisible People: Shadows and Light in Italian American Culture." *Anti-Italianism: Essays on a Prejudice*, edited by William J. Connell and Fred Gardaphé, Palgrave MacMillan, 2010, pp. 1–10.
"Gary Falk Papers, circa 1955–2013: Biographical Note." American Smithsonian Archives of American Art, https://www.aaa.si.edu/collections/gary-falk-papers-11157/biographical-note.
Gates, Henry Louis, Jr. *The Signifying Monkey: A Theory of African-American Literary Criticism*. Oxford University Press, 1988.
Gay, Roxane, editor. *The Selected Works of Audre Lorde*. W. W. Norton, 2020.
Gedalof, Irene. "Birth, Belonging, and Migrant Mothers: Narratives of Reproduction in Feminist Migration Studies." *Feminist Review*, vol. 93, Nov. 2009, pp. 81–100.
Giddings, Paula. *Where and When I Enter: The Impact of Black Women on Race and Sex in America*. Bantam Books, 1985.
Gieseking, Jen Jack. *A Queer New York: Geographies of Lesbians, Dykes, and Queers*. New York University Press, 2020.
Gilbert, Sandra. *Death's Door: Modern Dying and the Ways We Grieve*. W. W. Norton, 2006.
Giorgio, Adalgisa, Anastasia Christou, and Gill Rye. "Mothering and Migration: Interdisciplinary Dialogues, European Perspectives, and International Contexts." *Women's Studies International Forum*, vol. 52, Sept. 2015, pp. 49–52.
Giunta, Edvige. "Persephone's Daughters." *Women's Studies*, vol. 33, no. 6, 2004, pp. 767–86.
Guinta, Edvige and Joseph Sciorra, editors. *Embroidered Stories: Interpreting Women's Domestic Needlework from the Italian Diaspora*. University Press of Mississippi, 2014.
Gleason, William. "'I Dwell Now in a Neat, Little Cottage': Architecture, Race, and Desire in *The Bondswoman's Narrative*." *In Search of Hannah Crafts: Critical Essays on The Bondwoman's Narrative*, edited by Henry Louis Gates and Hollis Robbins, Perseus, 2004, pp. 145–74.
Glenn, Evelyn Nakano, Grace Chang, and Linda Rennie Forcey, editors. *Mothering: Ideology, Experience, and Agency*. Routledge, 1994.
Goeller, Alison D. "Persephone Goes Home: Italian American Women in Italy." *MELUS*, vol. 28, no. 3, Sept. 2003, pp. 73–90.
Gomez-Vega, Ibis. "Metaphors of Entrapment: Caribbean Women Writers Face the Wreckage of History." *Journal of Political and Military Sociology*, vol. 25, no. 2, Winter 1997, pp. 231–47.
Gordon, Avery F. *Ghostly Matters: Haunting and the Sociological Imagination*. University of Minnesota Press, 1997.
Grahn, Judy. *Another Mother Tongue: Gay Words, Gay Worlds*. Beacon, 1990.
Grames, Juliet. *The Seven or Eight Deaths of Stella Fortuna*. Ecco, 2019.

Green-Barteet, Miranda A. "'The Loophole of Retreat': Interstitial Spaces in Harriet Jacobs's *Incidents in the Life of a Slave Girl.*" *South Central Review*, vol. 30, no. 2, Summer 2013, pp. 53–72.

Grimm, Jacob and Wilhelm Grimm. *The Grimms' German Folk Tales*. Translated by Francis P. Magoun and Alexander H. Krappe, Southern Illinois University Press, 1960.

Grosz, Elizabeth. *Space, Time, and Perversion: Essays on the Politics of Bodies*. Routledge, 1996.

Guglielmo, Jennifer and Salvatore Salerno, editors. *Are Italians White? How Race Is Made in America*. Routledge, 2003.

Guglielmo, Thomas. "'No Color Barrier': Italians, Race, and Power in the United States." *Are Italians White? How Race Is Made in America*, edited by Jennifer Guglielmo and Salvatore Salerno, Routledge, 2003, pp. 29–43.

Gumbs, Alexis Pauline. *Survival Is a Promise: The Eternal Life of Audre Lorde*. Macmillan, 2024.

Guy-Sheftall, Beverly. *Daughters of Sorrow: Attitudes toward Black Women, 1880-1920*. Carlson, 1990.

Gwin, Minrose. *The Woman in the Red Dress: Gender, Space, and Reading*. University of Illinois Press, 2002.

Hackett, Joyce. "An Interview with Carole Maso." *Poets & Writers Magazine*, vol. 24, no. 3, May/June 1996, pp. 64–73.

Haizlip, Shirlee Taylor. *The Sweeter the Juice: A Family Memoir in Black and White*. Touchstone Books, 1994.

Halberstam, Judith [Jack]. *Female Masculinity*. Duke University Press, 1998.

Halperin, Laura. "Still Hands: Celia's Transgression in Cristina García's *Dreaming in Cuban*. *Latino Studies*, vol. 6, no. 2, 2008, pp. 418–35.

Harris, Charles B. "The Dead Fathers: The Rejection of Modernist Distance in *The Art Lover*." *Review of Contemporary Fiction*, vol. 17, no. 3, Fall 1997, pp. 157–74.

Harris, Middleton A., Morris Levitt, Roger Furman, and Ernest Smith, editors. *The Black Book*, foreword by Toni Morrison, 35th anniversary edition, Random House, 2009.

Harris, Victoria Frenkel. "Carole Maso: An Introduction and an Interpellated Interview." *Review of Contemporary Fiction*, vol. 17, no. 3, Fall 1997, pp. 105–11.

Hartman, Saidiya V. *Scenes of Subjection: Terror, Slavery and Self-Making in Nineteenth-Century America*. Oxford University Press, 1997.

Hawthorne, Nathaniel. *The Scarlet Letter*. Edited by Seymour Gross, Sculley Bradley, Richard Croom Beatty, and E. Hudson Long, 3rd edition, W. W. Norton, 1988.

Herrera, Andrea O'Reilly. "Women and the Revolution in Cristina García's *Dreaming in Cuban*. *Modern Language Studies*, vol. 27, nos. 3-4, Autumn–Winter 1997, pp. 69–91.

Herrera, Cristina. *Contemporary Chicana Literature: (Re)Writing the Maternal Script*. Cambria Press, 2014.

Higham, John. *Strangers in the Land: Patterns of American Nativism, 1860–1925*. 1955. Rutgers University Press, 2004.

Hirsch, Marianne. *The Generation of Postmemory: Writing and Visual Culture after the Holocaust*. Columbia University Press, 2012.

Hirsch, Marianne. *The Mother/Daughter Plot: Narrative, Psychoanalysis, Feminism*. Indiana University Press, 1989.

Hirsch, Marianne. "Mothers and Daughters." *Signs: Journal of Women in Culture and Society*, vol. 7, no. 1, 1981, pp. 200–22.

Holladay, Hilary. *The Power of Adrienne Rich: A Biography*. Nan A. Talese/Doubleday, 2020.

Holland, Sharon B. "To Touch the Mother's C(o)untry: Siting Audre Lorde's Erotics." *Lesbian Erotics*, edited by Karla Jay, New York University Press, 1995, pp. 212–26.

Horvitz, Deborah. "Nameless Ghosts: Possession and Dispossession in *Beloved*." *Studies in American Fiction*, vol. 17, no. 2, Autumn 1989, pp. 157–67.

Hurston, Zora Neale. *Their Eyes Were Watching God*. 1937. Harper, 1990.

Hutcheon, Linda. *A Poetics of Postmodernism: History, Theory, Fiction*. Routledge, 1988.

Hutcheon, Linda. *The Politics of Postmodernism*. Routledge, 1989.

Ifekwunigwe Jayne O., editor. *"Mixed-Race" Studies: A Reader*. Routledge, 2004.

Inscoe, John C. "Willa Cather's *Sapphira and the Slave Girl* in Appalachian Context: A Review Essay." *Appalachian Journal*, Fall 2011/Winter 2012, pp. 126–35.

Irigaray, Luce. "And the One Doesn't Stir without the Other." *Signs: Journal of Women in Culture and Society*, vol. 7, no. 1, Autumn 1981, pp. 60–67.

Irigaray, Luce. "This Sex Which Is Not One." *This Sex Which Is Not One*, translated by Catherine Porter with Catherine Burke, Cornell University Press, 1985, pp. 23–33.

Irigaray, Luce. "When Our Lips Speak Together." *This Sex Which Is Not One*, translated by Catherine Porter with Catherine Burke, Cornell University Press, 1985, pp. 205–18.

Jacobs, Harriet A. *Incidents in the Life of a Slave Girl: Written by Herself*. Edited by Jean Fagan Yellin, Harvard University Press, 1987.

Jacobs, Harriet A. *Incidents in the Life of a Slave Girl: Written by Herself*. Edited by Nellie McKay and Frances Smith Foster, 1st edition, W. W. Norton, 2001.

Jacobs, Harriet A. *Incidents in the Life of a Slave Girl: Written by Herself*. Edited by Jean Fagan Yellin, enlarged edition, Harvard University Press, 2009.

Jacobs, Harriet A. *Incidents in the Life of a Slave Girl: Written by Herself*. Edited by Frances Smith Foster and Richard Yarborough, 2nd edition, W. W. Norton, 2019, pp. 341–50.

Jacobson, Matthew Frye. *Whiteness of a Different Color: European Immigrants and the Alchemy of Race*. Harvard University Press, 1998.

Jackson, Kenneth T., editor. *The Encyclopedia of New York City*, 2nd edition, Yale University Press, 2010.

Jennings, La Vinia Delois, editor. *Margaret Garner: The Premier Performances of Toni Morrison's Libretto*. University of Virginia Press, 2016.

Jewett, Sarah Orne. *The Country of the Pointed Firs and Other Stories*. W. W. Norton, 1994.

Johnson, Eastman. *Old Kentucky Home—Life in the South*. 1859. New-York Historical Society.

Jones-Rogers, Stephanie E. *They Were Her Property: White Women as Slave Owners in the American South*. Yale University Press, 2019.

Jordan, June. "The Difficult Miracle of Black Poetry in America or Something like a Sonnet for Phillis Wheatley." *Wild Women in the Whirlwind: Afra-American Culture and the Contemporary Literary Renaissance*, edited by Joanne M. Braxton and Andrée Nicola McLaughlin, Rutgers University Press, 1990, pp. 22–34.

Kanzler, Katja. "*From* 'To Tell the Kitchen Version': Architectural Figurations of Race and Gender in Harriet Jacobs's *Incidents in the Life of a Slave Girl.*" *Incidents in the Life of a Slave Girl: Written by Herself*. Edited by Frances Smith Foster and Richard Yarborough, 2nd edition, W. W. Norton, 2019, pp. 341–50.

Kaplan, Caren. "Resisting Autobiography: Outlaw Genres and Transnational Feminist Subjects." *Decolonizing the Subject: The Politics of Gender in Women's Autobiography*, edited by Sidonie Smith and Julia Watson, University of Minnesota Press, 1988, pp. 115–38.

Kasinitz, Philip. "From Ghetto Elite to Service Sector: A Comparison of the Role of Two Waves of West Indian Immigrants in New York City." *Ethnic Groups*, vol. 7, 1988, pp. 173–203.

Kawash, Samira. "New Directions in Motherhood Studies." *Signs: Journal of Women in Culture and Society*, vol. 36, no. 4, Summer 2011, pp. 969–1003.

Keating, AnaLouise. "Making 'Our Shattered Faces Whole': The Black Goddess and Audre Lorde's Revision of Patriarchal Myth." *Frontiers: A Journal of Women's Studies*, vol. 13, no. 1, 1992, pp. 20–33.

Kennedy, V. Lynn. *Born Southern: Childbirth, Motherhood, and Social Networks*. Johns Hopkins University Press, 2010.

King, Katie. "Audre Lorde's Lacquered Layerings: The Lesbian Bar as a Site of Literary Production." *Cultural Studies*, vol. 2, no. 3, Oct. 1988, pp. 321–42.

Kingston, Maxine Hong. *The Woman Warrior: Memoirs of a Girlhood among Ghosts*. Vintage International, 1989.

Krieger, Georgia. "Playing Dead: Harriet Jacobs's Survival Strategy in *Incidents in the Life of a Slave Girl*." *African American Review*, vol. 42, nos. 3–4, Fall–Winter, 2008, pp. 607–21.

Laub, Dori. "Bearing Witness, or the Vicissitudes of Listening." *Testimony: Crises of Witnessing in Literature, Psychoanalysis and History*, by Shoshana Felman and Dori Laub, MD, Routledge, 1992, pp. 57–74.

Lauter, Paul. *Canons and Contexts*. Oxford University Press, 1991.

Lerner, Gerda, editor. *Black Women in White America: A Documentary History*. Vintage, 1972.

Lewis, Nghana. "We Shall Pave the Way: Willa Cather and Lillian Smith's Aesthetics of Civil Rights Politics." *The Arizona Quarterly*, vol. 60, no. 4, Winter 2004, pp. 33–64.

Li, Stephanie. "Becoming her Mother's Mother: Recreating Home and Self in Audre Lorde's *Zami: A New Spelling of My Name*." *Reclaiming Home, Remembering Motherhood, Rewriting History: African American and Afro-Caribbean Women's Literature in the Twentieth Century*, edited by Verena Theile and Marie Drews, Cambridge Scholars, 2009, pp. 139–63.

Li, Stephanie. "Motherhood as Resistance in Harriet Jacobs's *Incidents in the Life of a Slave Girl*." *Legacy: A Journal of American Women Writers*, vol. 23, no. 1, 2006, pp. 14–29.

Liscio, Lorraine. "*Beloved's* Narrative: Writing Mother's Milk." *Tulsa Studies in Women's Literature*, vol. 11, no. 1, Spring 1992, pp. 31–46.

A Litany for Survival: The Life and Work of Audre Lorde. Directed by Ada Gay Griffin and Michelle Parkerson. Third World Newsreel, 1995.

Lloyd, Susan Caperna. *No Pictures in My Grave: A Spiritual Journey in Sicily*. Mercury House, 1992.

Lombardi-Diop, Cristina. "Transoceanic Race: A Postcolonial Approach to Italian American Studies." *Transcending Borders, Bridging Gaps: Italian Americana, Diasporic Studies, and the University Curriculum*, edited by Anthony Julian Tamburri and Fred L. Gardaphé, John D. Calandra Italian American Institute, 2015, pp. 83–95.

López, Iraida H. "'And There Is Only My Imagination Where Our History Should Be': An Interview with Cristina Garcia." *Michigan Quarterly Review*, vol. 33, no. 3, Summer 1994, pp. 604–17.

López, Iraida H. *Impossible Returns: Narratives of the Cuban Diaspora*. University Press of Florida, 2015.

Lorde, Audre. *The Black Unicorn: Poems*. W. W. Norton, 1978.

Lorde, Audre. "An Interview: Audre Lorde and Adrienne Rich." *Sister Outsider: Essays and Speeches*, Crossing, 1984, pp. 81–109.

Lorde, Audre. "Poetry Is Not a Luxury." *Sister Outsider: Essays and Speeches*, Crossing, 1984, pp. 36–9.

Lorde, Audre. "Uses of the Erotic: The Erotic as Power." *Sister Outsider: Essays and Speeches*, Crossing, 2007, pp. 53–59.

Lorde, Audre. *Zami: A New Spelling of My Name, A Biomythography*. Crossing, 1982.

Loung, Ung. *First They Killed My Father*. HarperCollins, 2000.
Love, Heather. "Spoiled Identity: Stephen's Gordon's Loneliness and the Difficulties of Queer History." *GQL: A Journal of Lesbian and Gay Studies*, vol. 7, no. 4, Nov. 2001, pp. 487–519.
Luconi, Stefano. "Frank L. Rizzo and the Whiteness of Italian Americans." *Are Italians White? How Race Is Made in America*, edited by Jennifer Guglielmo and Salvatore Salerno, Routledge, 2003, pp. 177–91.
Maillard, Mary, editor. *Whispers of Cruel Wrongs: The Correspondence of Louisa Jacobs and Her Circle, 1879–1911*. University of Wisconsin Press, 2017.
Makkai, Rebecca. *The Great Believers*. Viking, 2018.
Makkai, Rebecca. "Other Types of Poison: Three Legends." *Harper's Magazine*, July 2013, https://harpers.org/archive/2013/07/other-types-of-poison/.
Makkai, Rebecca. "Rebecca Makkai: 2019 National Book Festival." Interview by Emily Eakin, *Library of Congress National Book Festival*, 6 Nov. 2019, https://www.loc.gov/events/2019-national-book-festival/schedule/item/webcast-8885/.
Makkai, Rebecca. "Rebecca Makkai on 'The Great Believers.'" Interview by Rich Fahle. *AWP Book Fair*, 1 Apr. 2019, https://www.youtube.com/watch?v=nYs98qZRd8c.
Marcus, Lisa. "'The Pull of Race and Blood and Kindred': Willa Cather's Southern Inheritance." *Willa Cather's Southern Connections: New Essays on Cather and the South*, edited by Ann Romines, University Press of Virginia, 2000, pp. 98–119.
Margaret Garner: An Opera in Two Acts. Composed by Richard Danielpour, libretto by Toni Morrison. 16 Sept. 2007, New York City Opera, NYC.
Marshall, Paule. *Brown Girl, Brownstones*. Feminist, 1981.
Maso, Carole. *The American Woman in the Chinese Hat*. Dalkey Archive Press, 1994.
Maso, Carole. *The Art Lover*. Ecco, 1990.
Maso, Carole. *AVA*. Dalkey Archive Press, 2002.
Maso, Carole. *Break Every Rule: Essays on Language, Longing, and Moments of Desire*. Counterpoint, 2000.
Maucione, Jessica. *Post-Neighborhood: Returning to Little Italy in American Narratives of the Globalization Age*. 2008. Washington State University, PhD dissertation.
McAuliffe, Samantha L. "Autoethnography and García's *Dreaming in Cuban*." *Comparative Literature and Culture*, vol. 13, no. 4, Dec. 2011, pp. 1–9.
McCormack, Leah. "Reclaiming Silenced & Erased Histories: The Paratextual Devices of Historiographic Metafiction." *Making Connections*, vol. 14, no. 2, Fall 2013, pp. 37–54.
McCracken, Ellen. *New Latina Narrative: The Feminine Space of Postmodern Ethnicity*. The University of Arizona Press, 1999.

McEntee, Grace. "The Ethos of Motherhood and Harriet Jacobs' Vision of Racial Equality in *Incidents in the Life of a Slave Girl*." *The Literary Mother: Essays on Representations of Maternity and Child Care*, edited by Susan C. Staub, McFarland, 2007, pp. 200–23.

McHale, Brian. *Postmodernist Fiction*. Routledge, 1987.

McKay, Nellie Y. "The Girls Who Become the Women: Childhood Memories in the Autobiographies of Harriet Jacobs, Mary Church Terrell, and Anne Moody." *Tradition and the Talents of Women*, edited by Florence Howe, University of Illinois Press, 1991, pp. 106–24. Reprinted in *Incidents in the Life of a Slave Girl*, edited by Nellie Y. McKay and Frances Smith Foster, W. W. Norton, 2001, pp. 236–53.

McKay, Nellie Y. "An Interview with Toni Morrison." *Contemporary Literature*, vol. 24, no. 4, Winter 1983, pp. 413–29.

McKay, Nellie Y. "The Narrative Self: Race, Politics, and Culture in Black American Women's Autobiography." *Women, Autobiography, Theory: A Reader*, edited by Sidonie Smith and Julia Watson, University of Wisconsin Press, 1998, pp. 96–107.

McKemmish, Sue. "Evidence of Me." *Australian Library Journal*, vol. 45, no. 3, Aug. 1996, pp. 174–87.

McKenzie, Marilyn Mobley. "'The Dangerous Journey': Toni Morrison's Reading of *Sapphira and the Slave Girl*." *Willa Cather's Southern Connections: New Essays on Cather and the South*, edited by Ann Romines, University Press of Virginia, 2000, pp. 83–89.

McKittrick, Katherine. *Demonic Grounds: Black Women and the Cartographies of Struggle*. University of Minnesota Press, 2006.

Mitchell, Angelyn. *The Freedom to Remember: Narrative, Slavery, and Gender in Contemporary Black Women's Fiction*. Rutgers University Press, 2002.

Mitchell, Juliet. *Psychoanalysis and Feminism: A Radical Reassessment of Freudian Psychoanalysis*. Basic Books, 2000.

Model, Suzanne. "Caribbean Immigrants: A Black Success Story?" *International Migration Review*, vol. 25, 1991, pp. 248–76.

Morgenstern, Naomi. "'Love Is Home-sickness': Nostalgia and Lesbian Desire in *Sapphira and the Slave Girl*." *Novel: A Forum on Fiction*, vol. 29, no. 2, Winter 1996, pp. 184–205.

Morris, Penelope and Perry Willson. "Motherhood in Post-1968 European Literature Network." *La Mamma Italiana: Interrogating a National Stereotype*, http://lamammaitaliana.wordpress.com/.

Morrison, Toni. *Beloved*. Alfred A. Knopf, 1987.

Morrison, Toni. "It Is Like Growing Up Black One More Time." *The New York Times*, 11 Aug. 1974, pp. 14–24.

Morrison, Toni. *Playing in the Dark: Whiteness and the Literary Imagination*. Harvard University Press, 1992.

Morrison, Toni. "Unspeakable Things Unspoken: The Afro-American Presence in American Literature." *Modern Critical Views: Toni Morrison*, edited with an introduction by Harold Bloom, Chelsea House, 1990, pp. 201-30.
Moyers, Bill. "A Conversation with Toni Morrison." *Conversations with Toni Morrison*, edited by Danille Taylor-Guthrie, University of Mississippi Press, 1994, pp. 262-74.
Muñoz, José Esteban. "Queerness as Horizon: Utopian Hermeneutics in the Face of Gay Pragmatism." *A Companion to Lesbian, Gay, Bisexual, Transgender, and Queer Studies*, edited by George E. Haggerty and Molly McGarry, Blackwell, 2007, pp. 452-63.
Murphy, Timothy F. "Testimony." *Writing AIDS: Gay Literature, Language and Analysis*, edited by Timothy F. Murphy and Suzanne Poirier, Columbia University Press, 1993, pp. 306-20.
Murray, Tony. "Edna O'Brien and Narrative Diaspora Space." *Irish Studies Review*, vol. 21, no. 1, 2013, pp. 85-98.
Musser, Amber Jamilla. "Coda: Elsewhere, Is Mother a Place?" *Sensual Excess: Queer Femininity and Brown Jouissance*, New York University Press, 2018, pp. 167-79.
Nayak, Suryia. *Race, Gender and the Activism of Black Feminist Theory: Working with Audre Lorde*. Routledge, 2015.
Naylor, Gloria. "A Conversation: Gloria Naylor and Toni Morrison." *Conversations with Toni Morrison*, edited by Danille Taylor-Guthrie, University of Mississippi Press, 1994, pp. 188-217.
Naylor, Gloria. *Mama Day*. Vintage, 1988.
Nelson, Maggie. *The Argonauts*. Graywolf, 2015.
Nevius, Marcus. *City of Refuge: Slavery and Petit Marronage in the Great Dismal Swamp, 1763-1856*. University of Georgia Press, 2020.
O'Brien, Sharon. "Enter William Cather." *Willa Cather: The Emerging Voice*, by Sharon O'Brien, Oxford University Press, 1987, pp. 96-116.
O'Hearn Chiawei, Claudine. *Half and Half: Writers on Growing Up Biracial and Bicultural*. Pantheon, 1998.
O'Loughlin, Michael J. "The Catholic Hospital That Pioneered AIDS Care." *America: The Jesuit Review*, 24 Jan. 2020, https://www.americamagazine.org/faith/2020/01/24/catholic-hospital-pioneered-aids-care.
O'Reilly, Andrea, editor. *Encyclopedia of Motherhood*. Sage, 2010.
O'Reilly, Andrea, editor. *From Motherhood to Mothering: The Legacy of Adrienne Rich's "Of Woman Born."* State University of New York Press, 2004.
O'Reilly, Andrea, editor. *Maternal Theory: Essential Readings*. Demeter, 2008.
O'Reilly, Andrea. *Rocking the Cradle: Thoughts on Feminism, Motherhood, and the Possibility of Empowered Motherhood*. Demeter, 2006.
O'Reilly, Andrea. *Toni Morrison and Motherhood: A Politics of the Heart*. State University of New York Press, 2004.

O'Reilly, Andrea, editor. *Mother Outlaws: Theories and Practices of Empowered Mothering*. Women's, 2004.
Orsi, Robert. *The Madonna of 115th Street: Faith and Community in Italian Harlem, 1880–1950*. Yale University Press, 1985.
Orsi, Robert. "The Religious Boundaries of an Inbetween People: Street Feste and the Problem of the Dark-Skinned Other in Italian Harlem, 1920–1990." *American Quarterly*, vol. 44, no. 3, Sept. 1992, pp. 313–47.
Ortiz, Fernando. "The Human Factors of Cubanidad." Translated by João Felipe Gonçalves and Gregory Duff Morton. *HAU: Journal of Ethnographic Theory*, vol. 4, no. 3, 2014, pp. 445–80.
Pauls, Elizabeth Prine. "Couvade." *Britannica Online Encyclopedia*, 15 July 2008, https://www.britannica.com/topic/couvade.
Pearl, Monica B. "'Sweet Home': Audre Lorde's *Zami* and the Legacies of American Writing." *Journal of American Studies*, vol. 43, no. 2, Aug. 2009, pp. 297–317.
Perez, Luis A. *Cuba: Between Reform and Revolution*. 1988. Oxford University Press, 2015.
Perez, Luis A. *The Structure of Cuban History: Meanings and Purpose of the Past*. University of North Carolina Press, 2013.
Pettersson, Inger. "Telling It to the Dead: Borderless Communication and Scars of Trauma in Cristina Garcia's *Dreaming in Cuban*." *Journal of Literary Studies*, vol. 29, no. 2, July 2013, pp. 44–61.
Piatote, Beth H. *Domestic Subjects: Gender, Citizenship, and Law in Native American Literature*. Yale University Press, 2013.
Pinto, Samantha. *Difficult Diasporas: The Transnational Feminist Aesthetic of the Black Atlantic*. New York University Press, 2013.
Pitts, Andrea J. "Gloria E. Anzaldúa's Autohistoria-teoría as an Epistemology of Self-Knowledge/Ignorance," *Hypatia*, vol. 31, no. 2, Spring 2016, pp. 352–69.
Pitts, Terry. "'There Is So Much Pain in the World': Carole Maso's *The Art Lover*." *Vertigo: Where Literature and Art Intersect, with an Emphasis on W. G. Sebald and Literature with Embedded Photographs*," 22 March 2016, https://sebald.wordpress.com/2016/03/22/there-is-so-much-pain-in-the-world.
Pollard, Tomas. "Political Science and His'try in *Sapphira and the Slave Girl*." *Willa Cather's Southern Connections: New Essays on Cather and the South*, edited by Ann Romines, University of Virginia Press, 2000, pp. 38–53.
Pomeroy, Barry. *Historiographic Metafiction or Lying with the Truth*. Bear's Carvery, 2015.
Porter, David H. "Cather on Cather III: Dust Jacket Copy on Willa Cather's Books." *Willa Cather Newsletter and Review*, vol. 48, no. 3, Spring 2005, pp. 51–60.
Provost, Kara. "Becoming Afrekete: The Trickster in the Work of Audre Lorde." *MELUS*, vol. 20, no. 4, 1995, pp. 45–59.

Ragusa, Kym. Email to Mary Jo Bona. 5 Jan. 2023.
Ragusa, Kym. "On Vulnerability and Risk: Learning to Write and Teach Memoir as a Student of Louise DeSalvo." *Personal Effects: Essays on Memoir, Teaching, and Culture in the Work of Louise DeSalvo*, edited by Nancy Caronia and Edvige Giunta, Fordham University Press, 2015, pp. 105–10.
Ragusa, Kym. *Fuori/Outside: A Video*. 1997. Third World Newsreel, 1997. www.twn.org.
Ragusa, Kym. *Passing*. Short. 1996. Third World Newsreel. www.twn.org.
Ragusa, Kym. *La pelle che ci separa*. Trans. Clara Antonucci and Caterina Romeo. Nutrimenti, 2008.
Ragusa, Kym. *The Skin Between Us: A Memoir of Race, Beauty, and Belonging*. W. W. Norton, 2006.
Randle, Gloria T. "Between the Rock and the Hard Place: Mediating Spaces in Harriet Jacobs's *Incidents in the Life of a Slave Girl*." *African American Review*, vol. 33, no. 1, Spring 1999, pp. 43–56.
Rankine, Claudia. "Adrienne Rich's Poetic Transformations." *The New Yorker*, 12 May 2016, https://newyorker.com/books/gage-turner/adrienne-rich-poetic-transformations.
Raynaud, Claudine. "'A Nutmeg Covered inside Its Covering of Mace': Audre Lorde's *Zami*." *Life/Lines: Theorizing Women's Autobiography*, edited by Bella Brodzki and Celeste Schenck, Cornell University Press, 1988, pp. 221–42.
Reinhardt, Mark. *Who Speaks for Margaret Garner?* University of Minnesota Press, 2010.
Reyes, Angelita Dianne. *Mothering across Cultures: Postcolonial Representations*. University of Minnesota Press, 2002.
Rich, Adrienne. *Collected Poems: 1950–2012*. Introduction by Claudia Rankine, W. W. Norton, 2016.
Rich, Adrienne. *Of Woman Born: Motherhood as Experience and Institution*. 10th anniversary edition, Norton, 1986.
Richards, David A.J. *Italian American: The Racializing of an Ethnic Identity*. New York University Press, 1999.
Rigney, Barbara Hill. *The Voices of Toni Morrison*. Ohio State University Press, 1991.
Roediger, David. "Guineas, Wiggers, and the Dramas of Racialized Culture." *American Literary History*, vol. 7, no. 4, Winter 1995, pp. 654–68.
Roediger, David. *Working toward Whiteness: How America's Immigrants Became White: The Strange Journey from Ellis Island to the Suburbs*. E-book edition, Basic Books, 2005.
Romines, Ann. "Explanatory Notes." *Sapphira and the Slave Girl*, by Willa Cather, edited by Charles W. Mignon, Kari A. Ronning, and Frederick M. Link, University of Nebraska Press, 2009, pp. 405–542.

Romines, Ann. "Historical Essay." *Sapphira and the Slave Girl*, by Willa Cather, edited by Charles W. Mignon, Kari A. Ronning, and Frederick M. Link, University of Nebraska Press, 2009, pp. 297–404.

Romines, Ann. "Losing and Finding 'Race': Old Jezebel's African Story." *Cather Studies*, vol. 8, 2010, pp. 396–411.

Romines, Ann. "Willa Cather's Civil War: A Very Long Engagement." *Cather Studies: History, Memory, and War*, vol. 6, 2006, pp. 1–27.

Roof, Judith. *Come as You Are: Sexuality and Narrative*. Columbia University Press, 1996.

Rowell, Charles H. and Audre Lorde. "'Above the Wind:' An Interview with Audre Lorde." *Callaloo*, vol. 23, no. 1, Winter 2000, pp. 52–63.

Rubin, Jennifer. "Florida Might Pay for MAGA Cruelty and Know-Nothingism." *The Washington Post*, July 14, 2023.

Ruddick, Sara. *Maternal Thinking: Toward a Politics of Peace*. Beacon, 1989.

Russell, Heather. *Legba's Crossing: Narratology in the African Atlantic*. University of Georgia Press, 2009.

Salas, Angela M. "Willa Cather's *Sapphira and the Slave Girl*: Extending the Boundaries of the Body." *College Literature*, vol. 24, no. 2, June 1997, pp. 97–108, https://go.gale.com/ps/i.do?p=AONE&u=googlescholar&id=GALE%7CA20378696&v=2.1&it=r&sid=googleScholar&asid=30379f49.

Scarry, Elaine. *The Body in Pain: The Making and Unmaking of the World*. Oxford University Press, 1985.

Schneiderman, Dave. "(One Generation) beyond Good and Evil: A Conversation with Rebecca Makkai." *Harper's Magazine*, 20 June 2013, https://harpers.org/2013/06/one-generation-beyond-good-and-evil-a-conversation-with-rebecca-makkai.

Scholes, Robert. "Language, Narrative, and Anti-Narrative." *Critical Inquiry*, vol. 7, no. 1, Autumn 1980, pp. 204–12.

Scholes, Robert. *Protocols of Reading*. Yale University Press, 1989.

Schultermandl, Silvia. "The Great Unresolved Mystique: Mother-Daughter Relationships in Feminist Literary Theory." *Transnational Matrilineage: Mother-Daughter Conflicts in Asian-American Literature*, by Silvia Schultermandl, LIT Verlag, 2009, pp. 33–56.

Schwab, Gabriele. *Haunting Legacies: Violent Histories and Transgenerational Traumas*. Columbia University Press, 2010.

Sciorra, Joseph. "'We Go Where the Italians Live': Religious Processions and Ethnic and Territorial Markers in a Multi-Ethnic Brooklyn Neighborhood." *Gods of the City: Religion and the American Urban Landscape*, edited by Robert Orsi, Indiana University Press, 1999, pp. 310–40.

Sedgwick, Eve Kosovsky. "Paranoid Reading, Reparative Reading: or, You're So Paranoid You Probably Think This Introduction Is about You." *Novel Gazing: Queer Readings in Fiction*, Duke University Press, 1997, pp. 1–37, http://

read.dukeupress.edu/books/book/chapter-pdf/604965/9780822382478-001.pdf.

Sharpe, Jenny. *Ghosts of Slavery: A Literary Archaeology of Black Women's Lives.* University of Minnesota Press, 2003.

Silbergleid, Robin Paula. *Narratives of Loss, Loss of Narrative: Crises of Representation in Twentieth-Century Fiction.* 2001. Indiana University, PhD dissertation.

Silbergleid, Robin Paula. "'Treblinka: A Rather Musical Word': Carole Maso's Post Holocaust Narrative." *MFS: Modern Fiction Studies,* vol. 53, no. 1, Spring 2007, pp. 1–26.

Silver, Brenda. "Mothers, Daughters, Mrs. Ramsay: Reflections." *Women's Studies Quarterly,* vol. 37, no. 3/4, Fall–Winter 2009, pp. 259–74.

Skaggs, Merrill Maguire. "The Return of the Native: *Sapphira and the Slave Girl.*" *After the World Broke in Two: The Later Novels of Willa Cather,* University Press of Virginia, 1990, pp. 164–89.

Smith, Barbara. "The Truth That Never Hurts: Black Lesbians in Fiction in the 1980s." *Wild Women in the Whirlwind: Afra-American Culture and the Contemporary Literary Renaissance,* edited by Joanne M. Braxton and Andrée Nicola McLaughlin, Rutgers University Press, 1989, pp. 213–45.

Smith, Sarah Stefana. "Keeping Time: Maroon Assemblages and Black Life in Crisis." *The South Atlantic Quarterly,* vol. 121, no. 1, January 2022, pp. 11–32.

Smith, Sidonie and Julia Watson. *Reading Autobiography: A Guide for Interpreting Life Narratives.* 2nd edition, University of Minnesota Press, 2010.

Smith, Valerie. "'Loopholes of Retreat': Architecture and Ideology in Harriet Jacobs's *Incidents in the Life of a Slave Girl.*" *Reading Black, Reading Feminist: A Critical Anthology,* edited by Henry Louis Gates, Jr., Meridian/Penguin, 1990, pp. 212–26.

Snow White and the Seven Dwarfs. Directed by Ben Sharpsteen, Larry Morey, Wilfred Jackson, David Hand, William Cottress, and Perce Pearce, Walt Disney Studios, 1937.

Solheim, Jennifer. "Part of a Bigger Conversation: An Interview with Rebecca Makkai." *Fiction Writers Review,* 6 Sept. 2018, https://fictionwritersreview.com/interview/part-of-a-bigger-conversation-an-interview-with-rebecca-makkai/.

Sontag, Susan. *AIDS and Its Metaphors.* Farrar, Straus, and Giroux, 1988.

Sontag, Susan. *On Photography.* 1977. Picador, 2001.

Sorisio, Carolyn. *Fleshing Out America: Race, Gender and the Politics of the Body in American Literature, 1833–1879.* University of Georgia Press, 2002.

Spillers, Hortense J. "Changing the Letter: The Yokes, the Jokes of Discourse, or, Mrs. Stowe, Mr. Reed." *Slavery and the Literary Imagination,* edited by Deborah E. McDowell and Arnold Rampersad, Johns Hopkins University Press, 1989, pp. 25–61.

Spillers, Hortense J. "Mama's Baby: Papa's Maybe: An American Grammar Book." *Diacritics*, vol. 17, no. 2, Summer 1987, pp. 64–81.

Stavans, Ilan. "Familia Faces." *The Nation*, vol. 10, February 2003, pp. 30–34.

Stirling, Grant. "Mourning and Metafiction: Carole Maso's '*The Art Lover*.'" *Contemporary Literature*, vol. 39, no. 4, Winter 1998, pp. 586–613.

Story, Kaila Adia, editor. *Patricia Hill Collins: Reconceiving Motherhood*. Demeter, 2014.

Stout, Janis P. "The Observant Eye, the Art of Illustration, and Willa Cather's *My Antonia*." *Cather Studies*, edited by Susan Rosowski, vol. 5, University of Nebraska Press, 2003, pp. 128–52.

Taronna, Annarita. "Shaping Transcultural Ethnographies of Southernness: *The Skin Between Us: A Memoir of Race, Beauty, and Belonging* by Kym Ragusa." *Scritture Migrante*, vol. 5, 2011, pp. 105–25.

Tate, Claudia. *Domestic Allegories of Political Desire: The Black Heroine's Text at the Turn of the Century*. Oxford University Press, 1992.

Tate, Claudia. *Psychoanalysis and Black Novels: Desire and the Protocols of Race*. Oxford University Press, 1998.

Tate, Claudia, editor. *Black Women Writers at Work*. Continuum, 1983.

Tate, Julee. "Matrilineal and Political Divisions in Cristina García's *Dreaming in Cuban* and *The Agüero Sisters*." *Letras Femeninas*, vol. 32, no. 2, invierno 2006, pp. 145–63.

Taylor, Ashley Coleman. "Religio-erotic Experience and Transoceanic Becoming at the Shoreline in Audre Lorde's *Zami*." *Journal of the American Academy of Religion*, vol. 20, March 2024, pp. 1–18.

Taylor-Guthrie, Danille, editor. *Conversations with Toni Morrison*. University of Mississippi Press, 1994.

Tenzer, Livia. "Documenting Race and Gender: Kym Ragusa Discusses *Passing* and *Fuori/Outside*." *Women's Studies Quarterly*, vol. 30, no. 1/2, Spring/Summer 2002, pp. 213–20.

Tomasi, Mari. *Like Lesser Gods*. 1949. New England Press, 1988.

Turner, Kay. "The Virgin of the Sorrows Procession: A Brooklyn Inversion." *Folklore Papers of the University Folklore Association*, vol. 9, 1980, pp. 1–26.

van der Kolk, B.A. and Onno van der Hart. "The Intrusive Past: The Flexibility of Memory and the Engraving of Trauma." *American Imago*, vol. 48, no. 4, Winter 1991, pp. 425–54.

Vásquez, Mary S. "Cuba as Text and Context in Cristina Garcia's *Dreaming in Cuban*." *The Bilingual Review*, vol. 20, no. 1, January–April, 1995, pp. 22–27.

Vellucci, Sabrina. "The Topographies of Ethnicity in Kym Ragusa's *Passing, Fuori/Outside*, and *The Skin Between Us*." *Contemporary Women's Cinema, Global Scenarios and Transnational Contexts*, edited by Veronica Pravadelli, Mimesis International, 2017, pp. 189–203.

Verdicchio, Pasquale. *Bound by Distance: Rethinking Nationalism through the Italian Diaspora*. Fairleigh Dickinson University Press, 1998.
Verdicchio, Pasquale. Email to Mary Jo Bona. 18 July 2020.
Vickerman, Milton. "Tweaking a Monolith: The West Indian Immigrant Encounter with 'Blackness.'" *Islands in the City: West Indian Migration to New York*, edited by Nancy Foner, University of California Press, 2001, pp. 237–56.
Wald, Gayle. "Race, Labor, and Domesticity in *Sapphira and the Slave Girl*." *Willa Cather's Southern Connections*, edited by Ann Romines, University of Virginia Press, 2000, pp. 90–97.
Walters, Tracey L. *African American Literature and the Classicist Tradition: Black Women Writers from Wheatley to Morrison*. Palgrave, 2007.
Warner, Anne Bradford. "Harriet Jacobs at Home in *Incidents in the Life of a Slave Girl*." *Southern Quarterly*, vol. 45, no. 3, 2008, pp. 30–47.
Warner, Oswald. "Black in America, Too: Afro-Caribbean Immigrants." *Social and Economic Studies*, vol. 61, no. 4, Dec. 2012, pp. 69–103.
Waters, Mary C. *Black Identities: West Indian Immigrant Dreams and American Realities*. Harvard University Press and Russell Sage Foundation, 1999.
Waters, Mary C. "Ethnic and Racial Identities of Second-Generation Black Immigrants in New York City." *International Migration Review*, vol. 28, no. 4, Winter 1994, pp. 795–820.
Watkins-Owens, Irma. *Blood Relations: Caribbean Immigrants and the Harlem Community, 1900–1930*. Indiana University Press, 1996.
Watkins-Owens, Irma. "Early Twentieth-Century-Caribbean Women: Migration and Social Networks in New York City." *Islands in the City: West Indian Migration to New York*, edited by Nancy Foner, University of California Press, 2001, pp. 25–51.
Waugh, Patricia. *Metafiction: The Theory and Practice of Self-Conscious Fiction*. 1984. Routledge, 2001.
Weiner, Annette B. *Inalienable Possessions: The Paradox of Keeping-while-Giving*. University of California Press, 1992.
Weisenburger, Steven. *Modern Medea: A Family Story of Slavery and Child-Murder*. Hill & Wang, 1998.
Weisenburger, Steven. "My Journey from 'Beloved.'" *New York City Opera: Playbill*, September 2007, pp. 10–12, 14, 40.
Welter, Barbara. "The Cult of True Womanhood: 1820–1860." *American Quarterly*, vol. 18, no. 2, Summer 1966, pp. 151–74.
Welter, Barbara. *Dimity Convictions: The American Woman in the Nineteenth Century*. Ohio University Press, 1976.
Wennerholm, Zoe. "'It's Your Future, Don't Miss It': Nostalgia, Utopia and Desire in the New York Lesbian Bar." 2019. Senior Capstone Projects, https://digitalwindow.vassar.edu./senior_capstone/897.

Whitford, Margaret. *Luce Irigaray: Philosophy in the Feminine*. Routledge, 1991.
Williams, Albert. "The 1980s AIDS Epidemic in Chicago Revisited in Rebecca Makkai's New Novel, *The Great Believers*." *Arts & Culture*, 14 June 2018, https://www.chicagoreader.com/chicago/rebecca-makkai-great-believers-AIDS-crisis-1980s-boystown/Content?oid=50305576.
Wilson, Harriet E. *Our Nig: Sketches from the Life of a Free Black*. 1859. Vintage Books, 2011.
Winnicott, D. W. *On the Child*. Introduction by T. Barry Brazelton, MD, Stanley I. Greenspan, MD, and Benjamin Spock, MD, Perseus, 2002.
Wolff, Cynthia Griffin. "'Margaret Garner': A Cincinnati Story." *Massachusetts Review*, vol. 32, no. 3, Autumn 1991, pp. 417–40.
Wolff, Cynthia Griffin. "Time and Memory in *Sapphira and the Slave Girl*: Sex, Abuse, and Art," *Cather Studies*, vol. 3, 1996, pp. 212–37.
"Women and the Law." *Women, Enterprise & Society*, Harvard Business School, 2010, https://www.library.hbs.edu/hc/wes/collections/women_law/.
Wong, Sau-ling Cynthia. "Immigrant Autobiography: Some Questions of Definition and Approach." *Women, Autobiography, Theory: A Reader*, edited by Sidonie Smith and Julia Watson, University of Wisconsin Press, 1998, pp. 299–315.
Woolf, Virginia. *A Room of One's Own*. 1928. Penguin Books, 1963.
Woolf, Virginia. *To the Lighthouse*. 1927. Harcourt, Brace & World, 1955.
Wyatt, Jean. "Giving Body to the Word: The Maternal Symbolic in Toni Morrison's *Beloved*." *PMLA*, vol. 108, no. 3, May 1993, pp. 474–88.
Yaeger, Patricia. "White Dirt: The Surreal Racial Landscapes of Willa Cather's South." *Willa Cather's Southern Connections*, edited by Ann Romines, University of Virginia Press, 2000, pp. 138–57.
Yellin, Jean Fagan. *Harriet Jacobs: A Life*. Basic Civitas Books, 2004.
Yellin, Jean Fagan, Joseph M. Thomas, Kate Culkin, and Scott Korb, editors. *The Harriet Jacobs Family Papers*. University of North Carolina Press, 2008.
Young, James E. "The Holocaust as Vicarious Past: Restoring the Voices of Memory to History." *Judaism: A Quarterly Journal of Jewish Life and Thought*, vol. 51, no. 1, Winter 2002, pp. 71–87.

Index

abandonment, 3, 5, 10, 65, 66, 69
   in *Dreaming in Cuban*, 63–64,
     178n21
   mothers, 63, 67–68, 74, 76–77,
     177n17
   trafficking and, 113–14
Abbott, Traci B., 35, 166n5, 172n42
abduction, 4, 20, 66, 77, 144, 159n4
   of daughter, 10, 12, 19, 21, 68–74
   experience of, 5
   narratives of, 68–69
   as slavery, 24
abolition, 23, 24, 47, 53, 183n51
absent father, 101–2
ACT UP protest, 125, 195n17, 198n32
Afrekete, 94, 112, 117, 155–56,
   190n42
African American, 17, 96–97, 169n25,
   185n11, 188n30, 189n35
African Caribbean, 104, 105–6, 110,
   188n33
African mythological gods, 190n42
Ahmed, Sara, 125
AIDS, 3, 19, 118–19, 148, 195n18,
   198n34
   antinarrative techniques in response
     to, 197n26
   in *The Art Lover*, 123, 125–26, 142,
     145
   Chinosole on, 186n18

Czerwiec memoir on, 199n40
   death by, 136, 140, 143, 147
   epidemic of, 123–24, 139, 149–50,
     193n4, 194n12, 195n19
   final-stage of, 127–28, 138
   in *The Great Believers*, 123–24, 125,
     127, 136, 139, 154, 197n24
   Holocaust and, 146–47
   Makkai on, 124–25, 127–28, 136–
     37, 138–39
   maternal care and, 122, 124, 138,
     141
   pandemic, 18, 121, 123–24, 193n4
   Reagan administration on, 194n12,
     195n16
American architectural vocabulary,
   169n27
American democracy, assaults on, 151
American narratives, in literary
   studies, 1–4, 6–11, 20, 151–52
American Reconstruction, 57, 58, 69,
   153, 175n6
American South, 24, 26, 33, 98
*The American Woman in the Chinese
   Hat* (Maso), 197n25
Ammons, Elizabeth, 52
Anderson-Minshall, Diane, 194n12
Andrews, William L., 40
"Antigone/Mother" (Bhattacharjee),
   160n5

223

antimaternalism, 23
antinarrative techniques, 144–45, 197n26
Anzaldúa, Gloria E., 164n34
apartheid structure, 97
Aphrodite, 116, 117
art, 18, 84, 122, 126–27, 135
  grief and, 131, 138–39
The Art Lover (Maso), 18–19, 127, 131, 136, 149–50, 154–55
  AIDS in, 123, 125–26, 142, 145
  caregivers in, 126
  "Hieroglyphs of Hope" in, 132–33
  Holocaust and, 146–48
  Matisse and, 132, 133–34, 135
  melancholia in, 197n25
  narratives in, 129–30
  othermothering in, 144
  queer kinship in, 121, 122, 124, 149
  queer maternality in, 128
Artavia, David, 194n12
assault, sexual, 33, 43–46, 48
Auden, W. H., 135
authority, maternal, 56
autobiography, 23, 65, 85, 99, 109, 130
  Cather, 50–52
  genre of, 13, 15, 88–89, 184n6
  Jacobs, 24, 31, 50, 173n49
  Maso, 145
autoethnography, 16, 85
autonomy, mobility and, 48, 171n36, 172n42

Bakhtin, Mikhail, 2
Baldo, Michela, 97, 188n32
Baldwin, James, 106
Ball, Charlene, 184n7, 190n40, 191n48
Barker, Wesley N., 159n1
Beloved (Morrison), 10, 15, 16, 70–72, 85, 179n30
  critical-race theories in, 84
  death in, 73
  diasporic time in, 81
  disremembered people in, 70, 179n31
  enslavement in, 174n4, 179n27
  ghosts in, 55, 57, 59
  home in, 60, 72, 81, 83
  literacy and slavery in, 178n25
  maternal plots in, 69
  milk in, 59, 60, 61, 73–74
  mother-daughter bonds in, 58, 68–69, 82
  motherhood in, 55–56
  othermothering in, 153–54, 157
  shame and pride in, 71, 73, 180n32
  slavery in, 58, 59, 60, 70, 72, 81, 83, 92
  trauma in, 179n29
  trees in, 58, 60, 62, 175n10, 179n28
Bhabha, Homi, 57, 58–59, 81, 175n6
Bhattacharjee, Tuhin, 160n5
biomythography
  in *Zami*, 89, 90, 91, 185n11
Birnbaum, Lucia Chiavola, 117
"birth-no-more" (Cavarero), 160n5
The Birthing Album (Faedo), 78
The Black Book (Morrison), 177n15
Black Feminist Thought (Collins), 160n7, 160n10
Black lesbians, 17, 91
  in *Zami*, 109, 110, 111, 165n35, 184n8, 190n39
Black motherhood, 5, 9, 23, 25, 26–27, 160n10
  Cather and, 31–35
  Morrison and, 59
Black space, 34–35, 110
Black women, 23, 24, 49, 54, 169n25
  enslavement of, 12, 26, 30, 185n11
  geographies of, 13, 35, 169n26
  othermothering and, 160n8
  portrayal of, 25, 36

in *Sapphira and the Slave Girl*, 171n38
  social reality for, 52–53
  subjectivity of, 25, 41, 45
Black Women and the Cartographies of Struggle (McKittrick), 163n25
body, 130, 132, 196n22
  grief in, 77
  maternal, 27, 64, 166n9, 176n14
  portrayal, 18–19
Boelhower, William, 68–69, 178n26, 186n23
Bolaki, Stella, 186n20
bondage, 3, 28, 36, 47, 50
bonds, 50
  maternal, 19, 87, 96, 118–19, 136
  matrilineal, 56, 80, 81, 87, 88
  mother-daughter, 5, 18, 58, 76, 79, 82, 122
  slaver and enslaved, 42
boomerang movement, 143
Bound by Distance (Verdicchio), 187n29
Bouson, J. Brooks, 142, 181n45, 199n42
Brah, Avtar, 12, 49, 164n30, 186n19
Braidotti, Rosi, 5
Braxton, Joanne M., 36
breasts, 61, 69, 75, 81, 181n44
  miscarriage and, 80
Brent, Linda (Jacobs's literary persona), 25, 27, 28–30, 36, 49–50, 166n4
  garret space of, 38, 39–40
bridges in *Dreaming in Cuban*, 81–82
Bromberger, Brian, 195n15
Brown, Gillian, 174n3
Brown Girl, Brownstones (Marshall), 187n25
Brown v. Board of Education, 93
Butler, Judith, 7, 111
Butler, Kim D., 189n34, 198n35

Butterfield, Sherri-Ann, 105–6

captivity, 13, 27, 34, 40, 53
care, maternal, 24, 122, 138, 141, 152, 157
caregivers, 125, 126, 127, 196n20
caretakers, 126, 138, 195n19, 196n20
Caribbean
  culture of, 96
  immigrants, 91, 104, 105–6
Carriacou, 90, 91, 94, 112, 118, 156
Castro, Fidel, 64, 76, 182n46
Cather, Willa, 14–15, 24–26, 41–42, 49–51, 167n15. See also *Sapphira and the Slave Girl*
  antimaternalism and, 23
  black motherhood and, 31–35
  Civil War and, 32, 53
  death and, 48
  maternal plots and, 44–45, 47
  "The Novel Démeublé," 171n35
  tropes used by, 46
  typescript of, 51
  use of topography, 43
  Wolff on, 52
Cavarero, Adriana, 4–5, 16, 20–21, 160n5, 160n6, 180n33
centrifugal reading (Scholes), 186n21
Challenger explosion, 147
chaperonage, antebellum custom of, 46–47
Chicago, IL, 137, 138
Chicago, Judy, 190n41
children, in slavery, 28–29, 36–37, 38
Chinosole, 17, 91, 96, 112, 186n18
Chodorow, Nancy, 8, 161n16
Chrysler, Caroline, 129
Cinderella, 67, 178n21
Cisneros, Sandra, 76, 164n33, 178n21, 180n37
Citheronia regalis (regal moth or walnut moth), 185n15

civil rights, autonomy and mobility as, 48
Civil War, 14, 24, 53
Cixous, Hélène, 21, 165n37
Collins, Patricia Hill, 4–6, 11, 55, 160n8, 164n31. *See also* othermothering
Black Feminist Thought, 160n7, 160n10
Coming to Jones Road #4 (Ringgold), 63
confession, feminist, 89, 96, 99, 111, 187n26
Cooley, Nicole, 128–29, 130
corporeality for Black women, 49
Covid-19 pandemic, 154, 170n30, 195n19
Crane, Stephen, 179n27
Crimp, Douglas, 198n34
critical-race theories, 84, 168n17
cross-dressing, 47–48, 53, 172n45
cross-over aesthetics, 181n41
Cuba, 66, 77, 79, 80, 98, 177n17
  as mother country, 81–82
Cuban Revolution (1959), 57, 63–64, 65, 66, 69, 175n7
Cuban Sea, 83, 155
cult of true womanhood, 6, 26, 28, 37, 160n9, 193n6
culture, antebellum, 3, 53, 162n22, 167n15
Czerwiec, MK, 199n40

Dalleo, Rafael, 76, 180n37
Darling, Martha, 180n36
Dartmouth, 10
Darwin, Charles, 189n36
daughterhood, 2, 20, 68, 74
daughtering, 3, 6, 13
daughters, 1, 14, 15, 41, 60, 154
  abandoned, 63, 68
  abduction of, 10, 12, 19, 21, 68–74

  genre-bending, 87–89
  mis-love and, 178n24
  motherless, 124
  wounds of mother and, 74–81
The Daughter's Seduction (Gallop), 6, 161n11
Davies, Carol Boyce, 96
Davis, Rocío, 8, 76
De Beauvoir, Simone, 191n45
De Veaux, Alexis, 185n12, 185n13, 185n16
death, 29, 37, 38, 73, 144, 196n21
  by AIDS, 136, 140, 143, 147
  Bhattacharjee on, 160n5
  Cather on, 48
  in *Dreaming in Cuban*, 67, 77, 83
DeGuzmán, María, 177n18, 182n48, 182n49, 182n50
Deleuze, Gilles, 179n28
Delirium (Chrysler), 129
Demeter (mythological character), 4–5, 42, 44, 45, 46
  myth of, 66, 71, 73–74, 114, 180n33
  plot of, 69, 139
Demonic Grounds (McKittrick), 12, 169n26
Derrida, Jacques, 184n6
DeSalvo, Louise, 189n37
Detail, Shipwreck in a Tree, Figurehead with Cloth (Perri), 156
devotional hymns, 115, 116
Di Prima, Diane, 189n37
diaspora, 12, 82, 104, 163n24, 177n16, 192n49
  matrilineal, 3, 16, 17
  in *The Skin Between Us*, 106
  time, 55, 81
  trajectories, 108
diasporan consciousness, 106, 118, 189n34, 198nn35
diasporic space, 12–15, 38, 39, 49

dictatorship
  motherhood and, 55
  slavery and, 56
Dictionary of Races or People (1911) (Dillingham Commission), 107
Dinner Party (Chicago), 190n41
discourse
  on mother-daughter relationship, 56–57, 66
  on motherhood, 2, 11, 59
disguises
  for escaping and enslaved persons, 47–48
  in *Sapphira and the Slave Girl*, 172n45
  social reality for Black women, 52–53
Dismal Swamp, 37, 170n30
distance, 55, 123–24, 132
  in *Sapphira and the Slave Girl*, 171n41
domestic fiction, of women, 164n29
domesticity after enslavement, 41
domination, 35, 38
double §, 42–43, 45, 171n37
Downing, Andrew Jackson, 169n27
Doyle, Laura A., 59
Doyle, Nora, 27, 166n9
Dreaming in Cuban (García), 15, 16, 55–57, 65–66, 68, 78–80
  abandonment in, 63–64, 178n21
  bridges in, 81–82
  critical-race theories in, 84
  death in, 67, 74, 77, 83
  diasporic time and, 81
  duende of the Cuban Sea and, 155–56
  exile in, 177n17, 181n42, 181n43, 182n46
  family trees in, 75–77
  The House on Mango Street influencing, 76, 180n37

  milk in, 77, 181n44
  trauma in, 181n42
Driver, Susan, 88, 183n5
Du Plessis, Rachel Blau, 18, 124, 125, 159n3, 194n13
Duany, Jorge, 182n46
duende, of the Cuban Sea, 83–84, 155, 157, 182n48, 182n49, 182n50
dynamics
  mother and daughter, 4, 16
  shame and pride, 71, 73, 180n32

Eakin, Emily, 138
Edelman, Lee, 18
Edenton, North Carolina, 28, 36
Ellis Island, 104
Emancipation Proclamation, 175n6
enslavement, 27, 28–29, 41, 56
  in *Beloved*, 174n4
  of Black women, 12, 26, 30, 185n11
  memories of, 58–59
  migration and, 169n23
  narratives of, 23, 31–32, 33, 34
  sexual, 36
  trauma of, 20
enslavers, 25–26, 28–29, 42
epidemic of AIDS, 123–24, 139, 149–50, 193n4, 194n12, 195n19
erotic, 152
  food as, 94, 190n41
  maternal, 17, 110, 112, 117, 118, 131, 165n35
  mothering, 3, 16, 88
ethic of motherhood, 157
ethnic identities, 96, 105, 192n2
ethnicity, race and, 96, 103, 105–6, 107–8
Evans, Stephanie Y., 40
exile, 5, 11, 64, 66, 72, 96
  Dreaming in Cuban and, 177n17, 181n42, 181n43, 182n46

experimentation narrative, 123

Faderman, Lillian, 195n16
Faedo, Maria, 78
Fahle, Rich, 198n36, 199n43
fairy tales, 34, 48, 67, 169n21, 178n21
Falk, Gary, 193n10
family court, 102
family trees, 58, 75–77, 97, 155, 180n38
Farrar, Margaret E., 39
Farwell, Marilyn, 143
fashion for women, 173n52
Felman, Shoshana, 165n36, 196n21
Felski, Rita, 99, 187n26
female enslavers, 25–26, 29, 32, 37
feminism, 2, 4, 6–11, 161n11
feminist, 84
  confession, 89, 96, 99, 111, 187n26
  diaspora studies, 12
  scholars, 7–8, 9, 12
Ferraro, Evelyn, 101, 187n28
fiction and reality, relationship of, 141
figures, maternal, 3, 5, 25, 121, 144, 149–50
Fiore, Teresa, 108, 189n38
Fitzgerald, F. Scott, 199n38
flying (Cixous), 21, 165n37
folktales, 34, 67, 84
Fortier, Anne-Marie, 96, 186n19, 186n20
Frank, Arthur, 19, 133, 165n36, 194n14, 196n22
freedom, 36, 37, 38, 40, 49–50
  mobility enabling, 53
Freeman, Elizabeth, 15, 19, 135, 148, 199n37
  on queer kinship, 192n1, 199n44
Freud, 10, 197n25
Fugitive Slave Act, 48–49, 172n47, 179n27
Fuori/Outside (Ragusa), 103

Gabaccia, Donna, 189n36

Gallop, Jane, 6, 161n11
García, Cristina, 15, 55–57, 65–67, 76–78, 83–85, 155. See also *Dreaming in Cuban*
  abduction narratives of, 68, 69
  breasts and, 80–81
  ideologies in *Dreaming in Cuban*, 182n48
  maternal stories of, 74–75
  on mother-daughter bonds, 82
  on unmothering, 63–64
  use of polyphony by, 174n2
  Vanishing Maps, 182n47
Gardaphé, Fred, 189n35
Garner, Margaret, 56, 84, 153, 173n1, 174n4, 183n51
garret space, 37–38, 39–40, 163n26, 170n31
Gedalof, Irene, 12, 72
gender, 4, 6, 20, 33, 143, 162n22
  race and, 44, 59
  roles in, 111
genealogy, 58, 69, 70, 97
  of miscegenation, 28, 35
  of mother lines, 89
generations, 58, 75, 100–101, 139, 149
  of mother-daughter ties, 16, 17
  through plantations, 15, 55–56
genre
  of autobiography, 13, 15, 88–89, 184n6
  feminist confession, 89, 96, 99, 111
  of historiographic metafiction, 121, 122, 126, 136
  of life writing, 10, 13, 88
  of novel, 18, 33
geographies, 13, 35, 117–19, 163n27, 169n26
ghosts, 20, 54, 55, 59, 68
  in *Beloved*, 69, 70, 176n13
  in *Dreaming in Cuban*, 78–79, 155
  in *The Great Believers*, 141
Gilbert, Sandra, 196n21

Giunta, Edvige, 104, 152
Gleason, William, 169n27
Glissant, Édouard, 76
Gomez-Vega, Ibis, 64
Gordon, Avery, 57, 169n24, 175n6, 176n11, 176n13, 178n25
  on names in *Beloved*, 179n30
grandmothers, 99, 101, 103, 114, 142–43
  in *Incidents in the Life of a Slave Girl*, 167n13
  maternal, 29, 36, 66, 70, 108
The Great Believers (Makkai), 3, 18, 19–20, 140, 147–50, 154
  AIDS and, 123–24, 125, 127, 136, 139, 197n24
  antinarrative techniques in, 144–45
  Bromberger on, 195n15
  caretakers in, 138
  Holocaust and, 146
  melancholia in, 127, 141–42, 143, 197n25
  queer kinship in, 121, 122
  queer maternality in, 137
  trauma in, 196n24
Green-Barteet, Miranda, 27, 38–39, 163n26, 170n31
Grenada, 105, 110
grief, 77, 130, 131, 132, 138–39
  narratives of, 122
  patriarchy and, 133
Grimm brothers, 169n21
Guattari, Félix, 179n28
Guglielmo, Jennifer, 189n35
Guglielmo, Thomas, 107
Gwin, Minrose, 13, 35, 163n27

Halberstam, Jack, 47, 111
Halperin, Laura, 177n19, 178n21, 182n48
Harlem, 17, 97, 104–9, 112
  Italian, 101, 115–16
  race riots, 93

Harris, Charles B., 130, 198n29
Harris, Victoria Frenkel, 130
haunting, 55, 57, 58, 67, 176n12, 176n14
Hawthorne, Nathaniel, 180n34
Herrera, Andrea O'Reilly, 80–81, 178n21, 181n44
heteronarrative, 128, 143, 197n27
heterosexual, 10, 26, 50, 111, 130, 142
  plot, 143
"Hieroglyphs of Hope" (Maso), 132–33
Hirsch, Marianne, 6, 7, 9, 10, 15–16, 164n32, 176n13
  on postmemory, 196n23
  reference to Spivak, 179n29
  on rememory, 196n24
historical trauma, 13, 164n32
histories
  matrilineal, 57, 70–71, 72, 91
  migration, 107
historiographic metafiction, 121, 122, 124, 126, 136
HIV, 140, 193n4, 195n17, 195n18
Holocaust, 18, 122, 126, 127, 139, 146–48
  narratives of, 146
Homan, Margaret, 176n14
home, 12, 20, 41, 50, 58, 156
  in *Beloved*, 60, 72, 81, 83
  Bolaki on, 186n20
  freedom and, 36
  in *Sapphira and the Slave Girl*, 49
  Sweet, 60, 62, 63, 71, 153, 176n11
  in *Zami*, 183n1
homeland, 198n35
  matrilineal, 66, 94
homophobia, 92, 109, 111
homosexuality, 124, 143, 195n17
  Jews and, 135, 146, 147
Horvitz, Deborah, 179n31
The House on Mango Street, 76, 180n37

Hurston, Zora Neale, 178n24
Hutcheon, Linda, 123, 193n8
hyperassimilation, 181n43

"I Dwell Now in a Neat" (Gleason), 169n27
identities, 76, 88, 91, 102–3, 110–11, 186n20
　ethnic, 96, 105, 192n2
　of immigrants, 105–6
　of Lorde, 185n12, 187n29
ideology
　of daughterhood, 20
　in *Dreaming in Cuban*, 182n48
　of motherhood, 84, 183n5
　of womanhood, 48
illnesses, 121–22, 125–26, 130, 132, 135, 139
　in *The Great Believers* (Makkai), 136–37
　narratives of, 196n22
imagery
　African, 115
　maternal, 92
"Imitation and Gender Insubordination" (Butler), 7
immigrants, 49, 66, 104
　African Caribbean, 105–6, 188n33
　identities of, 105–6
　Italian, 104, 106, 113, 115, *116*, 188n30
　parents as, 17, 91, 93–94, 97
Immigration Act (1965), 107
Immigration Restriction Act (1924), 186n22
In Spite of Plato (Cavarero), 4
Incidents in the Life of a Slave Girl (Jacobs), 14, 30, 36–38, 91, 166n4, 166n13
　caretaking in, 27
　death in, 29, 37
　diasporic space in, 39–40

　maternal plots in, 23–26
　motherhood in, 41
　sensory deprivation in, 170n32
　slavery in, 28–29
innuendos for gender and race, 44
institution, 50, 56, 59
　mental, 64, 65, 177n19
　of motherhood, 5, 9, 11, 160n10, 161n15
　of slavery, 24, 25, 31, 38, 48, 174n3
interdisciplinarity, of motherhood, 7, 9
intersectional approach to maternality, 10
Irigaray, Luce, 160n6, 162n21, 180n33
Irigarayan, 94–95
Italian Americans, 97, 106–7, 113, 186n19, 189n35
　in Harlem, 101, 115–16, 191n43
　woman carrying heavy bundle on head, *116*

Jacobs, Harriet, 13, 14–15, 23–25, 39, 167n11, 167n13
　autobiography of, 24, 31, 50, 173n49
　Black characters and, 35
　Jacobs, L. and, 153
　literary persona of, 28–30, 36, 49–50, 166n4, 170n32, 193n6
　Lorde and, 90–91
　motherhood and, 41
　Tubman and, 40
　use of garret space, 37–38
Jacobs, Louisa, 153, 166n8, 170n33, 170n34
Jews, 192n2
　homosexuality and, 135, 146, 147
Jim Crow, 108, 111, 186n22
Jones-Rogers, Stephanie E., 162n22
Jordan, June, 169n23

Kanzler, Katja, 37
Kaplan, Caren, 89, 184n6
Kawash, Samira, 6-7, 11
kinship, queer, 18, 119, 121, 122, 124, 149
  Freeman on, 192n1, 199n44
Kleinman, Arthur, 194n12
Kore. See Persephone

lamentation, 71
language, as navigation through space and time, 27
Laub, Dori, 196n21
Lauter, Paul, 2
The Law of Genre (Derrida), 184n6
Lefebvre, Henri, 163n27
lens, for analysis of narrative, 1-2, 10, 15, 19, 25
  race as, 30, 32
lesbian bars, 17, 109-10, 190n39
lesbians, 91, 96, 110-11, 126, 133, 165n35
LGBTQ*, 4, 138, 190n39
Li, Stephanie, 27-28, 166n4, 170n29, 185n14
life writing, 10, 13, 88
  in *Zami*, 96, 109, 117, 183n1, 183n5
liminality of space, 13, 37, 103, 187n28
Liscio, Lorraine, 176n11
literacy of Brent, 29, 39, 40, 114
literary persona, 25, 27, 28, 36, 49, 88
  of Jacobs, 166n4, 170n32
literary studies, American narratives in, 1-4, 6-11, 20, 151-52
live entombment, 37, 48
living death on plantation space, 38, 48
Lombardi-Diop, Cristina, 108
López, Iraida H., 174n2

Lorca, García, 67, 83, 182n50
Lorde, Audre, 9-10, 13, 16-17, 87-96, 104-6, 109-12, 117-19. See also *Zami*
  Cover design for *Zami*, 95
  identities of, 185n12, 187n29
  interview with, 184n10
  Jacobs and, 90-91
  othermothering and, 165n35
  Rich and, 162n18
  Smith, B. on, 184n8
  "Uses of the Erotic," 152, 183n2
  X-ray machines and, 185n16
Los Angeles Times, 186n22
Love, Heather, 162n22

Madonna of Mount Carmel, 112-13, 115, 116-17
Maillard, Mary, 170n34
Makkai, Rebecca, 13, 18, 19-20, 127-28, 148-50, 154. See also *The Great Believers*
  AIDS and, 124-25, 127-28, 136-37, 138-39
  conversation with, 194n11
  HIV and, 140
  Holocaust and, 146-47
  interview of, 198n36, 199n43
  Jews and, 192n2
  Maso and, 121-23, 126
  othermothering and, 144
  relationship of fiction and reality in, 141
  Windy City Times, 123, 138, 141, 199n41
male power, 57, 61, 64
Marcus, Lisa, 171n37
Márquez, Gabriel García, 75
Marshall, Paule, 187n25
Maso, Carole, 18, 19-20, 126-27, 149-50. See also *The Art Lover*
  AIDS and, 146-48

Maso, Carole *(continued)*
  The American Woman in the Chinese Hat, 197n25
  autobiography of, 145
  break from *The Art Lover*, 193n5
  critique of modernism, 198n29
  death and, 144
  ethnic identity and, 192n2
  fear and, 198n33
  "Hieroglyphs of Hope," 128–36
  Makkai and, 121–23, 126
  maternality and, 154–55
  othermothering and, 125
  reparenting and, 124
Massey, Doreen, 35
maternal, 12–14, 38, 92, 104, 136
  authority, 56
  body, 27, 64, 166n9, 176n14
  bonds, 19, 87, 96, 118–19, 136
  care, 24, 122, 138, 141, 152, 157
  erotic, 17, 110, 112, 117, 118, 131, 165n35
  figures, 3, 5, 25, 121, 144, 149–50
  love, 20–21, 64, 66, 68
  memory, 16, 59, 60, 68, 83, 95
  movements, 108
  narratives of, 18
  plots, 18, 23–26, 44, 47, 69, 72, 75, 123
  practices, 2, 5, 25, 48
  representation, 6, 11, 14, 26–27, 57, 84
  stories, 56, 57, 72, 74–75, 105, 118
  subjectivity in, 1, 3, 8, 13, 26, 61, 73
  trauma, 3, 16, 55, 60
  violation of, 61, 62
Maternal Theory (O'Reilly), 7
maternality, 5, 32, 157, 159n1, 165n35, 175n5
  Black women and, 23–24
  intersectional approach to, 10

  motherhood and, 1–4
  queer, 20, 110, 121, 127, 128, 136–37
  reconceptualizations of, 16
  slavocracy and, 23, 50
Matisse, 132, 133–34, 135
matrilineal
  bonds, 56, 80, 81, 87, 88
  diaspora, 3, 16, 17
  history, 57, 70–71, 72, 91
  homeland, 66, 94
Maucione, Jessica, 107
McAuliffe, Christa, 147
McAuliffe, Samantha L., 183n52
McCarthyism, 93
McCracken, Ellen, 79–80, 181n41, 181n43
McEntee, Grace, 50
McKay, Nellie, 173n1
McKemmish, Sue, 66, 178n20
McKenzie, Marilyn Mobley, 43, 173n51
McKittrick, Katherine, 12–13, 163n25, 169n26
melancholia
  in *The Art Lovers*, 197n25
  in *The Great Believers*, 127, 141–42, 143, 197n25
memoir, 19, 25, 96–97, 99, 107
memory, 61, 65, 71, 89
  of enslavement, 58–59
  maternal, 16, 59, 60, 68, 83, 95
metafiction, 122–23, 128, 141
Metamorphosis (Ovid), 118
metaphors, Ragusa using, 103
migration, 7, 66, 82, 104–5, 107, 113
  to America, 77, 80
  enslavement and, 169n23
  movement and, 12, 98
  separation as result of, 98, 187n24
milk
  in *Beloved*, 59, 60, 61, 73–74
  in *Dreaming in Cuban*, 77, 181n44

mis-love (Hurston), 178n24
miscarriage, 66, 77, 80, 84, 181n39
miscegenation, genealogy of, 28, 35
mixed-race, 17, 44, 97, 107, 108
Modern Language Association (MLA), 91
Molly Horniblow's House, 39
moral mother, 27, 33, 41, 51
Morgenstern, Naomi, 171n41
Morrison, Toni, 10, 13, 15–16, 60–62, 71, 82–85. See also *Beloved*
  on abandonment and abduction, 68–69
  The Black Book, 177n15
  disremembered people in *Beloved*, 70, 179n31
  ghosts and, 55, 81
  interview of, 180n35, 183n51
  maternal plot and, 72–73
  metafictional techniques and, 56
  on motherhood, 175n5, 175n6
  rememory, 176n13
  on *Sapphira and the Slave Girl*, 171n40
  Song of Solomon, 178n26
  trauma and, 59
  use of polyphony by, 173n1
mother-daughter, 7, 8, 9, 20, 25, 31
  bonds, 5, 18, 58, 76, 79, 82, 122
  dynamics of, 4, 16
  plots, 10, 14, 19, 138, 176n11
  separation, 15, 47, 54
The Mother/Daughter Plot (Hirsch), 10
mother lines, 70, 89
motherhood, 1–4, 5–11, 20, 26–27, 125, 166n6
  in *Beloved*, 55–56
  concept of, 19, 25
  dictatorship and, 55
  ethic of, 157
  ideology of, 84, 183n5
  institution of, 160n10, 161n15

Morrison, 175n5, 175n6
movement and, 2
sentimental, 27, 28, 40–41
studies of, 2, 4, 6–11, 151, 161n15
mothering
  long-distance, 54, 55
  narratives, 20–21
mothers. *See specific topics*
mourning, 136–44, 197n25
movement, 1, 11
  of enslaved persons, 25, 35
  migration and, 12, 98
  motherhood and, 2
movements of Black women, 24, 26, 48, 53, 152
Moyers, Bill, 183n51
Muñoz, José Esteban, 200n45
Murphy, Timothy F., 135, 198n34
Murray, Tony, 164n30, 187n24
mythography, 87, 91, 94, 105
myths, 4–5, 66, 114, 117–18, 180n33

"New Directions in Motherhood Studies" (Kawash), 6–7
normativity, 2, 60, 123, 136, 143, 157
nuclear family, 6, 105, 128, 129, 130

O'Brien, Sharon, 52
OED (1743), 159n1
Oedipal crisis, 10, 159n3, 194n13
Of Woman Born (Rich), 9–10, 11
Ohio River, 62, 82
O'Loughlin, Michael J., 195n18
One Hundred Years of Solitude (Márquez), 75
ontological framework, 159n1
oppression, 94, 152
  systems of, 11, 87, 99
"Ordinary Seductions" (García), 64–65
O'Reilly, Andrea, 7, 9, 59, 61, 161n15, 175n5

organizing principle, of pairing texts (Lauter), 2
Origins of Species (Darwin), 189n36
Orsi, Robert, 191n46
othermothering (Collins), 4, 5, 12, 67, 93, 152
   in *The Art Lover*, 144
   in *Beloved*, 153–54, 157
   Black women and, 160n8
   Lorde and, 165n35
   memory of, 71
   in *Zami*, 156
Our Nig (Wilson), 184n9
outlaw genres (Kaplan), 89
Ovid, 118

pairing texts, 2, 3, 4
pandemic
   AIDS, 18, 121, 123–24, 193n4
   Covid-19, 154, 170n30, 195n19
Panic of 1873, 57
paradigm shift, about maternality, 1
parents as immigrants, 17, 91, 93–94, 97
Passing (Ragusa), 103, 188n31
paternalism, 166n5
patriarchy, 5, 8, 67, 69, 181n41
   cruelties of, 83
   grief and, 133
   prerogative of, 33
patterns, in maternality, 3
Pearl, Monica B., 90, 183n1, 185n11
Pearl Harbor bombing, 93
peculiar institution, 29, 174n3
Penelope (mythological character), 5, 41, 65, 72, 153, 180n33
perceptions of time, 5, 15
Perri, Christine, 156
Persephone (mythological character), 4–5, 42, 44, 45, 46, 117–18
   myth of, 66, 71–72, 73–74, 114, 180n33
   plot of, 69, 139

Pettersson, Inger, 181n41, 181n42
Pinto, Samantha, 12, 163n24
Pitts, Terry, 193n9
plantation, 24, 36, 48, 58, 169n24
   generations through, 15, 55–56
plateau *(al'maida)*, 75
plots
   heterosexual, 143
   maternal, 18, 23–26, 44, 47, 69, 72, 75, 123
   mother-daughter, 10, 14, 19, 138, 176n11
   rape, 24, 46, 172n42
   seduction, 14, 44, 45
Pollard, Tomas, 173n50
polyphony, 173n1, 174n2
portrayal
   Black lesbian bar scene, 190n39
   Black women, 25, 36
   body, 18–19
   motherhood, 166n6
   peculiar institution, 174n3
post-Holocaust narratives, 127, 196n24
postbellum America, 52, 56, 59, 82, 153
postmemory, 15–16, 71, 146, 164n32, 176n13
   Hirsch on, 196n23
power
   judicial, 29
   male, 57, 61, 64
   of motherhood, 11
"practiced place," 13
Pratt, Mary Louise, 85, 183n52
property, people as, 25, 29
Provost, Kara, 190n42
psychoanalysis, feminism and, 161n11
Puritans, 180n34

Quakers, 47, 172n43
queer, 4, 96, 138, 186n20, 199n37, 200n45
   kinship, 18, 119, 121, 122, 124, 149

maternality, 20, 110, 121, 127, 128, 136–37
space, 19–20, 92, 109–17, 190n39

race, 17, 30, 32, 44, 59
 ethnicity and, 96–97, 103, 105–6, 107–8
 Harlem race riots, 93
racial violence, 175n6
racism, 52, 102–3, 106–7, 111, 152, 199n43
Ragusa, Kym, 16–17, 87–89, 96–104, 106–9, 112–17, 156. See also *The Skin Between Us*
 arranged marriages and, 191n45
 email from, 187n27
 identities of, 187n29
 Passing, 103, 188n31
Randle, Gloria T., 30, 38
rape, 66, 77, 79–80
 plot, 24, 46, 172n42
Raynaud, Claudine, 185n17
Reagan, Ronald, 124, 147, 194n12, 195n16
reconceptualizations of maternality, 16
Reconstruction. *See* American Reconstruction
recovery project, 15, 55, 82
The Red Badge of Courage (Crane), 179n27
relationship, mother-daughter, 7, 8, 20, 25, 31
 in *The Art Lover* (Maso), 129, 131
 discourse on, 56–57, 66
 in *Sapphira and the Slave Girl* (Cather), 42, 173n51
religious processions, 109, 191n47
rememory, 15, 55, 59, 61, 154
 Hirsch on, 196n24
 Morrison and, 176n13
reparenting, 3, 18, 124, 125, 159n3, 194n13

representation, maternal, 6, 11, 14, 26–27, 57, 84
reproduction of mothering, 18, 21
The Reproduction of Mothering (Chodorow), 8
resistance, of authors about motherhood, 20
rhizome, 76, 179n28
Rich, Adrienne, 9–10, 11, 161n17, 162n18, 184n10
Rigney, Barbara Hill, 173n1
Ringgold, Faith, 63
Roediger, David, 107
Romines, Ann, 31, 167n15, 168n18, 172n43, 173n52
Roof, Judith, 128, 197n27
Rubin, Jennifer, 151

Sapphira and the Slave Girl (Cather), 14, 23–26, 27, 31–35, 41, 168n16
 Black women in, 171n38
 distance in, 171n41
 double $ in, 42–43, 45, 171n37
 mobility and autonomy in, 171n36
 Morrison on, 171n40
 Nancy's strength in, 45
 Pollard on, 173n50
 Quakers in, 47, 172n43
 rape plots in, 24, 46, 172n42
 Romines on, 168n18
 scholarly editions of, 165n2
 slavery in, 165n3, 168n20
 topography in, 43
 typescript of, 51
 white supremacy in, 15, 24, 42
The Scarlet Letter (Hawthorne), 180n34
Scarry, Elaine, 144
Scholes, Robert, 144, 186n21
Sedgwick, Eve, 192n3
seduction plot, 14, 44, 45
segregation, 17, 52, 110, 186n22
sentimental motherhood, 27, 28, 40–41

separation, 74, 85, 159n4
  mother-daughter, 15, 47, 54
  as result of migration, 98, 187n24
sexual assault, 33, 43–46, 48
sexual enslavement, 36
sexual liaison, 30
sexual violence, 24, 25, 35, 40, 46
shame, 71, 73, 180n32, 181n45
Sharpe, Jenny, 12, 35
shed space, 38, 39, *39*, 40
Signs (Hirsch), 6, 9
Silbergleid, Robin, 142, 197n25
SILENCE=DEATH, 133–34, *134*
Silver, Brenda, 161n17
Sister Outsider(s), 106, 110, 113
Skaggs, Merrill Maguire, 171n41
The Skin Between Us (Ragusa), 87–89, 102–4, 107–9, 113–15, 156
  arranged marriages and, 191n45
  Baldo on, 188n32
  diaspora in, 106
  immigrants and migration in, 98–99
  Madonna and Aphrodite in, 116–17
  race and ethnicity in, 96–97
  Spillers and, 101
  Title page design, *100*
skin tone, 34, 101, 191n46
slavery, 23, 42, 165n3, 168n18, 171n38
  in *Beloved*, 58, 59, 60, 70, 72, 81, 83, 92
  children in, 28–29, 36–37, 38
  dictatorship and, 56
  institution of, 24, 25, 31, 38, 48, 174n3
  literacy and, 178n25
  mothers and, 170n29
  in *Sapphira and the Slave Girl*, 165n3, 168n20
  trauma of, 58, 59

slavocracy, 25, 28, 40, 169n23, 176n11
  on double $, 46
  maternality and, 23, 50
  narratives of, 79
Smith, Barbara, 17, 90, 103, 184n8
Smith, Sarah Stefana, 170n30
Smith, Sidonie, 183n1
Snow White (Grimm), 34, 67, 169n21
social change, movements for, 152
"Someone Puts a Pineapple Together" (Stevens), 76
Song of Solomon (Morrison), 178n26
Sontag, Susan, 193n4
Sorisio, Carolyn, 170n29
Southern antebellum, 35
Southern apparel, 52–53
Southern white women, 53, 162n22
Southern womanhood, 32–33, 42, 45
space, 41–48
  Black, 34–35
  of bridge, 82
  diaspora, 12–15, 38, 39, 49
  garret, 37–38, 39–40, 163n26, 170n31
  liminality of, 13, 37, 103, 187n28
  plantation, 24, 36, 48, 58, 169n24
  queer, 19–20, 92, 109–17, 190n39
  shed, 38, 39, *39*, 40
  time and, 2, 5, 14, 16, 25, 153
  urban, 17
Spillers, Hortense, 29, 37, 56, 57, 60, 61, 101, 171n38, 174n3, 176n11
Spivak, Gayatri C., 179n29
Stavans, Ilan, 164n33
Stevens, Wallace, 75–76
Stirling, Grant, 197n25
stories, maternal, 56, 57, 72, 74–75, 105, 118
storytellers, wounds of, 19, 198n31
studies of motherhood, 2, 4, 6–11, 12, 151, 161n15

subjectivity
    of Black lesbians, 111
    of Black women, 25, 41, 45
    maternal, 1, 3, 8, 13, 26, 61, 73
survivorship, 139, 154
Sweet Home, 60, 62, 63, 71, 153, 176n11
synesthetic experience, 144
systems of oppression, 11, 87, 99

Taronna, Annarita, 97–98, 155
Tate, Claudia, 91, 161n12, 181n40, 184n9
Tate, Julee, 8–9, 77
Tenzer, Livia, 103, 108, 188n31
"The Novel Démeublé" (Cather), 171n35
They Were Her Property (Jones-Rogers), 162n22
time, 15, 27, 35–36, 180n33
    diaspora, 55, 81
    movement and, 75
    rememory and, 176n13
    space and, 2, 5, 14, 16, 25, 153
To the Lighthouse (Woolf), 131
topography, in *Sapphira and the Slave Girl*, 43
trafficking, abandonment and, 113–14
trauma, 66, 140, 149, 154
    in *Beloved*, 179n29
    Bouson on, 199n42
    in *Dreaming in Cuban*, 181n42
    of enslavement, 20
    in *The Great Believers*, 196n24
    historical, 13, 164n32
    maternal, 3, 16, 55, 60
    of slavery, 58, 59
traumatic memory, 61, 142
trees, 58, 60, 62, 175n10, 179n28
tropes
    in *Beloved*, 60
    Cather use of, 46

Truth, Sojourner, 40
Tubman, Harriet, 40

underground railroad, 31, 42, 47, 48
unfreedom, 24, 26, 27, 29, 31, 49
unhousing, 11, 12, 17, 25, 140, 162n22
unmothering, 59, 63–64, 71, 74, 138
urban spaces, 17
"Uses of the Erotic" (Lorde), 152, 183n2

Vanishing Maps (García), 182n47
Vásquez, Mary S., 177n18, 178n22
Vellucci, Sabrina, 103
Verdicchio, Pasquale, 187n29
violation of maternal, 61, 62
violence, 61–62
    racial, 175n6
    sexual, 24, 25, 35, 40, 46
Virgin and Child (Matisse), 133–34
Virginia, 31–32
virtuous womanhood, 40, 41, 45
voices, in *Zami*, 109, 183n7

Wald, Gayle, 171n38
Warner, Anne Bradford, 48
Warner, Oswald, 188n33
Washington Post, 151
Watkins-Owens, Irma, 187n25
Watson, Julia, 90, 103, 109, 183n1
Welter, Barbara, 160n9, 167n10
Wenzel, Hélène Vivienne, 162n21
Wheatley, Phillis, 169n23
white supremacy, 23, 106, 189n35
    in *Sapphira and the Slave Girl*, 15, 24, 42
Williams, Albert, 199n39
Wilson, Harriet E., 184n9
Windy City Times (Makkai), 123, 138, 141, 199n41

Wolff, Cynthia Griffin, 46, 52, 165n3
womanhood, 35, 36, 39, 47, 48, 94
  Southern, 32–33, 42, 45
  virtuous, 40, 41, 45
Wong, Sau-ling Cynthia, 186n23
Woolf, Virginia, 131, 198n30, 199n37
Working toward Whiteness (Roediger), 107
World War I, 139, 142
World War II, 14, 53, 93
The Wounded Storyteller (Frank), 196n22
wounds, 60, 61, 82, 177n15
  daughter-mother, 74–81
  mother, 68–74
  of storytellers, 19, 198n31
Writing beyond the Ending (Du Plessis), 124, 159n3, 194n13
Wyatt, Jean, 176n12, 176n14

X-ray machines, Lorde and, 185n16

Yaeger, Patricia, 42, 171n41
Yellin, Jean Fagin, 91, 153, 166n4, 167n14, 169n28, 170n32
  biography of Jacobs, H., 167n11, 167n13, 175n9

Zami (Lorde), 10, 17, 87–96, 109–12, 117–19
  African mythological gods in, 190n42
  biomythography of, 89, 90, 91, 185n11
  Black lesbians in, 109, 110, 111, 165n35, 184n8, 190n39
  Brown Girl comparison to, 187n25
  concept of home in, 183n1
  Cover design for, 95
  erotic food in, 94, 190n41
  scenes in, 185n17
  voices in, 109, 183n7

www.ingramcontent.com/pod-product-compliance
Lightning Source LLC
Chambersburg PA
CBHW022005220426
43663CB00007B/974